THE GREEK QABALAH

THE
GREEK
QABALAH

Alphabetic Mysticism and Numerology
in the Ancient World

KIEREN BARRY

SAMUEL WEISER, INC.
York Beach, Maine

First published in 1999 by
SAMUEL WEISER, INC.
Box 612
York Beach, ME 03910-0612
www.weiserbooks.com

Library of Congress Cataloging-in-Publication Data

Barry, Kieren.
    The Greek Qabalah : alphabetic mysticism and numerology in the ancient world / Kieren Barry.
        p. cm.
    Includes bibliographical references and index.
    ISBN 1-57863-110-6 (pbk. : alk. paper)
    1. Numerology—Greece—History.   2. Greek language—Alphabet—History.   3. Cabala—History. I. Title.
    BF1623.P9B397 1999
    133.3'35'0938—DC21   99-22783
                                           CIP

EB
Typeset in 11 point Adobe Garamond
Cover and text design by Kathryn Sky-Peck

PRINTED IN THE UNITED STATES OF AMERICA

08 07 06 05 04 03 02 01 00 99
10 9 8 7 6 5 4 3 2 1

CONTENTS

v

LIST OF ILLUSTRATIONS
AND TABLES

vii

Nullum numen habes si sit prudentia; nos te,
nos facimus, Fortuna, deam caeloque locamus.

—JUVENAL, SATIRE X

You have no divinity Fortune, if we are wise; it is we,
we, who make you into a deity, and set you in heaven.

ACKNOWLEDGMENTS

THE HELP AND ASSISTANCE of the following people and institutions for their contributions in preparing this work is gratefully acknowledged: The library staff at the University of Hong Kong, and at Berkeley Library, Trinity College for permission to use their resources; the Bodleian Library, University of Oxford and my learned friend Mark Hickford for securing an introduction there; the British Museum Press and Quest Books for their permission to use the illustrations in this book; Stephen Ronan of Chthonios Books for consent to use his translation of Theodorus, and many helpful early references; the Classics Department of the University of Auckland for historical method and inspiration generally, and, in particular, Dr. Bill Barnes for sparing his valuable time to read an early draft, and for numerous corrections and suggestions; publishers E. J. Brill of the Netherlands for permission to quote excerpts from their edition of the *Nag Hammadi Codices*; Princeton University Press for permission to quote excerpts from *Proclus' Commentary on the First Book of Euclid's Elements*; Aristarchos Papadopoulos, Evangelos Rigakis, and Nyk Ashlin for their encouragement, support, and feedback in the early stages of the project; my good friend Antony George for patient and generous technical and software support; Cynthia Crosse for her kind assistance in researching sources at Auckland University Library; all the editorial staff at Samuel Weiser; and most especially my Muse, Michelle, for enduring so many hours of research and writing.

PREFACE

IT IS NECESSARY TO BEGIN WITH an apology. It is, in fact, anachronistic and misleading to use the term *Greek Qabalah*. The word *Qabalah* (derived from Hebrew *QBL*, "to receive") in rabbinic Hebrew simply means "tradition." It came to be used to name a specific Jewish mystical philosophy that emerged in France and Spain in the 13th century of the current or Christian era (C.E.). This philosophical school believed in spiritual illumination from a "received" knowledge, or *gnosis*. The Qabalists are probably best known for their use of a technique known as "literal Qabalah" that involved the interpretation of Jewish sacred scriptures according to the number, shape, and mystical attributions of each letter of the Hebrew alphabet. The term *Qabalah* (sometimes Anglicized as *Kabbalah* or *Cabala*) is used so often to refer to this technique of literary analysis, rather than to Qabalistic philosophy as a whole, that it has become practically synonymous with it in the West. It is only in this more restricted sense that the word is used in this book.

Qabalistic philosophy formed a principal school of thought within Judaism. It became well-known in Christian Europe due to its influence during the Middle Ages. The resultant widespread awareness of Hebrew Qabalah in the West has often led to the mistaken belief that the Jews were the original founders of the literal Qabalah, and even that it was the Jews who first used letters as numbers. The main thesis of this book is that *Qabalah* is, in fact, a late Jewish term for a gnosis that was already ancient when it emerged in Jewish mysticism. It was, in fact, the Greeks who, as early as the eighth century B.C.E., invented alphabetic numerals, the very essence of Qabalistic numerology. They introduced the idea to the Middle East only after the conquests of Alexander the

Great in the fourth century B.C.E. Examples of Greek Qabalah can also be found outside of mainland Greece well before the third century C.E. in Egyptian amulets, Roman graffiti, Gnostic philosophy, and early Christian writings. This is the earliest likely date of the first known work in Hebrew Qabalah, the *Sefer Yezirah,* or *Book of Formation.*[1] This early work was essentially a product of the impact of Greek Gnosticism on Jewish mysticism, and shows the influence of numerous concepts, such as the Gnostic theory of creation by emanations, the Pythagorean decad, Platonic philosophy, Ptolemaic astrology, and the four elements of Empedocles, all of which were already part of existing Greek alphabetical symbolism. It is this earlier Greek gnosis, anachronistically called here by the later Hebrew term *Qabalah,* that is investigated and presented in this book.

In recent times, numerology, Hebrew Qabalah, enneagrams, divination, and similar topics have experienced a renaissance as part of the esoteric doctrines of interest to the so-called New Age movement. As part of this process, many books have been written on these subjects without any deep awareness of their origins or past development. As a consequence, many fundamental misconceptions and misunderstandings have been introduced and repeated. One of the secondary functions of this book is to restore the factual historical basis of alphabetic numerology and symbolism in order to provide a background upon which further writings on these topics can draw. To that end, as many relevant examples and excerpts from ancient writings and inscriptions as possible have been collated, translated, and presented here, so as to form a sourcebook of material. Important quotations and facts have been footnoted so that they can be checked or further investigated, and so that further debate

---

[1] Third to sixth century C.E. G. Scholem, "*Sefer Yezirah,*" in *Encyclopedia Judaica* (Jerusalem: Keter Publishing House, 1972).

or research can be launched from a firm foundation of textual sources. The book is, therefore, necessarily academic in style, but it has been addressed to readers without any prior knowledge of Greek, ancient history, Qabalah, numerology, or related areas. In each chapter, some basic historical background is given to illuminate the context, as well as to provide an introduction to the period concerned and a general understanding of the various forces at work. The temptation to interpret the material presented with any individual theory has, hopefully, been resisted, and, apart from some general summations of the evidence, it has been left to the readers to draw their own conclusions.

Another purpose of this book, particularly in view of the recent resurgence of interest in Qabalah and numerology in the West, is to remove the perception that these subjects are particularly esoteric in any way. As will be shown, in the ancient world, the attribution of numerical values to letters was unexceptional, simply because it was the standard system of numeration. There were no separate symbols for numerals such as those we now use. Because of this, there are widespread instances of numerical wordplay in ancient writings, as well as references to other symbolism attached to the letters of the alphabet in common folklore and superstition. In addition, the massive importance accorded to numbers and their perceived qualities after Pythagoras pervades the works of many of the later Greek philosophers. It is, therefore, impossible for us to translate and interpret these writings properly, unless we have first studied and understood the techniques of alphabetic numerology and symbolism that were employed by Greek authors. The ill-informed alphabetical gymnastics applied by past generations to the famous "Beast 666" in the biblical book of Revelation is but one example illustrating this need. It shows how much the interpretation of ancient writings has suffered because of a lack of academic resources and respectability in the area. As will be seen, Martianus Capella's *Marriage of Philology and Mercury* is another case of a work that was long misunderstood for the same reason.

Even today, cryptic Greek Qabalistic passages in Valentinus' *Pistis Sophia* remain unsolved. The extensive discussion of Greek Qabalah in the recently discovered *Marsanes* codex, among those celebrated Gnostic scrolls found at Nag Hammadi in Egypt in 1945, again shows that we simply cannot afford to ignore a branch of knowledge considered so important to the Gnostics, as well as to the early Christians, the Neoplatonists, and others. This knowledge was so widespread throughout the ancient Graeco-Roman world that it appeared in common graffiti. It is a mistake to discount a technique as frivolous or superstitious simply because it is found in amulets and oracles, when we know it was also used by leading ancient commentators in the interpretation of major philosophical and sacred writings, from Plato to the Bible. In short, you don't have to subscribe to the use of Qabalah or numerology in the modern world to appreciate its benefits in fully understanding the old.

The renaissance of Qabalah in recent times is evident in the number of books on the topic that can be found in almost any bookstore. To a certain extent, this is due to the New Age movement and its interest in the mystical, magical, and religious beliefs of other cultures and ages. With specific reference to the Qabalah, however, this phenomenon has also been interpreted as being indicative of an increasing number of people (Christians in particular) seeking to add a more mystical or magical element to their faith, but who, at the same time, do not want a philosophy that might challenge their fundamental religious beliefs. For those people, the Qabalah is not a historical study but a living practice. The appendices at the end of this book have been included with them in mind, rather than for an academic audience.

— KIEREN BARRY, HONG KONG

chapter one

HISTORY OF THE ALPHABET

efore commencing with the study of alphabetic symbolism, let us first briefly review the history of the invention of writing itself, and the evolution of the alphabet. Examining the origins of the alphabet will serve as a useful means to introduce the early history of the Greeks and other peoples and cultures relevant to our story. It will also provide us with a complete picture of the full range of ideas behind alphabetic symbols, right from their inception. This will, in turn, provide a useful backdrop against which to consider the range of their subsequent use.

Many examples of as-yet-undeciphered scripts dating from several thousands of years B.C.E., plainly independent in origin, have been found at several neolithic sites, such as Banpo in China,

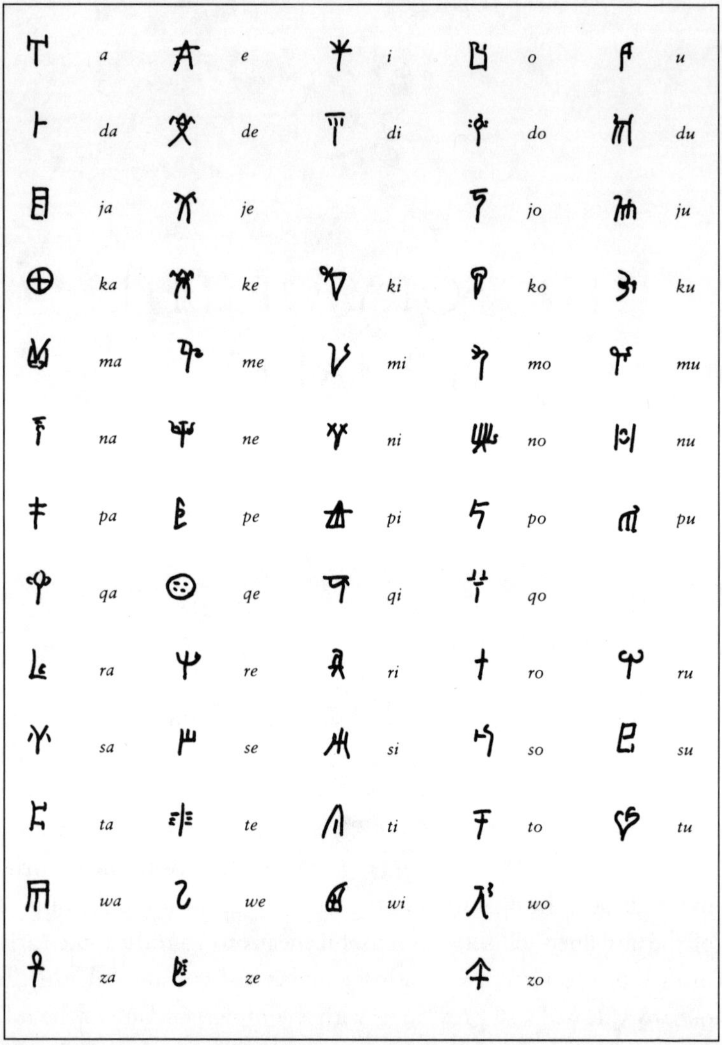

Figure 1. Linear B signs. (Reprinted from John Chadwick, *Linear B and Related Scripts,* 1987 © the British Museum, British Museum Press, used by permission.)

and Moenjodaro in Pakistan. In the oldest civilizations of the world, the earliest forms of writing were basically pictographic. The characters were ideograms or pictograms, ideas or objects each represented by a single stylized symbol. The earliest widespread and enduring example of such a system is found in the ancient civilization of Mesopotamia (modern Iraq), where writing first appeared around 3000 B.C.E. as a cuneiform or "wedge-shaped" script consisting of marks made by a reed stylus on clay tablets. Not long afterward, a basically similar system, known as hieroglyphics or "sacred pictures," arose in Egypt. These symbols then came to represent syllables, and were used in conjunction with other pictograms to denote the sound and meaning of various other words. A similar methodology lies behind Chinese characters and their composite pictophonetic radicals.

In Mycenaean Greece during the second millennium B.C.E., writing also consisted of pictographic scripts. The best-documented versions known to historians today are called Linear A and Linear B (see figure 1, page 2). These were based on the pictographic writing brought to Mycenae and other Greek cities by traders from the kingdom of Minos on the nearby central island of Crete, an island closely connected with early Mycenaean Greece. An example of early Minoan pictographic writing appears on the famous Phaistos disc from Crete, which, in spite of extensive research, remains undeciphered to this day. An account of the use of this type of writing is also preserved in Homer's *Iliad*, where Bellerophon is sent away bearing a letter from the king in symbols "on a folded tablet" containing a message that the bearer should be killed—an idea copied by Shakespeare in *Hamlet*.[1] The Mycenaean Linear B script (1400-1200 B.C.E.) contained eighty-eight different phonetic signs, and was deciphered by Ventris and Chadwick only as recently as 1953 (see figure 2, page 4).

Such systems were obviously cumbersome, and there was much experimentation in the ancient Near East aimed at producing a simpler method of representing language in writing. The ori-

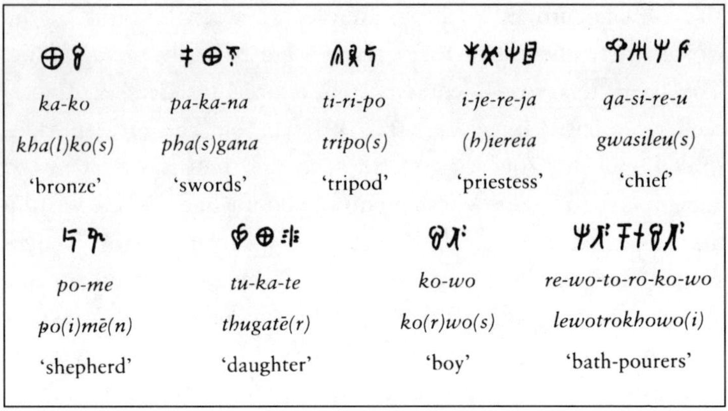
ka-ko
kha(l)ko(s)
'bronze'
pa-ka-na
pha(s)gana
'swords'
ti-ri-po
tripo(s)
'tripod'
i-je-re-ja
(h)iereia
'priestess'
qa-si-re-u
gwasileu(s)
'chief'
po-me
po(i)mē(n)
'shepherd'
tu-ka-te
thugatē(r)
'daughter'
ko-wo
ko(r)wo(s)
'boy'
re-wo-to-ro-ko-wo
lewotrokhowo(i)
'bath-pourers'

Figure 2. Examples of Linear B signs with English translation. (Reprinted from John Chadwick, *Linear B and Related Scripts,* 1987 © the British Museum, British Museum Press, used by permission.)

gin of the alphabet, in which each sound is denoted by a single sign, is generally attributed to the region forming the land bridge between the great cultures of Egypt and Mesopotamia. This area is also known to historians and archaeologists as the Fertile Crescent, and was home to the kingdoms of Phoenicia, Aram, and Israel. In addition to the land trade routes that passed through the region, maritime trade transformed coastal trading ports in this area into centers of great commercial activity. All available evidence suggests that it was in this part of the world that some person or persons, dissatisfied with the various cumbersome existing methods of transcribing words, first had the idea of representing each sound with one symbol only.

It is likely that the inventor of the first alphabet knew of and was influenced by the scripts and symbols then used for writing by surrounding cultures. The earliest example of a syllabic alphabet occurs in 1400 B.C.E. in the form of a 32-letter alphabet from the Phoenician coastal city of Ugarit (Ras Shamra), with the letters written in a cuneiform script, showing Mesopotamian influence (see figure 3, page 5).[2] For many centuries, Egypt had maintained

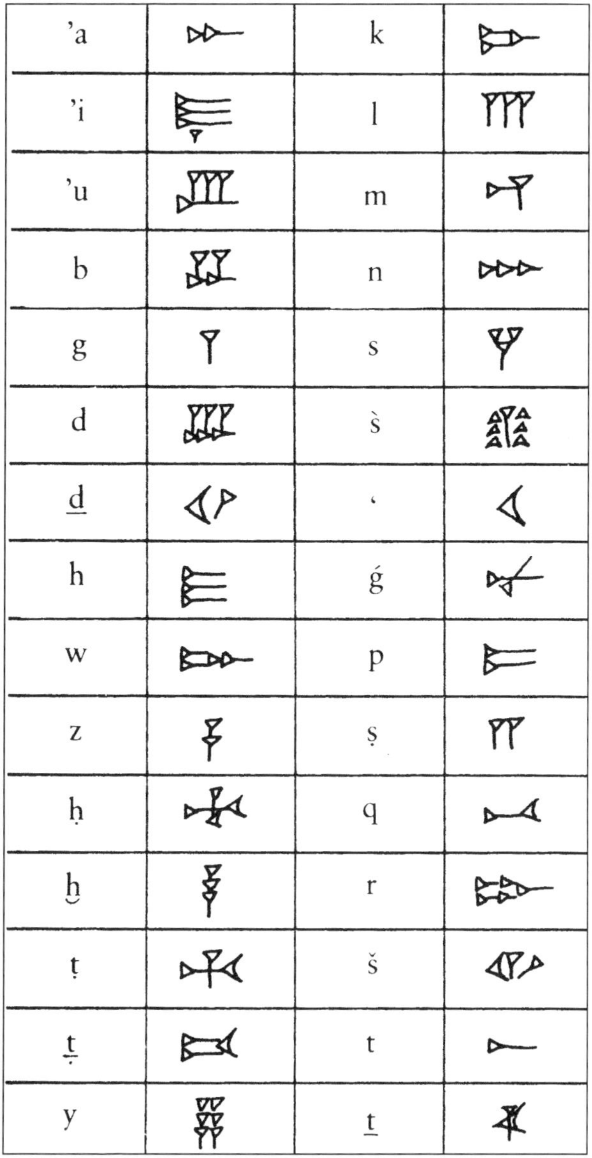

Figure 3. Ugaritic cuneiform alphabet. (Reprinted from John Healy, *The Early Alphabet,* 1990 © the British Museum, British Museum Press, used by permission.)

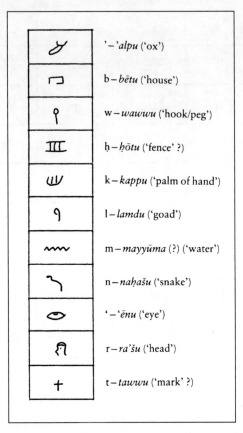

ʾ	ʾ – ʾalpu ('ox')
	b – bētu ('house')
	w – wawwu ('hook/peg')
	ḥ – ḥōtu ('fence' ?)
	k – kappu ('palm of hand')
	l – lamdu ('goad')
	m – mayyūma (?) ('water')
	n – naḥašu ('snake')
	ʿ – ʿēnu ('eye')
	r – raʾšu ('head')
	t – tawwu ('mark' ?)

Figure 4. Some proto-Sinaic signs. (Reprinted from John Healy, *The Early Alphabet*, 1990 © the British Museum, British Museum Press, used by permission.)

close ties with the coastal Phoenician cities, and Egyptian influence can also be seen in several letters (see figure 4).[3] The Egyptian hieroglyphic for water (≈), for example, was simplified in shape to become the Phoenician letter *mem*. Its wave-like shape is still visible in our own form of that letter, M. Likewise, the Phoenician letter O is traceable to the Egyptian hieroglyph for an eye; the letter Y can perhaps be traced to that of a prop. The Phoenician

6

script was written from right to left, like hieroglyphics, as is still the practice in Arabic and Hebrew. It is not unlikely that some Phoenician symbols were also derived from the pictographic script used by the early Minoans, who were also engaged in regular trade with the coastal cities of the Levant.

The invention of the syllabic alphabet in the area of Phoenicia occurred just before the period in Greek history known as the Dark Age (1200-800 B.C.E.). This is the period of the Trojan War, recounted by Homer in the *Iliad*. Scholars generally agree that the Trojan War occurred around 1200 B.C.E., a time when mighty walled cities like King Agamemnon's Mycenae dotted mainland Greece. On the island of Crete, the kingdom of Minos thrived on maritime trade between the nations surrounding it, and its ships dominated the Aegean. Shortly after this period, however, it seems as if Greek history stops, and archaeologists find centuries of little else but destruction, as Greece's walled cities apparently fell to invaders and wars. When the Dark Age of Greece ended, the kingdoms of Mycenae and Minos had been reduced to mere myths, remembered only in legend and in heroic works like the songs of Homer.

After the collapse of Minoan culture and sea power, Phoenician vessels, originating from cities on the coast of present-day Lebanon, came to dominate the Mediterranean. A passage in the *Odyssey* records the Greeks' perception of their neighbors from across the sea: "Thither came the Phoenicians, mariners renowned, greedy merchant men, with countless gauds in a black ship."[4]

The Phoenicians became famous traders, colonists and sailors, and even circumnavigated Africa around 600 B.C.E. on behalf of the Pharaoh Necoh.[5] They carried their alphabet with them to most of the lands of the ancient world, while another form of the same parent North Semitic alphabet, Aramaic, spread eastward by land routes toward India. In this fashion, the 22-letter North Semitic alphabet became the source of almost every script used in the world today, except those of the Far East (see fig-

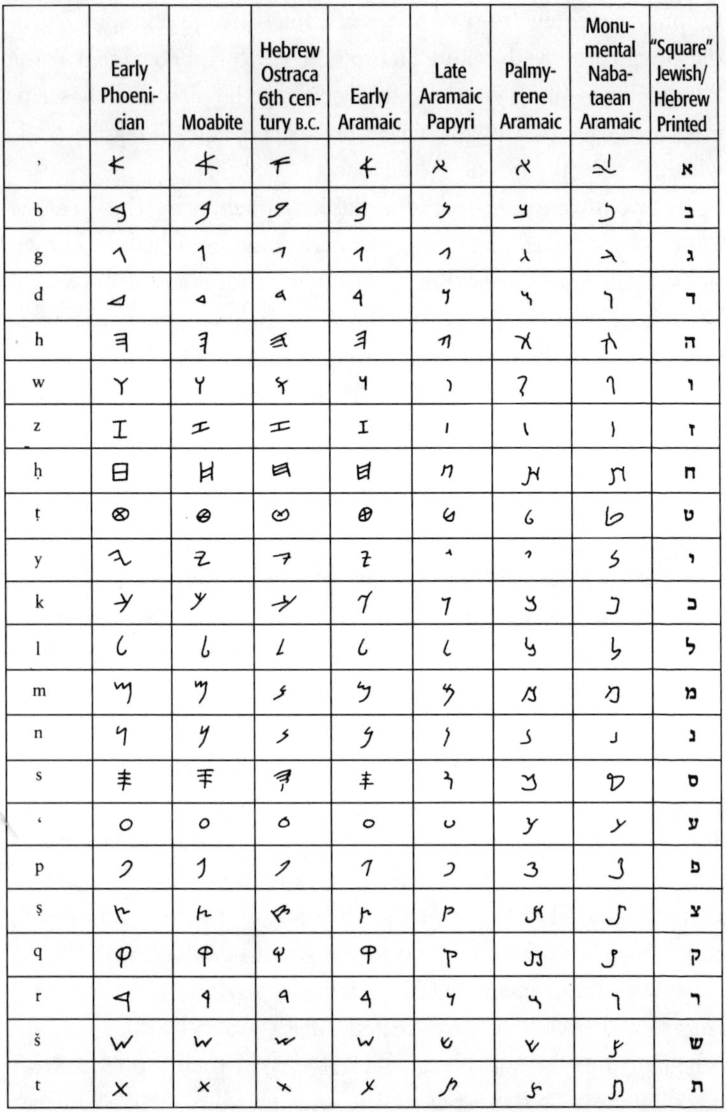

	Early Phoeni-cian	Moabite	Hebrew Ostraca 6th cen-tury B.C.	Early Aramaic	Late Aramaic Papyri	Palmy-rene Aramaic	Monu-mental Naba-taean Aramaic	"Square" Jewish/ Hebrew Printed
'	𝕂	𝕂	𝖥	𝕂	א	א	⅃	א
b	⅁	⅁	⅁	⅁	⅁	⅁	⅃	ב
g	⋀	⋀	⅂	⅂	⋀	λ	⋋	ג
d	◿	◢	◣	4	⅂	⅂	⅂	ד
h	ⅎ	ⅎ	⅏	ⅎ	𝑛	Ӿ	⅄	ה
w	Y	Y	Ӻ	Ꮞ	ⅰ	⅀	⅂	ו
z	I	𝖨	⊑	I	ⅰ	ⅼ	ⅰ	ז
ḥ	日	Ħ	⊟	日	𝑛	Ӿ	⅀	ח
ṭ	⊗	⊝	⊗	⊕	ⅆ	6	⅀	ט
y	⅄	ⅎ	ⅎ	⅋	⌐	⅀	⅀	י
k	⅄	⅄	⅄	⅂	⅂	⅀	⅃	כ
l	⅃	⅃	⅃	⅃	⅃	⅄	⅃	ל
m	⅏	⅏	⅄	⅄	⅄	ⅆ	⅂	מ
n	⅄	⅄	⅄	⅄	ⅰ	⅃	⅃	נ
s	ⅎ	ⅎ	ⅎ	ⅎ	⅀	⅂	⅂	ס
'	○	○	○	○	⅄	У	У	ע
p	⅂	⅂	⅂	⅂	⅂	ⅲ	⅃	פ
ṣ	⅄	⅄	ⅾ	ⅼ	⅂	⅀	⅀	צ
q	φ	φ	φ	φ	⅂	⅀	⅀	ק
r	⅂	⅂	⅂	⅂	⅄	ⅼ	ⅰ	ר
š	W	w	ⅳ	w	ⅴ	ⅴ	ⅆ	ש
t	×	×	ⅹ	ⅹ	�ⅰ	ⅾ	ⅅ	ת

Figure 5. Phoenician, Hebrew, and Aramaic scripts. (Reprinted from John Healy, *The Early Alphabet,* 1990 © the British Museum, British Museum Press, used by permission.)

ure 5, page 8). Among the alphabetic scripts of the world that can be traced to this one original parent alphabet are Phoenician, Aramaic, Arabic, Hebrew, Greek, Coptic, Russian, Latin, Runes, Gothic, English, Mongol, Tibetan, Korean, and Sanskrit (see figure 6, page 10).

Some time around 850 B.C.E. when the Dark Age of Greece was drawing to a close, the Greeks, like other Mediterranean cultures, adopted the new alphabetic script from the Phoenicians.[6] This was around the time of Homer and Hesiod, whose compositions are the earliest surviving works in Greek preserved with the aid of the new alphabet. This fact has even led to the suggestion that Homer's poems were actually the impetus and instrument for the adaptation and diffusion of the Phoenician alphabet throughout Greece.[7] The pictographic writing used earlier in mainland Greece appears to have vanished from common use during the Dark Age, along with the cities that had used it. It is unlikely that any kind of literacy survived through the turmoil of Greece during this period.

Recently, Roger Woodard, in his work *Greek Writing from Knossos to Homer,* has used linguistic analysis to propose the theory that the Greek adaptation of the Phoenician consonantal alphabet took place in a bilingual setting on the island of Cyprus, where scribes were still using a syllabic script probably evolved from Minoan Linear A. Much academic debate still surrounds the date, location, and speed of the Greek adaptation of the Phoenician alphabet, but there is general consensus that the Greek historian, Herodotus, was essentially correct when he recorded in his *Histories* (written about 450 B.C.E.) that:

> The Greeks were taught these letters by the Phoenicians and adopted them, with a few alterations, for their own use, continuing to refer to them as "Phoenician things" [*phoinikeia*]—as was only right, as the Phoenicians had introduced them.[8]

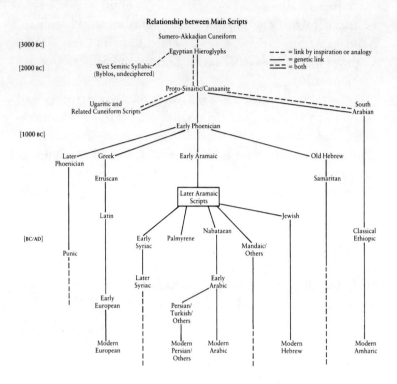

Figure 6. Relationship between main scripts. (Reprinted from John Healy, *The Early Alphabet,* 1990 © the British Museum, British Museum Press, used by permission.)

Greek tradition, as recounted by Herodotus, went even further and attributed the alphabet to a specific Phoenician individual named Cadmus, the founder of Thebes. Hence the letters came to be known as Cadmean letters (*kadmeia grammata*).[9] Other legends arose concerning the origin of the Greek alphabet, including a story that they were invented by Hermes, who allegedly saw a flight of cranes and decided that similar shapes could be used to represent sounds. Cranes fly in a V-like formation that readily evokes the angular characters of the early alphabets.[10] Hermes' counterpart in Egypt was the god Thoth, called Hermes Trismegistus by the Greeks, whose symbol was the crane-like white ibis, and to whom was also attributed the invention of writing. Another version is recorded by the Roman writer Caius Julius Hyginus, who wrote that the Moirai, or Fates, invented the first seven letters (the vowels); Palamedes, son of Nauplius, later invented eleven more; Epicharmus of Sicily then added two; and Simonides of Ceos contributed a further four.[11] Pliny wrote in his *Natural History* that Palamedes added four letters to the sixteen brought by Cadmus. These traditions indicate there may have been a specific individual named Palamedes who perfected the Greek alphabet by making changes to the Phoenician system.[12]

The Phoenicians gave each of their letters names, some derived from their pictographic origin, others simply as a mnemonic or memory aid, similar to our modern nursery alphabets; A for apple, B for bee, and so on.[13] Thus, the letter *aleph* in Phoenician means ox, *beth* means house, and *gimel* means a camel. In Greek, these foreign names had no meaning, and so they became slightly altered in pronunciation over time, so that *aleph, beth,* and *gimel* became *alpha, beta,* and *gamma.* The names of the first two letters give us our word *alphabet,* from *alphabetum,* a term first used by Tertullian (155-230 C.E.), one of the early Christian apologists generally known as the Church Fathers.[14]

			Ionia	Athens	Corinth	Argos	Euboea (cf. Etruscan)
A	α	a	AA	AA	AA	AA	AA
B	β	b	B	B	⊔	Ϲ	B
Γ	γ	g	Γ	Λ	<C	ΓΛ	<C
E	δ	d	Δ	Δ	Δ	D	DD
E	ε	e	ßE	ßE	B	ßE	ßE
F	ϝ	w	—	ß	ß	ßF	ß
Z	ζ	z	I	I	I	I	I
H	η	ē	⊟H	—	—	—	—
	|h|	h	—	⊟H	⊟H	⊟H	⊟H
Θ	θ	th	⊗⊕O	⊗⊕O	⊗⊕O	⊗⊕O	⊗⊕O
I	ι	i	I	I	ξ	I	I
K	κ	k	K	K	K	K	K
Λ	λ	l	ΓΛ	V	ΓΛ	⊢	V
M	μ	m	ΜM	ΜM	ΜM	ΜM	ΜΜM
N	ν	n	ΝN	ΝN	ΝN	ΝN	ΝN
Ξ	ξ	x	Ŧ	(XS)	Ŧ	ŦHH	X
O	o	o	O	O	O	O	O
Π	π	p	Γ	Γ	Γ	Γ	ΓΓ
M	—	s	—	—	M	M	M(?)
Q	ρ	q	φ	φ	φ	φ	φ
Π	ρ	r	PD	PR	PR	PR	P
Σ	σ ς	s	ξ	ς	—	ξ	ς
T	τ	t	T	T	T	T	T
Y	υ	u	VY	ΥΥV	ΥΥV	ΥΥV	ΥΥV
Φ	φ	ph	φ	φⅢ	φⅢ	φⅢ	φⅢ
X	χ	kh	X	X	X	X	ΥΨ
Ψ	ψ	ps	ΨV	(φS)	ΨV	V	(φS)
Ω	ω	ō	∩Ω	—	—	—	—

Figure 7. Some archaic Greek alphabets from the 8th to the 7th centuries B.C.E. (Reprinted from B. F. Cook, *Greek Inscriptions*, 1987 © the British Museum, British Museum Press, used by permission.)

It was the Greeks who invented the first real alphabet in the form we now use in the West by adding something the Phoenician system lacked—a set of pure vowels. In the Semitic consonantal alphabet, each of the letters could represent several sounds, depending upon the vowel sound (e.g., *ba, be, bi, bo, bu*) that was later denoted by diacritical points or marks between the letters. By separating the syllable into two distinct parts, consonant and vowel, the Greeks fundamentally improved on the syllabic alphabet. They adapted a few Phoenician letters representing consonants they did not use to use as the vowel sounds.

A form of *waw* became the letter *upsilon* (Y). This was used to represent the vowel sound U, and added to the end of the alphabet after *tau* (T). The Greeks also invented new signs for the double consonants *phi*, *chi*, and *psi* (Φ, X, Ψ), probably adapted from early forms of the letters *theta* and *kappa*, which they also added to the end of the alphabet.[15] The Ionic form of the alphabet included separate characters for the long and short forms of the letters O and E, one of the changes attributed by some to Simonides of Ceos (556–467 B.C.E.), a well-known Greek poet who supposedly first introduced the new letters into his manuscripts.[16] The Ionic dialect had no use for the Phoenician aspirant *cheth* (H), known as *heta* by many Greeks, and they therefore used this letter for the long form of E and called it *eta*. The O was opened at the bottom to produce Ω, "big O" (*o-mega*), in contrast to the old "little O" (*o-mikron*), and this letter was also added to the end of the alphabet. In adopting the Phoenician alphabet, the Greeks also seem to have assigned the wrong names to the Phoenician sibilants: *zayin*, *tzaddi*, *samekh*, and *shin*.[17] Other letters, such as *digamma*, *qoppa*, and *sanpi*, were dropped when their relative sounds were not used (see figure 7, page 12).[18]

At first, the Greeks wrote from right to left, in the fashion of the Phoenicians. They soon began to write in the opposite direction, however, if this proved more convenient. Some ancient Greek vases show writing in both directions. In several carved stone inscriptions, each new line begins under the last letter of the line above and runs in the opposite direction. Occasionally, the letters even face the other way. Since this method recalled the way in which a field was plowed, with the ox-drawn plow turning at the end of each furrow, it was called "ox-turning" (*boustrophedon*). Eventually, the Greeks came to write uniformly in the fashion we now use, from left to right only. Writing from left to right made it easier for a right-handed person to avoid smudging and to see the most recently formed characters.

Numerous variations in letter pronunciation arose as the Phoenician alphabet was adapted for different Greek dialects. The Ionic alphabet of Miletus was officially adopted at Athens in 403 B.C.E., and eventually became the standard throughout the Greek world. Another development was the use of accent marks, introduced by Aristophanes of Byzantium in the middle of the third century B.C.E. to assist students in pronunciation.[19] Lowercase forms of the Greek letters, or minuscules, were derived from the cursive style of writing, and are evidenced as early as the third century B.C.E.[20]

Greek writing had an important offshoot in Egypt, called Coptic. Following Alexander the Great's conquest of Egypt in the fourth century B.C.E., the Macedonians ruled there for three centuries, until Cleopatra, the only one of her line who bothered to learn the Egyptian language, was defeated, along with Antony, by Roman forces at Actium in 31 B.C.E. While upper-class Egyptians, therefore, spoke and wrote in Greek, the lower classes used Coptic. Coptic based 25 of its 32 letters on the Greek alphabet and added an extra seven letters from demotic, a cursive form of hieroglyphics, used for the Egyptian language. Both words "Coptic" and "Egypt" share the same etymology, each derived from the Egyptian *he-ku-Ptah*, meaning "the house of the spirit of Ptah," the Egyptian creator god. The use of Coptic was much advanced by the spread of Christianity in Egypt, and an extensive body of Coptic Christian magical papyri, incorporating numerous examples of Greek Qabalah, has recently been published.[21]

Another form on the Greek alphabet came to Rome. Colonists from the Greek island of Euboea carried their particular version of the alphabet to Italy, where it was adopted and modified by the resident Etruscans. This was, in turn, adopted later by their conquerors, the Romans, around the sixth century B.C.E. (see figure 8, page 15). The earliest Latin inscription, found on a

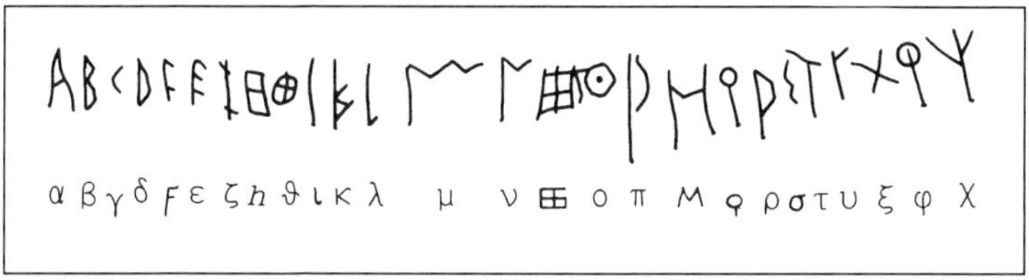

Figure 8. Greek alphabet from a vase at Formello, north of Rome. (Reprinted from A. O. Dilke, 1987 © the British Museum, British Museum Press, used by permission.)

brooch known as the Praeneste fibula (though some scholars regard it as a 19th-century forgery), is written from right to left, although another example from the sixth century B.C.E. is written *boustrophedon*. Like every race that received the alphabet, the Romans altered it to suit their own tongue.[22] Of the twenty-six Etruscan letters, the Romans adopted twenty-one, while some letters for which they had no use were retained as numbers.[23] After their conquest of Greece, the Romans added the letters Y and Z to assist in pronouncing Greek words. The Emperor Claudius, during his brief reign from 51 to 54 B.C.E., tried unsuccessfully to introduce three new letters, including an equivalent of the Greek letter *psi*, and another for the sound of our letter W.[24]

It is from this Roman alphabet that our own is derived, the letters J, U, and W being later additions. W was added in Anglo-Saxon writings of the seventh century C.E., derived by doubling the letter V, a fact reflected in its name, "double-U," as well as by its shape. Both J and U became established during the 16th century; J was developed from I, and U from V. Thus the English alphabet evolved through the medium of the Greek, Etruscan, and then Roman adaptations. Ultimately however, it derived from the Phoenician script in use over 3,000 years ago.

Notes to Chapter One

1 Homer, *Iliad*, VI; 168–9; Shakespeare, *Hamlet*, V, ii.

2 D. Diringer, *The Alphabet* (London: Hutchinson, 1948), p. 203.

3 D. Diringer, *Writing* (London: Hutchinson, 1962), p. 120; J. F. Healy, *The Early Alphabet* (London: British Museum Press, 1990), pp. 57–59.

4 Homer, *Odyssey*, XV; 415–6, S. H. Butcher and A. Lang, (trans.) (London: MacMillan, 1930), p. 253.

5 Herodotus, *Histories*, IV; 42.

6 A. R. Burn, *The Pelican History of Greece* (London: Pelican Books, 1966), p. 80; R. Woodard, *Greek Writing from Knossos to Homer* (New York: Oxford University Press, 1997), p. 219.

7 B. Powell, *Homer and the Origin of the Greek Alphabet* (Cambridge: Cambridge University Press, 1991); contra, see R. Woodard, *Greek Writing from Knossos to Homer*.

8 Herodotus, *Histories*, V; 60, A. de Selincourt (trans.) (London: Penguin, 1974), p. 361.

9 The name of Cadmus appears often in Greek legend, where his origin is generally connected with the East; see R. Graves, *The Greek Myths* (London: Pelican Books, 1955), chapters 58–59, and original sources there cited. K. Koutrovelis (*About Kadmos: Was he a Phoenician or a Greek?*, in *Davlos*, No. 137 (Athens: May 1993)) has interpreted the mythological evidence as suggesting a Greek origin; but since the Phoenician derivation of the Greek letter-forms is plain, Cadmus' origin is irrelevant.

10 R. Graves, *The White Goddess*, p. 227.

11 Hyginus, *Fables*, 277.

12 B. Powell, *Homer and the Origin of the Greek Alphabet*, p. 235.

13 D. Diringer, *The Alphabet*, p. 219.

14 D. Diringer, *The Alphabet*, p. 195.

15 A. C. Moorhouse, *The Triumph of the Alphabet* (New York: H. Schuman, 1953), p. 131; B. F. Cook, *Greek Inscriptions* (Berkeley: University of California Press, 1987), p. 9.

16 R. Graves, *The White Goddess*, p. 225.

17 The "confusion hypothesis" is propounded by Lillian Jeffrey in her authoritative work, *The Local Scripts of Archaic Greece* (Oxford: Oxford University Press, 1961). The Phoenician letter *samekh* was called *shin*, which, in Greek, became shortened in pronunciation to *xi* (Ξ); while the zig-zag letter *shin* was tilted on its side and called *samekh*, which became pronounced in Greek as *sigma* (Σ). The Phoenician letter *zayin* was wrongly called *tzaddi*. In Greek this came to be pronounced as *zeta* (Z); while *tzaddi* (originally written similar to the letter M) was wrongly called *zayin*, which came to be pronounced as *san*, but was not used in Ionic and was therefore dropped. Contra, see R. Woodard, *Greek Writing from Knossos to Homer*, pp. 138–156. Woodard proposes that the Greeks made no confusion with regard to the names of the Phoenician sibilant let-

ters, but created new names in the process of assigning altered sound values to them (compare the names *eta* and *zeta*; *pi* and *xi*).

18 A variant form of the Phoenician letter *waw*, known as the *digamma* because its shape resembled two letters *gamma* (Γ) placed on top of one another (F), came to be used to represent a consonantal U, similar to English W. The *digamma* letter was gradually discarded in Classical times, as the sound fell into disuse in the Ionic (Eastern Greek) dialect, and was retained as a numerical sign. It became gradually simplified in form until it was no more than a large comma, the *episemon* or *stigma* (ς), almost identical in appearance to a semi-compound letter known as *stau*, that was used in later Greek to represent the sound of S and T together. Derived from *tzaddi*, the archaic letter *sanpi* or *sampi* had its name coined by grammarians of the Byzantine period after the fact that this letter was in shape "like *pi*" (ως αν πι; [*h*]*os an pi*); it was dropped in later times in favor of *xi* or double *sigma*. Most local Greek alphabets used either *sigma* or *san*, but not both.

19 D. Diringer, *Writing*, p. 153.

20 A. C. Moorhouse, *The Triumph of the Alphabet*, p. 140. In this way, the letter *sigma* (Σ) also developed its alternate cursive form (C), in which the angles are removed and replaced with a simple curve, as also appears in its minuscule final form (ς).

21 M. Meyer and R. Smith (ed.), *Ancient Christian Magic—Coptic Texts of Ritual Power* (New York: HarperCollins, 1995).

22 On the Praeneste fibula, the sound F is represented by the combined letters FH, although, later, the H was dropped following Etruscan influence. Thus the Romans came to use the *digamma* (F), that represented a W sound in Greek, for the sound F, and instead used the letter *waw* (V) for both the consonant W and the vowel U. The Etruscans did not differentiate between the C and G sounds, so the Romans created the letter G by adding a tail to the cursive Etruscan form of *gamma* (C). They generally had no use for the letter *kappa* (K), and therefore this was dropped by Appius Claudius Censor in 312 B.C.E.

23 D. Diringer, *Writing*, pp. 165–166.

24 A. C. Moorhouse, *The Triumph of the Alphabet*, p. 139.

chapter two

THE ALPHABET AS NUMBER

y further extending the brilliant idea of the alphabet, the Greeks developed a symbolic system that employed the letters as number symbols. In the early history of all the great cultures of the ancient world, including Egypt and Mesopotamia, counting was accomplished by representing each unit with a single symbol repeated a set number of times. When this limit was reached, that set was replaced by a separate symbol. These symbols were then combined as required to express larger numbers. The division into sets and subsets was usually based on groups of ten (denary) to replicate counting on one's fingers. Some early Ugaritic, Aramaic, Arabic, and Phoenician inscriptions show numerals by means of such denary symbols; others spell out the numbers in full. This is

Figure 9. Moabite stone inscription of King Mesha, circa 850 B.C.E. (Reprinted from John Healy, *The Early Alphabet*, 1990 © the British Museum, British Museum Press, used by permission.)

true on the Moabite Stone, a famous early Semitic inscription from the ninth century B.C.E. commemorating the victory of King Moab over the Israelites (see figure 9, page 20).[1] Likewise, numerals are always spelled out in full in the Old Testament.

Alphabetic numerals were invented by the Greeks, perhaps at the eastern Greek city of Miletus on the coast of modern Turkey, possibly as early as the eighth century B.C.E.[2] The oldest surviving examples have been traced to vase graffiti from the sixth century B.C.E.[3] In ancient Greece there were in fact two significant types of numeration widely used—the Attic (also known as the Herodianic or acrophonic) and the Ionian (also known as the Milesian, Alexandrian, or alphabetic).

The Herodianic system derives its name from the fact it appears in inscriptions in Athens described by a second century C.E. grammatist named Herodianus. It may have developed as early as the seventh century B.C.E, but is best known in Attica from the middle of the fifth century B.C.E.[4] A single stroke, *iota* (I), was repeated for numbers up to four, then the letter *pi* (Π), for *pente* (five), was used; at ten, the symbol *delta* (Δ), as the initial letter of *deka* (ten), was used. Because the system was denary, a new letter was used for each power of ten: *eta* (H) for *hekaton* (100); *chi* (X) for *chilioi* (1,000); and *mu* (M) for *myrioi* (10,000). Thus the number 21,335 would be written as MMXHHHΔΔΔΠ. The Greeks also combined these symbols with the letter *pi* (Π) to create new symbols for multiples based on five. For 50, a tiny Δ (10) was placed inside the Π (5); for 500, a small H (100) was written inside the Π (see figure 10, page 22). The Herodianic system is also known as the acrophonic (*akro* means "topmost" or "upper," and *phone* means "sound"), since the letters used to represent numbers are the initial letters or sounds for those numbers.

The older and simpler Milesian, or alphabetic, system used every letter in the alphabet to represent a number. It came into general use during the Alexandrian age and continued beyond the Roman period into the Byzantine era. Three archaic letters (*digam-*

1 I		500 𐅅			*Examples*
5 Γ	(*pente*)	1000 X	(*khilioi*)		11 ΔI
10 Δ	(*deka*)	5000 𐅆			63 𐅄ΔIII
50 𐅄, 𐅄, 𐅄		10,000 M	(*myrioi*)		128 HΔΔΓIII
100 H	(*hekaton*)	50,000 𐅇			1601 X𐅅HI

Figure 10. Milesian alphabetic numerals. (Reprinted from A. O. Dilke, *Mathematics and Measurements,* 1987 © the British Museum, British Museum Press, used by permission.)

ma as 6, *qoppa* as 90, and *sanpi* as 900) continued to be used with the twenty-four of the classical Greek alphabet. This gave twenty-seven letters, enough symbols to represent the nine integers, nine multiples of ten, and nine multiples of a hundred (see figure 11).

The innovative idea of using sound symbols to denote numbers was later carried across the Mediterranean, during the period that followed the massive conquests of Alexander, known as the Hellenistic Age (338 to 30 B.C.E.). In Egypt, it seems to have been adopted officially at Alexandria during the reign of Ptolemy Philadelphus (246-221 B.C.E.).[5] The Milesian numerical system replaced all others in the lands of the Middle East during the centuries of Greek rule that followed the Macedonian conquest.

1 α	10 ι	100 ρ	1000 ͵α
2 β	20 κ	200 σ	10,000 M
3 γ	30 λ	300 τ	20,000 $\overset{\beta}{M}$
4 δ	40 μ	400 υ	
5 ε	50 ν	500 φ	*Examples*
6 ϝ	60 ξ	600 χ	11 ια
7 ζ	70 ο	700 ψ	63 ξγ
8 η	80 π	800 ω	128 ρκη
9 θ	90 ϙ	900 ϡ	1601 ͵αχα

Figure 11. Attic acrophonic numerals. (Reprinted from A. O. Dilke, 1987 © the British Museum, British Museum Press, used by permission.)

Egyptians, Persians, Phoenicians, Arabs, and Jews all eventually adopted the Greek system of using letters as numerals.

In addition to the acrophonic and alphabetic systems, a third form of numeration should also be mentioned. This uses the letters of the alphabet as the ordinal numerals 1 to 24: A = 1, B = 2, and so on, up to Ω = 24. This system was used in manuscripts to enumerate chapter numbers, as instanced, for example, in Aristotle's *Metaphysics*. This can also be seen on coins from Athens and Ptolemaic Egypt. The satirist Lucian (125-180 C.E.) tells how letters of the alphabet were used in similar fashion as lots at the Olympic Games, where competitors drew letters to determine their opponents and the order of their matches.

> A silver urn dedicated to the god is placed before them. Into this are thrown small lots, the size of beans, with letters on them. Two are marked *alpha*, two *beta*, two *gamma*, and so on in the same way, if there are more competitors, two lots always having the same letter. Each of the competitors comes up, offers a prayer to Zeus, puts his hand into the urn, and picks one of the lots. After him another does the same. A policeman stands by each one and holds his hand, not letting him read what the letter is which he has drawn. When all now have their own, the chief police officer, I think it is, or one of the National Judges themselves (I don't remember now) goes round the competitors, who are standing in a circle, and inspects their lots. In this way he matches one who has *alpha* to the other one who has drawn the other *alpha* for the wrestling or the pancratium. Similarly he matches the two *betas*, and the others with the same letter in the same way.[6]

The use of the Greek alphabetic system of numerals endowed every word written in the ancient alphabets, such as Greek, Arabic and Hebrew, with a numerical significance, since each of the letters could be added up to form a single number. The Greeks called this phenomenon *isopsephos* (*iso*- means "equal"; *psephos*, "pebble"), since it was common practice among the early Greeks to use patterns of pebbles or stones to learn arithmetic. Another word for pebbles (*kalkuli*) is the origin of our word "calculate."

A system of numerical word measures appears to have existed among the Babylonians as well. A single example occurs during the reign of Sargon II (727-707 B.C.E.) in an inscription on a clay tablet stating that the king built the wall of Khorsabad "equivalent to the value of his name" (*dur sharrukin*), calculated as 16,283 cubits.[7] The use of isopsephy was widespread in the writings of magicians and by the interpreters of dreams in the Hellenistic Age, when tradition held that Pythagoras had used isopsephy for the purposes of divination.[8]

Under the Roman Empire, the more cumbersome system of Roman numerals, which was similar to the Herodianic system, became widespread. The numerical ciphers D, M, C, and L used by the Romans were probably all derived from early Greek letter forms.[9] The use of Roman numerals was eventually replaced by the so-called "Arabic" numerals we now use. Arabic numerals are, in fact, letters belonging to an Indian alphabet brought to Spain by Arabs under Islam in the 12th and 13th centuries C.E. From Spain, their use spread into Europe. Our numeral 5 is actually the Indo-Bactrian letter P, the initial letter of Sanskrit *panchan*, or five (Greek, *pente*). Our numeral 4 is the letter "ch," the initial letter of Sanskrit *chatur* (Latin, *quatuor*); 7 is the letter S, the initial letter of *saptan*, seven (Latin, *septem*). Thus evolved the present separation between our alphabetic signs and our numerals. Our numerals were originally letters of an obscure Indo-Bactrian alphabet introduced to India 2400 years ago by the conquests of the Persian king, Darius.

Notes to Chapter Two

[1] D. Diringer, *Writing* (London: Hutchinson, 1962), p. 133; compare the account in *2 Kings* 3:4–27.

[2] W. Halsey (ed.), *"Numerals and Systems of Numeration,"* in *Collier's Encyclopaedia*.

[3] L. Jeffrey, *The Local Scripts of Archaic Greece* (Oxford: Oxford University Press, 1961), p. 327.

[4] B. F. Cook, *Greek Inscriptions* (Berkeley: University of California Press, 1987), p. 12.

[5] W. Halsey (ed.), *"Numerals and Systems of Numeration,"* in *Collier's Encyclopaedia*.

[6] Lucian, *Hermotimus*, vol. VI, 40. A. M. Harmon, trans. (London: William Heinemann Ltd., 1925), pp. 337–339.

[7] M. Farbridge, *Studies in Biblical and Semitic Symbolism* (Hoboken, NJ: Ktav Publishing House, 1970), p. 94.

[8] Iamblichus, *The Life of Pythagoras*, 19, in K. Guthrie, (trans.), *The Pythagorean Sourcebook and Library* (Grand Rapids, MI: Phanes Press, 1988), p. 81; B. Powell, *Homer and the Origin of the Greek Alphabet* (Cambridge: Cambridge University Press, 1991), p. 108.

[9] The topic is subject to ongoing debate, but one suggestion is that the letter *omega* (ω) was inverted to become M (the initial of *mille* = 1000); *phi* (Φ = 500) was halved to become D; *theta* (Θ) was halved to become C (the initial of *centum* = 100); and L was a bisected early form of the letter *chi* (X). Possibly it was the outspread fingers of the hand that gave the shape of the Roman figure V, and two such figures joined at their apexes gave X. See D. Diringer, *Writing*, p. 166; and M. Farbridge, *Studies in Biblical and Semitic Symbolism*, p. 92.

chapter three

PYTHAGORAS

nter Pythagoras, the son of a stone-cutter from the island of Samos, who lived around 580-500 B.C.E. Pythagoras was the first recorded figure in history to elevate numbers into the sphere of philosophy and religion. Pythagoras left no major writings behind him, but we have biographies of his life from later writers such as Porphyry and Iamblichus. There are also the so-called *Golden Verses of Pythagoras*, sayings preserved by the Neoplatonist Hierocles of Alexandria, a contemporary of Proclus. Pythagoras reputedly formulated the famous theorem that the square of the hypotenuse of a right-angled triangle was equal in area to the sum of the squares of the other two sides, although, in fact, this was already well-known in Egypt and Mesopotamia. He is also reputed to have studied the connection between music and number, probably noting the mathematical correlation obtained by stopping a lyre string at various points along its length.[1]

From this and other observations of the "sacred" geometry to be found in nature, and probably influenced by the importance of sacred numbers in Orphic mysticism, Pythagoras developed the idea that numbers were the key to the nature of the universe. He is quoted in his biography by Iamblichus as having laid down, in his *Sacred Discourse,* that "number is the ruler of forms and ideas, and the cause of gods and demons."[2] The teachings of Pythagoras drew a large following in the Greek colony of Croton in southern Italy where he went to live. Here, a kind of freemasonry evolved among the aristocracy, a fraternity with Pythagoras as its master. Its members dominated the politics of Croton, until they were massacred in a riot long after Pythagoras had died. His followers, however, spread the principles of Pythagoras' thought to other parts of the Greek world. The learned Aristotle (384-322 B.C.E.), who studied under Plato at Athens and later served as tutor to Alexander the Great, said in his *Metaphysics*:

> Pythagoreans applied themselves to mathematics, and were the first to develop this science; and through studying it, they came to believe that its principles are the principles of everything. And since numbers are by nature first among these principles, and they fancied that they could detect in numbers, to a greater extent than in fire and earth and water, many analogues of what is and comes into being—such and such a property being Justice, and such and such Soul or Mind, another Opportunity, and similarly, more or less, with all the rest—and since they saw further that the properties and ratios of the musical scales are based on numbers, and since it seemed clear that all other things in nature were modelled upon numbers, and that numbers are the ultimate things in the whole physical universe, they assumed the ele-

ments of number to be the elements of everything, and the whole universe to be a proportion or number.[3]

The Pythagoreans viewed the numbers from one to ten as the primordial powers that formed the base of all possible numbers. Aristotle expresses these ten principles in two columns of related qualities—limited and unlimited, odd and even, one and plurality, right and left, male and female, resting and moving, straight and crooked, light and darkness, good and bad, square and oblong. The number one was identified with the creator, and so represented male and strength; two represented the female and weakness; three was the number of the whole (beginning, middle, and end), four portrayed righteousness and stability; five was marriage as the combination of odd and even, male and female; six represented wholeness, peace, and sacrifice; seven was identified with joy, love, and opportunity; eight indicated steadfastness and balance; while nine signified completion.[4] The Pythagoreans regarded the number ten as especially sacred, and the decad was pictorially represented in the form of a four-tiered triangular pattern of ten dots known as the *tetraktys*, a sacred symbol upon which oaths were sworn. The *tetraktys* (from *tetra*, four, after its four levels) was drawn thus:

The triangular representation of the decad in the *tetraktys* probably had its origins in the arrangements of pebbles used to study mathematics, as well as in the fact that the first letter in the Greek word for the decad (ΔEKA, *deka*) was itself a triangle, and was used in the Herodianic numerical system as a symbol for the number ten.

The study of the mystical properties of the numbers in the decad became a separate branch of arithmetic known to the

Greeks as arithmology. Arithmology dealt with the attributes, epithets, and magical powers of these numbers, and identified them with a variety of animate and inanimate objects, as well as with gods and goddesses. There are frequent references to arithmology in the *Timaeus* of Plato (427–347 B.C.E.), and numerous accounts of it, including three books devoted wholly to the subject, have survived in more or less complete form.[5] As will be apparent to those familiar with the Hebrew Qabalah, the ten *sefiroth* are nothing other than abstract forms of the Pythagorean decad, further dramatic evidence of Greek influence on that school.

In astronomy, the Pythagoreans recognized the Earth, the Sun, the Moon, five other planets, and the "sphere of the fixed stars," as well as a supposed "counter-earth" revolving on the far side of a central fire at the heart of the universe, thus completing the sacred number ten. The distances and speeds of the planets' orbits created a harmony known as "the music of the spheres," that sounded to human ears like silence.[6] An interesting account of Pythagorean cosmogony and the music of the spheres has been preserved by the Roman lawyer and statesman Cicero (106–43 B.C.E.) in *The Dream of Scipio*, a work similar in many respects to "The Myth Of Er" found in *The Republic* by Plato, who provides us with the earliest discussion of astronomical matters.[7]

The intimate connection between letter and number made by the Greeks meant that the letters of the alphabet automatically inherited Pythagorean numerical symbolism. According to the biography of Pythagoras written by the eminent Neoplatonist, Iamblichus of Chalcis (242-326 C.E.), this enabled Pythagoras to invent divination by isopsephy, known today simply as Pythagorean numerology. This he taught to an elderly Scythian priest of Apollo by the name of Abaris.

> Abaris stayed with Pythagoras, and was compendiously taught physiology and theology; and instead of divining by the entrails of beasts, he revealed to him the art of prognos-

ticating by numbers, conceiving this to be a method purer, more divine, and more kindred to the celestial numbers of the Gods.[8]

The identification of number with the divine is also attributed to the Pythagoreans, as we know from the Greek historian Plutarch of Chaeronea (45-125 C.E.), in his work *On Isis and Osiris*.

> I myself believe that when these people called the monad Apollo, the dyad Artemis, the hebdomad Athena [the "virginal" prime number], and the first cube Poseidon [8 = 2 x 2 x 2], it is like what is established and assuredly enacted and written in sacred rites.[9]

This list of correspondences is much expanded in a work of the fourth century C.E. called *The Theology of Arithmetic*, commonly attributed to Iamblichus. In fact, the text is more a series of notes preserved by Iamblichus, and has been derived largely from a treatise on arithmology by the famous Pythagorean mathematician, Nicomachus of Gerasa (circa 100 C.E.), whose *Introduction to Arithmetic*, the first book to use Arabic numbers, became a standard textbook for a thousand years.[10] The monad is here variously described as akin to Zeus, Prometheus, and chaos; the dyad is the muse Erato (*Love*), and also Isis, justice, nature, and Rhea; the triad is prudence, and Hecate, the goddess of the Moon with its three phases; the tetrad is justice, Herakles, the four elements and the four seasons; the pentad is Nemesis, providence, Aphrodite, justice, Pallas, and aethyr, the fifth element or quintessence; the hexad is harmony, the universe (since *Kosmos* by isopsephy = 600, whose root is 6), and the muse Thaleia (*abundance*); the heptad is Athena, as the "virgin" prime number, and chance; the octad is the muse Euterpe (*delight*), and thus changeable (*eutreptos*) in nature; and the ennead is variously Oceanus, Prometheus, Hephaestus, Hera, and Hyperion.[11] The connection between deities and numbers was also made by the Babylonians, who attributed the number 20 to Shamash, or Utu, the god of the Sun; 30 to Sin, the Moon god; 40 to Ea, or Enki, the god of water; 50 to Bel, the patron god of Babylon; and 60 to the sky god, Anu.[12]

Pythagoreanism was to have a major influence on later Greek philosophy. The very word "philosophy" was, in actual fact, coined by Pythagoras, who was the first to describe himself as a "lover of wisdom" (*philo-sophos*). Pythagoreanism also formed the basis of Platonism. Late in the Hellenistic Age, it enjoyed a renaissance in what became known as Neopythagoreanism. The Neopythagoreans included Philo of Alexandria (circa 20 B.C.E.-40 C.E.), Apollonius of Tyana (circa 20-90 C.E.), and Numenius of Apamea (second century C.E.). Pythagorean doctrines flourished again in the form of Neoplatonism, an amalgam of Pythagoreanism and Platonism developed in the third century C.E. by Plotinus (204-270 C.E.). In all its various forms, the number mysticism of Pythagoras and his followers continues to recur throughout the history of the evolution of the Qabalah, and must be acknowledged as its ultimate origin.

Notes to Chapter Three

[1] A. R. Burn, *The Pelican History of Greece* (London: Pelican Books, 1966), p. 138.

[2] R. Graves, *The White Goddess* (London: Faber & Faber, 1961), p. 251, fn. 1.

[3] Aristotle, *Metaphysics*, 985b, in H. Treddenick, (trans.) (Cambridge: Harvard University Press, 1962), p. 33.

[4] W. Burkert, *Lore and Science in Ancient Pythagoreanism* (Cambridge: Harvard University Press, 1972), p. 467.

[5] F. E. Robbins, in D'Ooge (trans.), *Nicomachus* (New York and London: Macmillan, 1926), pp. 90–91, lists thirteen accounts.

[6] Aristotle, *On the Heavens*, II 9. For a lengthy citation of ancient authorities on the topic, see A. E. Pease, ed., *M. Tulli Ciceronis De Natura Deorum* (Cambridge: Harvard University Press, 1958), p. 1020.

[7] P. Bullock (trans.), *The Dream of Scipio* (London: Aquarian Press, 1983), p. 25; Plato, *Republic*, X 617b; *Timaeus*, VII 37.

[8] Iamblichus, *The Life of Pythagoras*, 19, in K. Guthrie (trans.), *The Pythagorean Sourcebook and Library* (Grand Rapids, MI: Phanes Press, 1988), p. 81.

[9] Plutarch, *On Isis and Osiris*, IX; 254f, in John Gwynn Griffiths (trans.) (Cardiff: Great Britain: University of Wales Press, 1970), p. 133. See also C. J. De Vogel, *Pythagoras and Early Pythagoreanism* (Assen: Van Gorcum and Co., 1966), p. 200.

[10] W. Rutherford, *Pythagoras—Lover of Wisdom*, (London: Aquarian Press, 1984), p. 104.

[11] R. Waterfield (trans.), *The Theology of Arithmetic* (London: Phanes Press, 1988).

[12] M. Farbridge, *Studies in Biblical and Semitic Symbolism* (Hoboken, NJ: Ktav Publishing House, 1970), p. 142.

chapter four

THE VOWELS AND
THE PLANETS

The earliest observers of the heavens noted a group of "stars" that, unlike the constellations (or "fixed" stars), moved. These were called "wanderers" (*planetes*) by the Greeks, from whence we derive our word "planet." Babylonian astronomers eventually observed the five nearest "wanderers." When considered together with the Sun and Moon, this gave a group of seven planets. The Greeks received their facts about the planets from the Babylonians, including the association of the planets with individual gods that is still preserved in the names of the Graeco-Roman deities given to the planets. The seven planets were quickly associated with the fact that there were seven Greek vowels. These came to represent the powers of the planetary gods. The connection first occurs in an arithmological treatise, *On Sevens*, attributed to the famous physician Hippocrates (circa 460-377 B.C.E.), from whom the Hippocratic Oath takes its name.[1] Not long afterward, Aristotle (384-322 B.C.E.) refers to the fact that the vowels and other letters of the Greek alphabet had various sets of symbolic correspondences, including the planets and musical notes.

> There are seven vowels, seven strings to the scale, seven Pleiades . . . and seven heroes who attacked Thebes . . . [The Pythagoreans] also assert that *xi*, *psi* and *zeta* are concords . . . because there are only three double consonants, and . . . there are three concords. . . . And they point out that the interval from *alpha* to *omega* in the alphabet is equal to that from the lowest note of a flute to the highest, whose number [twenty-four] is equal to that of the whole system of the universe.[2]

The above passage from Aristotle provides us with our earliest reference to a complete set of nonnumerical correspondences for each of the twenty-four letters of the Greek alphabet, namely the musical notes of the flute. It will be remembered that Aristotle also recorded that the connection between music and the heavens had been made by the Pythagoreans. The three "double letters," *zeta*, *xi*, and *psi* (Z, Ξ, and Ψ) were so called because they each represented the sounds of two other letters combined (*ds*, *ks*, and *ps*) and could be written as ΔΣ, ΚΣ, and ΠΣ respectively. The sounds of the letters Ξ and Ψ, introduced by Simonides of Ceos and adopted at Athens in 403 B.C.E., had previously been written in this way as two letters, ΚΣ and ΠΣ.

The other change Simonides made to the Greek alphabet was the distinction between the long and short forms of the vowels E (*eta* and *epsilon*) and O (*omicron* and *omega*). Therefore, the association between the vowels and the planets could not have been made before 403 B.C.E., when the additional vowels *epsilon* and *omega* were adopted into the alphabet, since, before that time, there were only five vowels. This explains the comment in Hyginus' *Fables* that the letters added by Simonides were "connected with Apollo's lyre," which had seven strings.[3]

Because the orbits of the planets created the "music of the spheres," according to Pythagoras, and, following him, were also equated with the seven notes of the major scale by Plato in "The Myth of Er," the seven vowels were naturally seen as corresponding to the musical scale.[4] We therefore find magical invocations from Alexandrian Egypt containing statements such as: "In your seven-lettered name is established the harmony of the seven sounds";[5] and "I hymn your holy power in a musical hymn, ΑΕΗΙΟΥΩΩΩ."[6] One ritual even sets out instructions for the recitation of the seven vowels, and also incorporates a further set of correspondences, namely the seven directions of east, north, west, south, up, down, and center.

> Speaking to the rising sun, stretch out your right hand to the left and your left hand likewise to the left and say "A." To the North, putting forward only your right fist, say "EE." Then to the West, extending both hands in front of you, say "HHH." To the South, holding both on your stomach, say "IIII." To the Earth, bending over and touching the ends of your toes, say "OOOOO." Looking into the Air, having your hands on your heart, say "**YYYYYY**." Looking up to Heaven, having both hands on your head, say "**ΩΩΩΩΩΩΩ**."[7]

A first account of the usage of such a chant is found in the writings of the first century B.C.E. Alexandrian philosopher Demetrius, who, when discussing the elision of vowels and hiatus in his essay *On Style*, wrote:

> In Egypt the priests, when singing hymns in praise of the gods, employ the seven vowels, which they utter in succes-

sion; and the sound of these is so euphonious that men listen to it in place of the flute and lyre.[8]

Philo Judaeus (circa 30 B.C.E.–45 C.E.) expands on the connection in his essay, *On the Creation of the World*, while adding observations on grammar.

> The number seven exerts its influence . . . in those noblest of sciences, grammar and music. For the seven-stringed lyre, corresponding to the choir of the planets, produces notable melodies, and it is not going too far to say that the lyre is the rule to which the making of all musical instruments conforms. And among the letters in grammar there are seven properly called vowels or "vocals," since as is obvious they can be sounded by themselves, and when joined with others can produce articulate sounds; for on the one hand they fill up what is lacking in the "semi-vowels," rendering the sounds full and complete, and on the other hand they change the nature of the "voiceless" (the consonants) by breathing into them something of their own power, that it may now be possible to pronounce letters before incapable of pronunciation.[9]

In his *Manual of Harmony*, Nicomachus of Gerasa provides us with a similar passage regarding the connection between the vowels, the planets, and music.[10]

> And the tones of the seven spheres, each of which by nature produces a particular sound, are the sources of the nomenclature of the vowels. These are described as unpronounceable in themselves and in all their combinations by wise men since the tone in this context performs a role analogous to that of the monad in number, the point in geometry, and the letter in grammar. However, when they are combined with

the materiality of the consonants just as soul is combined with body and harmony with strings—the one producing a creature, the other notes and melodies—they have potencies which are effacious and perfective of divine things. Thus whenever the theurgists are conducting such acts of worship they make invocation symbolically hissing, clucking, and inarticulate and discordant sounds.[10]

The ancient connection between the seven Greek vowels and music, reflected in the symbolism attached to Apollo's lyre and the music of the spheres, has been well researched and documented in two recent books on the Pythagorean-Platonic conception of the harmonic universe: *The Music of the Spheres*, by New York music critic Jamie James, and *The Mystery of the Seven Vowels*, by Joscelyn Godwin, Professor of Music at Colgate University.

Although we know from Hippocrates and Aristotle that the seven vowels were attributed to the planets by the early fourth century B.C.E., we have to look further to find which vowel was connected with any given planet. The Greek historian Plutarch of Chaeronea (45–125 C.E.), who held a priesthood at Delphi when Greece was under Roman rule, wrote an essay titled *On the E at Delphi*, in which he records that, in addition to the well-known inscriptions at the famous Delphic oracle and ancient temple of Apollo ("know thyself" and "avoid extremes"—ΓΝΩΘΙ ΣΑΥΤΟΝ and ΜΗΔΕΝ ΑΓΑΝ), there was also a representation of the letter *epsilon* (E). Greek coins have also been found that show the E suspended between the middle columns of the temple (see figure 12, page 40).[11] Among the reasons put forward by Plutarch's speaker for the existence of the E on Apollo's is the following:

> There are seven vowels in the alphabet and seven stars that have an independent and unconstrained motion; E is the second in order of the vowels from the beginning, and the

Sun the second planet after the Moon, and practically all Greeks identify Apollo with the Sun.[12]

To understand this passage, it must be remembered that early Greek philosophers, such as Plato and Aristotle, thought of the universe as geocentric, with the Moon orbiting next to the Earth, followed by the Sun, then the "wandering stars" (Venus, Mercury, Mars, Jupiter, and Saturn), and last, the "fixed stars."[13] The planets were arranged according to how long it took them to make a circuit through the zodiac, with a longer time corresponding to a greater distance. The association of the letter E at Apollo's ancient temple in Delphi with the Sun, as recounted by Plutarch, accords with this early Platonic order of the planets, in which the Sun was "the second planet after the Moon."

A different geocentric system, in which the Sun was placed as the fourth of the planets, is first recorded in the time of Archimedes (287–212 B.C.E.).[14] This later order (Earth, Moon, Mercury, Venus, Sun, Mars, Jupiter, Saturn, and fixed stars) is often referred to as the Ptolemaic system, after its codification by the famous ancient astrologer Claudius Ptolemaeus (100–178 C.E.) in his influential collection of astronomical and astrological

Figure 12. Coins from Delphi with the letter E and the Temple of Apollo. (Reprinted from F. W. Imhoof-Blumer and Percy Gardner, *Ancient Coins Illustrating Lost Masterpieces of Greek Art,* Chicago: Argonaut, 1964.)

lore known as the *Almagest* and *Tetrabiblos*. The Ptolemaic system, the same as that we find in Cicero's *Dream of Scipio*, became the standard in astronomy until Copernicus re-asserted the heliocentric theory of the Pythagoreans. Because the seven vowels as symbols of the planets almost always appear as a collective group, the exact planetary attribution of specific vowels was probably not static, but is likely to have changed along with the ancients' perception of the order of the planets, from the Platonic to the Ptolemaic.[15]

A specific set of correspondences is made to the seven heavens of the Gnostics by Marcus, who, according to the early Church Father Irenaeus of Lyons (125–203 C.E.), connected these heavens to the vowels in the following order:

> And the first heaven indeed pronounces *Alpha*, the next to this *Epsilon*, the third *Eta*, the fourth, which is also in the midst of the seven, utters the sound of *Iota*, the fifth *Omicron*, the sixth *Upsilon*, the seventh, which is also fourth from the middle, utters the element *Omega*.[16]

The seven heavens were loosely connected to the spheres of the planets and were ruled by various angels or powers, whose order, names, and qualities varied widely in different Gnostic texts. The supreme deity was seen as living above the sphere of the seven planets in an eighth region, called the Ogdoas.

Another writer bearing the name of Porphyry (not to be confused with the famous Neoplatonist of that name) wrote a commentary on Dionysius of Thrace's *Art of Grammar*, in which he records that *alpha* was consecrated to Venus, *iota* to the Sun, *omicron* to Mars, *upsilon* to Jupiter, and *omega* to Saturn.[17] The consecration of the first vowel, *alpha,* to Venus is curious, unless it was done under the acrophonic principle known as *notarichon*, as the initial letter of Aphrodite (ΑΦΡΟΔΙΤΗ)—in which case, *epsilon* (Ε) could have been connected either to the Moon, as the initial letter of Hecate (EKATH), or Mercury, as the initial letter of Hermes (ΕΡΜΗΣ). Joscelyn Godwin is probably correct in his conclusion that the attribution of the letter *alpha* to Venus is an error, and that the following set of attributions, with the letters following their natural sequence in relation to the Ptolemaic order, was that usually used in the Hellenistic Age and thereafter:[18]

Greek Letter	Gnostic Heaven	Planet	God or Goddess
A	First	Moon	Selene or Hecate
E	Second	Mercury	Hermes
H	Third	Venus	Aphrodite
I	Fourth	Sun	Helios
O	Fifth	Mars	Ares
Y	Sixth	Jupiter	Zeus
Ω	Seventh	Saturn	Chronos

It is worth noting here that the planets were also assigned to the 24 hours of the day, and this arrangement determined the order of the days in our week, as explained by O. Neugebauer in *The Exact Sciences in Antiquity*:

> The Greek system . . . follows the model which arranges the planets in depth according to their periods of sidereal rotation. This is reflected even in the arrangement of days of the

planetary week which we still use today. Here the Sun is placed between Mars and Venus, and the Moon below Mercury. Every one of the 24 hours of a day is given a "ruler" following this sequence. Beginning, e.g., with the Sun for the first hour one obtains:

DAY 1	hour 1 Sun	hour 2 Venus	hour 3 Mercury	hour 4 Moon	hour 5... Saturn	hour 24 Mercury
DAY 2	hour 1 Moon	hour 2 Saturn	hour 3 Jupiter	... ...	... ...	hour 24 Jupiter
DAY 3	hour 1 Mars	hour 2 Sun ...	... ...	... ...	... ...	... ...

The "ruler" of the first hour is then considered to be the ruler of the day and thus one obtains for seven consecutive days the following rulers:

• Sun • Moon • Mars • Mercury
• Jupiter • Venus • Saturn

which is the sequence of the days of the week and also the arrangement of the planets in Hindu astronomy. Here we have a system which is obviously Greek in origin not only because it is based on the arrangement of the celestial bodies according to their distance from the earth but also because it supposes a division of the day into 24 hours, a form of reckoning which is not Babylonian but a Hellenistic product of ultimately Egyptian origin. It is totally misleading when this order is called "Chaldean" in modern literature.[19]

The seven-day week, which took its arrangement from the seven planets, came into widespread use in the Mediterranean world only during the first and second centuries C.E. M. H. Farbridge has noted that the importance of the number seven in Greek and Semitic symbolism predates the astrological conception of a group of seven planets (as opposed to five), and that, therefore, the seven-day week probably originated from dividing the lunar month of twenty-eight days into quarters.[20] In different parts of the Roman Empire, the names of the days followed different sequences in accordance with various astrological schemes, but Sunday eventually became established as the first day of the week when the Emperor Constantine recognized it as the official day of rest in 321 C.E.[21] Not suprisingly, the days of the week were also subject to numerological interpretation, in terms of Pythagorean number symbolism, according to their sequence. Thus John Lydus, a civil servant and antiquarian who lived during the first half of the sixth century C.E. in the late Roman Empire or Byzantine Age, used Pythagorean sources to associate the fourth day with the fourth planet, the tetrad, the four positions of the Sun, and the four phases of the Moon.[22]

The connection between the vowels and the planets imme-diately made these seven Greek letters part of a vast range of plan-etary "sympathies" used in ancient astrology, alchemy, and magic, including incenses, precious stones, metals, flowers, herbs, colors, musical notes, emotions, virtues, and vices. Alchemy, for instance, which originated in Hellenistic Egypt, was among the major con-tributors to the extensive system of Qabalistic correspondences of which the letters of the alphabet were part. The works of the early Hellenistic alchemists show strong influences from magic and Gnosticism, and were often filled with strange symbols or were deliberately written in cryptic alphabets.[23] As noted by the French scientist Marcellin Berthelot, in his study of chemistry in the ancient world:

> Alchemy steadily extended itself, at first by the connection established between the metals and the planets, drawn from the fact that they were alike in lustre, colour and number.

We then join to this late discovery an earlier one: that is the number seven, a sacred number which one finds everywhere, in the days of the week, in the number of the planets and their heavenly zones, in their corresponding metals, the colours, the strings of the lyre and their musical notes, the vowels of the Greek alphabet, and also in the number of stars in the Great Bear, the sages of Greece, and the gates of Thebes and the leaders who besieged them, after Aeschylus.[24]

An example of this association between the planets, metals, colors and the days of the week is found in an account of Mithraism given by the pagan author Celsus in his *True Doctrine*, an attack on Christianity written around 178 C.E. Plutarch records that the rites and mysteries of the cult of the bull-slaying solar god, Mithra or Mithras, descended from Persian Zoroastrianism, were introduced into the Roman world by pirates from Cilicia (modern Turkey).[25] The values of self-sacrifice, truth, loyalty, and honor in Mithraism appealed greatly to the sailors, officers, and soldiers of the Roman legions, who, by the second century C.E., had established temples to Mithras the Redeemer, also known as the Unconquered Sun (*Sol Invictus*), throughout the Roman Empire. This widespread influence made Mithraism the main contender with Christianity for the title of official religion of the Roman Empire, until the conversion of the Emperor Constantine settled the issue in 337 C.E. Traces of the long struggle with Mithraism survive in the celebration of the birth of the Redeemer on December 25th, which, in the Julian calendar, was reckoned as the winter solstice and was celebrated by the Egyptians as the birth of the newborn Sun. Since Mithras was identified with the Sun, this date was also used by his followers to celebrate his nativity, Mithramas. In view of the popularity of this nativity festival, the early Christians, who did not know or celebrate the birthday of Jesus, decided to adopt it as well, rather than be upstaged annually by their competitors.[26] This is the origin of the festival today celebrated as Christmas.

To return to the matter of planetary correspondences, Celsus describes the ascent of the soul through the seven heavens according to the Mithraic mysteries. This ascent was also reflected in seven stages of Mithraic initiation: Raven, Nymphus, Soldier, Lion, Persian, Courier of the Sun, and Father. Much of what Celsus wrote was preserved by Origen (circa 185-254 C.E.). Generally viewed as the preeminent theologian among the early Church Fathers, Origen eventually died an old man, after lengthy torture during persecutions in Caesarea. Origen lived a life so austere that he even castrated himself, reputedly on the strength of Matthew 19:12— "There are eunuchs who have made themselves eunuchs for the kingdom of heaven's sake. He who is able to accept it, let him accept it." In reply to Celsus' *True Doctrine*, Origen wrote *Against Celsus*, perhaps the greatest early Christian apology, in which the following account of planetary correspondences to the metals appears:

These truths are obscurely represented by the teaching of the Persians and by the mystery of Mithras which is of Persian origin. For in the latter there is a symbol of two orbits in heaven, the one being that of the fixed stars and the other that assigned to the planets, and of the soul's passage through these. The symbol is this. There is a ladder with seven gates and at its top is an eighth gate. The first of these gates is of lead, the second of tin, the third of bronze, the fourth of iron, the fifth of an alloy, the sixth of silver, and the seventh of gold. They associate the first with Kronos (Saturn), taking lead to refer to the slowness of the star; the second with Aphrodite (Venus), comparing her with the brightness and softness of tin; the third with Zeus (Jupiter), as the gate that has a bronze base and which is firm; the fourth with Hermes (Mercury), for both iron and Hermes are reliable for all works and make money and are hard-working; the fifth with Ares (Mars), the gate which as a result of the mixture is uneven and varied in quality; the sixth with the Moon as the silver gate; and the seventh with the Sun as the golden gate, these metals resembling their colours.[27]

The earliest authentic and reliable author on alchemy is Zosimus of Panopolis in Egypt (present day Akhmim), whose writings date from around 300 C.E.[28] The works of Zosimus were divided into sections designated under letters of the alphabet, including one entitled *On the Letter Omega*, in which Zosimus uses the technique of *notarichon* (abbreviation) to connect *omega* with the ocean, as the initial letter of the Greek god Oceanus, from which the associated English word is clearly derived. He also confirms the connection between the vowel, *omega,* and Chronos, or Saturn:

> The letter Omega is round, formed of two parts, and belongs to the seventh zone, that of Saturn according to the language of corporeal beings; but according to the language of the incorporeal it is something other, inexplicable, which only Nicotheus the Hidden has known. Now, in the language of corporeal beings, this letter is called Ocean, the origin and seed of all the gods.[29]

The Greeks used the same word, *stoicheia* (from στειχω, "to march in a row"), to denote not only atomic elements as the order of essential constituents of matter, but also alphabetic letters, since they occurred in a sequence and were the essential constituents of speech.[30] The vowels, ΑΕΗΙΟΥΩ, also became known as the elements (*stoicheia*), since they represented the combined forces of the seven planets or "elements" in the Kosmos of Hellenistic theology.[31] These powers or elements are among those referred to by Paul in Galatians 4:8–9:

47

But then, indeed, when you did not know God, you served those which by nature are not gods. But now after you have known God, or rather are known by God, how is it that you turn again to the weak and beggardly elements [*stoicheia*], to which you desire again to be in bondage?[32]

As the mystic signs of the planets, the seven vowels, ΑΕΗΙΟΥΩ, are repeated in many spells and charms. They also appear in the great *Mithras Liturgy*, unearthed by Dieterich from a magical papyrus in Paris, as "the Seven Deathless Lords of the Universe."[33] They are also called "the seven letters of the magicians,"[34] or "the heptagram." Often, they are represented in the form of a square, a diamond, or a triangle, thus:

$$A$$
$$E\ E$$
$$H\ H\ H$$
$$I\ I\ I\ I$$
$$O\ O\ O\ O\ O$$
$$Y\ Y\ Y\ Y\ Y\ Y$$
$$\Omega\ \Omega\ \Omega\ \Omega\ \Omega\ \Omega\ \Omega$$

The seven-voweled name of ΑΕΗΙΟΥΩ also appears in Greek and Coptic magical papyri in conjunction with the oft-invoked Jewish god, IAO or IEOU. This derived from the Greek attempt to write what they called the *tetragrammaton,* or four-lettered name used by the Jews for their supreme deity, IHVH (יהוה) or Yahweh, wrongly rendered in Elizabethan English as "Jehovah."[35] Due to the fact that it was compiled entirely of the mystic vowels, the name IAΩ readily lent itself to symbolic analysis. The letter *iota*, being the middle of the seven vowels, could be seen as representing the Sun or God of Light, while the last two letters, *alpha* and *omega*, signified the beginning and end.[36] In the Gnostic text known as the *Pistis Sophia*, Jesus gives the following analysis of the name IAO to his disciples:

48

This is its interpretation: Iota, the Universe came out; Alpha, they will turn them; Omega, will become the completion of all completions.[37]

In a later Coptic Christian papyrus from around 600 C.E., God the Father even appears with the Greek vowels tattooed across his chest.[38] Another manuscript from the same collection, designed to protect a pregnant woman from evil forces, sets out seven words of power and the seven archangels as magically associated with the vowels.[39]

A	EIA	Michael	Peace
E	EIIAK	Gabriel	Grace
H	MIIAK	Raphael	Power
I	SEMIIAK	Suriel	Will
O	ARTORE	Raguel	Truth
Y	ARTORAN	Anael	Glory
Ω	NARTORAK	Saraphuel	Healing

In later Christian ceremonial magic, the archangels came to be used in place of the planets in invocations and amulets. Of the seven archangels, only Michael and Gabriel are mentioned in the Bible, and Raphael appears in the apocryphal book Tobit.[40] The names of the other archangels are taken from Jewish sources, but there are many variations on the above list.[41]

Notes to Chapter Four

1 J. Mansfield, *The Pseudo-Hippocratic Tract ΠΕΡΙ ΕΒΔΟΜΑΔΩΝ Ch. 1–11 and Greek Philosophy* (Assen: Van Gorcum and Co., 1971), pp. 138–146.

2 Aristotle, *Metaphysics*, Book N, 1093a-b, in H. Treddenick (trans.), (Cambridge: Harvard University Press, 1962), pp. 300–301.

3 R. Graves, *The White Goddess* (London: Faber & Faber, 1961), p. 227.

4 Plato, *Republic*, X; 617b; J. James, *The Music of the Spheres* (London: Abacus, 1995), pp. 46–51.

5 K. Preisendanz (ed.), *Papyri Graecae Magicae* (Leipzig: Teubner, 1928); republished by H. D. Betz (ed.), *The Greek Magical Papyri in Translation* (Chicago: University of Chicago Press, 1986); often abbreviated, including hereafter, as "*PGM*"; *PGM*, XII; 775–6.

6 *PGM*, XIII; 630.

7 *PGM*, XIII; 824–842.

8 Demetrius, *On Style*, 71, in W. Rhys Roberts (trans.), (London: William Heinemann Ltd., 1973), p. 347.

9 Philo Judaeus, *On the Creation of the World*, 126, in F. H. Colson and G. H. Whitaker (trans.), (London: William Heinemann Ltd., 1929), p. 99.

10 Nicomachus, *Harmonicum Enchiridion*, in Jan, Carl (ed.), *Musici Scriptores Graeci*, p. 276, in S. Gersh (trans.), *From Iamblichus to Eriugena* (Leiden: Brill, 1978), p. 295.

11 F. W. Imhoof-Blumer and P. Gardner, *A Numismatic Commentary on Pausanias* (Chicago: Argonaut, 1964), plate x, nos xxii–xxiii, p. 119; originally published in *Journal of Hellenic Studies*, vols. 6–8 (1885–7).

12 Plutarch, *Moralia*, V; 386, in F. C. Babbitt (trans.) (London: William Heinemann, Ltd., 1936), p. 207.

13 Plato, *The Republic*, X; 616–7.

14 W. Burkert, *Lore and Science in Ancient Pythagoreanism* (Cambridge: Harvard University Press, 1972), p. 318.

15 See for example Macrobius, *Commentary on the Dream of Scipio*, I; 6, 70.

16 Irenaeus, *Against Heresies*, I; 16, in R. M. Grant (trans.), *Irenaeus of Lyons* (London: Routledge, 1985), p. 82.

17 J. Bidez, *Vie de Porphyre* (Hildesheim: G. Olms, 1964), appendix, p. 72.

18 J. Godwin, *The Mystery of the Seven Vowels* (Grand Rapids, MI: Phanes Press, 1991), pp. 20–21, 64.

19 O. Neugebauer, *The Exact Sciences in Antiquity* (New York: Dover, 1967), p. 169.

20 M. H. Farbridge, *Studies in Biblical and Semitic Symbolism* (Hoboken, NJ: Ktav Publishing House, 1970), pp. 132–134.

21 M. Maas, *John Lydus and the Roman Past* (London: Routledge, 1992), pp. 57–58.

22 Johannis Lydus, *On the Months*, II; 9.

23 M. Berthelot and C. Ruelle, *Collection des Anciens Alchimistes Grecs* (Paris: 1888), p. 156, fig. 29.

24 M. Berthelot, *La Chimie Des Anciens et du Moyen Age* (Paris: 1893), p. 74, translation by this author.

25 Plutarch, *Life of Pompey*, XXIV; 1–8. For a useful collection of the ancient authorities, see also M. Meyer (ed.), *The Ancient Mysteries—A Sourcebook* (San Francisco: HarperSanFrancisco, 1987), pp. 197–221.

26 J G. Frazer, *The Golden Bough* (London: Macmillan Press, 1922), chapter 37.

27 Origen, *Against Celsus*, VI; 22, in H. Chadwick (trans.) (Cambridge: Cambridge University Press, 1980).

28 R. Patai, *The Jewish Alchemists* (Princeton: Princeton University Press, 1994), p. 52; J. Doresse, *The Secret Books of the Egyptian Gnostics* (Rochester, VT: Inner Traditions International, 1986), p. 99.

29 Zosimus, *Upon the Letter Omega*, in M. Berthelot and C. Ruelle, *Collection des Anciens Alchimistes Grecs*, p. 221; from J. Doresse (trans.), *The Secret Books of the Egyptian Gnostics*, p. 100. The Greek writings attributed to Zosimus are transcribed and translated into French by Berthelot and Ruelle; and an annotated English translation has been made by H. M. Jackson, *Zosimus of Panopolis on the Letter Omega* (Missoula, MT: 1978). It is misleading to say that "he devoted a treatise to every letter of the alphabet" (J. Doresse, *The Secret Books of the Egyptian Gnostics*, p. 278). Zosimus was simply using the Greek letters according to their ordinal system of numbering, although sometimes (as here) alluding in his text to the symbolism attached to the relevant letter.

30 B. Powell, *Homer and the Origin of the Greek Alphabet* (Cambridge: Cambridge University Press, 1991), pp. 235–236.

31 G. Murray, *Five Stages of Greek Religion* (London: Watts and Co., 1935), p. 142.

32 Professors Robert Eisenman and Michael Wise see Paul as referring to the observation of calendrical notations by various Jewish sects; *The Dead Sea Scrolls Uncovered* (New York: Penguin Books, 1992), p. 223.

33 G. Murray, *Five Stages of Greek Religion*, p. 146.

34 *PGM*, LXIII; 6–7; *PGM*, XIII; 760.

35 Another substitute for the tetragrammaton was "PIPI," probably because of the physical resemblance of the Greek letters ΠΙΠΙ to the Hebrew letters יהוה; S. Lieberman, *Greek in Jewish Palestine* (New York: The Jewish Theological Seminary, 1942), p. 120 fn. 38; cited in H. Betz, *The Greek Magical Papyri in Translation* (Chicago: University of Chicago Press, 1986), p. 49 fn. 85. Regarding the name IAO, see also G. Scholem, *Origins of the Kabbalah* (Princeton: Princeton University Press, 1990), pp. 32–33, fn. 55, and the sources cited there.

36 J. Godwin, *The Mystery of the Seven Vowels*, pp. 63–67.

37 G. Horner (trans.), *Pistis Sophia* (London: Macmillan, 1924), p. 180.

[38] M. Meyer and R. Smith (ed.), *Ancient Christian Magic—Coptic Texts of Ritual Power* (New York: HarperCollins, 1995), p. 280.

[39] Meyer and Smith (ed.), *Ancient Christian Magic,* pp. 124 and 316.

[40] Tobit, IV; 1.

[41] Meyer and Smith (ed.), *Ancient Christian Magic,* p. 388.

chapter five

THE CONSONANTS, THE ELEMENTS, AND THE ZODIAC

eferences to the elements can be found in the teachings of the earliest Greek philosophers. Thales (circa 624–546 B.C.E.) thought that the basic matter of the universe was water; Anaximenes (circa 585–524 B.C.E.) believed it was air; and Heraclitus (circa 544–484 B.C.E.) considered it to be fire. The elements were first considered as a group of four by Empedocles (circa 495–435 B.C.E.): earth (*ge*); fire (*pyr*); water (*hydor*); and air (*aither*). It needs to be noted, in view of later developments, that Empedocles did not use the word *aer* (AHP) to refer to the element we know as air (from which its name is clearly derived). Instead, he used the word *aither* (AIΘHP). The word *aither* meant "air" in Greek until the fourth century B.C.E., whereas *aer* referred only to moist air, mist, or cloud. Later, *aither* came to refer only to the highest and most exalted form of air, and eventually, with the Stoics, even to a form of fire. The meaning of *aer* expanded correspondingly to the sense in which we now understand it.[1] The element *aer* (AHP) also formed an anagram with the name of the goddess Hera (HPA), and is so used in a pun by Homer in the *Iliad*.[2]

Plato later ascribed the four elements to the regular polyhedrons, also known as the Platonic, or perfect, solids because each of their faces are polygons of the same shape and size. Euclid (circa 300 B.C.E.) proved the geometrical fact that only five solids fit this description: the cube, with four square faces; the tetrahedron, octahedron, and icosahedron, having four, eight, and twenty equilateral triangles, respectively; and the dodecahedron, with twelve pentagons. Plato attributed the cube to earth, the pyramid (or tetrahedron) to fire, the octahedron to air, and the icosahedron to water, The dodecahedron was "used for embroidering the constellations on the whole heaven."[3] Proclus, in his commentary on the first book of Euclid's *Elements*, records that the four elements were connected to the gods by Philolaos, a Pythagorean of Croton, or Metapontum, during the late fifth century B.C.E.

> Rightly, then, Philolaos dedicated the angle of the triangle to the four gods Kronos, Hades, Ares and Dionysus, since he includes within their province the entire fourfold ordering of the cosmic elements derived from the heavens or from the four segments of the zodiacal circle. Kronos gives being to all the moist and cold essences, Ares engenders every fiery nature, Hades has control of all terrestrial life, and Dionysus supervises moist and warm generation, of which wine, being moist and warm, is a symbol.[4]

A different set of correspondences between the gods and the elements, attributed to the Egyptian priest and historian Manetho (third century B.C.E.) is recorded by Eusebius (264–340 C.E.), bishop of Caesarea, the Roman capital of Judea:

> The Egyptians say that Isis and Osiris are the Moon and the Sun; that Zeus is the name which they give to the all-pervading Spirit, Hephaestus to Fire, and Demeter to Earth. Among the Egyptians the moist element is named Ocean and their own river Nile; and to him they ascribed the origin of the Gods. To Air, again, they give, it is said, the name of Athena.[5]

Aristotle further systemized the four elements, and added *aither* as a fifth element, representing the highest elemental principle underlying the other four. In Latin, this fifth substance was known as *quinta essentia* (from whence our word "quintessence"). This refinement gained great importance in ancient and later medieval alchemy, in which this purest of essences was supposed to have the power to rejuvenate the old and to cure all kinds of illnesses.[6] The alchemist Zosimus of Panopolis provides us with an example of acrostic or *notarichon* when writing about Adam, the first man, explaining how the four elements and the four cardinal points correspond with the four letters A—Δ—A—M:

> The first man, who amongst us is called Thoth, has been called ADAM by the Chaldeans, the Parthians, the Medes and the Hebrews, a name taken from the language of angels. Moreover, those people named him thus for the symbolic value of the four letters, that is, the four elements, which correspond to the cardinal directions of the whole of the sphere. In effect, the letter A in his name designates the East [*anatole*] and the Air [*aer*]. The letter D stands for the setting sun in the West [*dusis*], which goes down by reason of its weight. The letter M corresponds to midday [*mesembria*, South] the fire of the burning which produces the matura-

tion of bodies, the fourth zone and the middle zone. . . . Therefore the carnal Adam is named Thoth as regards his external shape; as for the man who dwells within Adam— the spiritual man—he has both a proper name and a common name. His proper name is still unknown to me today; indeed, only Nicotheus the Hidden knew these things. As for his common name, it is Phos [ΦΩΣ; light, fire].[7]

In his writings, Zosimus also represents the planet Mars by an arrow with a point and the letter *theta* (Θ), for *thouras* ("the rushing one"). He sometimes adds a *pi* (Π) as an abbreviation for the epithet *pyroeis* ("the fiery one").[8] The abbreviations recorded by Zosimus therefore provide evidence that at least two of the four elements were denoted by their initial letter; air (A) and fire (Π). This explanation of the name of Adam reflected the Gnostic myth, found in the Apocryphon of John, regarding Adam's creation from the four elements, emphasizing man's enslavement in the material world of the Demiurge.[9] In the *Sibylline Oracles*, the name ADAM is also explained as a *notarichon* composed of the initials of the four directions; *anatole* (east), *dusis* (west), *arktos* (north), and *mesembria* (south).[10] It should be mentioned that the Jews had their own acrostic interpretation of the name Adam, which, as Hebrew did not use vowels, was written ADM (אדם). In the second century C.E., Rabbi Yohanan used the Greek technique of *notarichon* (transliterated in Hebrew as *notariqon*), to explain the name Adam as the initials of the words *afer*, *dam*, and *marah*, being dust, blood, and gall.[11]

The various qualities accorded to the five elements by Aristotle were continually added to and extended throughout the Hellenistic Age. Like the planets, they formed the basis for a wide range of correspondences. Letters became part of these when it was noted by the ancients that the Greek words for the five elements—air, water, fire, earth, and ether (αηρ, υδωρ, πυρ, γη, αιθηρ)—used only five consonants altogether (Ρ, Δ, Π, Γ, and

Θ).[12] These consonants would logically equate to the five elements and their Aristotelian attributes as follows:

Greek Letter	Element	Qualities	Greek God	Platonic Solid
Γ	Earth	Cold and Dry	Hades	Cube
Δ	Water	Cold and Wet	Chronos	Icosahedron
Θ	Ether	All	Zeus	Dodecahedron
Π	Fire	Hot and Dry	Ares	Tetrahedron
Ρ	Air	Hot and Wet	Dionysus	Octahedron

The connection between the stars and the Greek alphabet is also very old and takes a variety of forms. Stars and star-groups appear in the very earliest Greek writings, for instance, in Homer's description of the engravings on Achilles' shield, which included the Pleiades, the Hyades, Orion, and the Great Bear.[13] We have seen that by the fourth century B.C.E., the vowels were already connected with the seven stars in the Pleiades, or the Seven Sisters (Alcyone, Maia, Electra, Merope, Taygeta, Celeno and Sterope), as recorded by Aristotle in his *Metaphysics*.[14] The fourth century B.C.E. tract, *On Sevens*, attributed to Hippocrates, also notes both the Great Bear and the Pleiades as having seven stars.[15] Franz Dornseiff, the German academic who, earlier this century, wrote the still leading work on ancient letter symbolism, *Das Alphabet in Mystik und Magie*, mentions an ancient papyrus with a magical invocation to the "ΑΕΗΙΟΥΩ which rise in the night," apparently referring to the seven stars of Ursa Major, the Great Bear.[16]

This early connection between the letters of the alphabet and constellations was inevitably extended to the twelve signs of the zodiac. An early system of zodiacal correspondences is recorded by Vettius Valens (second century C.E.) who wrote that the Hellenistic astrologers used a system in which all twenty-four letters of the Greek alphabet were allocated to the twelve zodiacal signs in pairs as set out below.[17]

♈	♉	♊	♋	♌	♍	♎	♏	♐	♑	♒	♓
Α Ν	Β Ξ	Γ Ο	Δ Π	Ε Ρ	Ζ Σ	Η Τ	Θ Υ	Ι Φ	Κ Χ	Λ Ψ	Μ Ω

This formed the foundation for a system known as onomantic astrology that included a number of different techniques. Using the zodiacal attributions of each Greek letter, the name of the party concerned could be converted to a pseudo-astrological chart, on the basis of which answers were made to questions.[18]

The numerous correspondences attached to the signs of the zodiac meant that they could be divided into different groups. According to the four elements of Empedocles, each sign was ruled by fire, air, water or earth. In the Graeco-Roman astrology recorded by Ptolemy (100–178 C.E.) the signs were classified as human-shaped, animal-shaped, or polymorphic.[19] Dionysius of Thrace (second century B.C.E.), in his *Ars Grammatica,* divided the Greek alphabet into seven vowels and seventeen consonants, and further divided the seventeen consonants into eight semi-vowels (Ζ, Λ, Μ, Ν, Ξ, Ρ, Σ, Ψ) and nine voiceless consonants, or mutes (Β, Γ, Δ, Θ, Κ, Π, Τ, Φ, Χ).[20] The signs of the zodiac were then classified as corresponding to these "voiced" (φων–ηεντα), "semi-voiced" (ημιφωνα), and "voiceless" (αφωνα) letters.[21]

Voiced	A E H I O Y Ω	♈ ♉ ♊ ♍ ♒
Semi-voiced	Z Λ M N Ξ P Σ Ψ	♌ ♐ ♑
Voiceless	B Γ Δ Θ K Π T Φ Ξ	♋ ♎ ♏ ♓

Although it is impossible for us now to ascertain the reasons for this allocation of the signs, it appears that the signs of the Fish, the Scales, the Scorpion, and the Crab (♋ ♎ ♏ ♓) were attributed to the so-called "mute" letters (*a-phona*) because they were also unable to make any sound, unlike the other animal, human, and anthropomorphic zodiacal signs.

There was probably a fourth system of allocating the twenty-four letters of the Greek alphabet to the stars, that employed the elements and the planets. The ancient connection between the seven vowels and the "wandering stars," or planets, as well as to other numerically corresponding star-groups, very likely led to consideration of whether the remaining seventeen consonant letters could be attributed to the remaining constellations. Extending the early planet/vowel association to include the other stars and letters would have been a predictable Hellenistic conjecture— one easily developed into a complete system of alphabetic symbolism by ascribing the remaining seventeen letters of the Greek alphabet to the twelve zodiacal constellations and the five elements. The five consonants in the Greek names for the five elements, referred to earlier, left exactly twelve consonants for the zodiac, together with the seven vowels, giving a set of attributions such as were later attributed to the Hebrew alphabet in the *Sefer Yezirah*, about which more will be said later. Franz Dornseiff concurs that the system of combined planetary, zodiacal, and elemental correspondences found in the *Sefer Yezirah* was probably first made by the Greeks, although no evidence of its use has survived.[22] Assuming a sequential allocation of the zodiacal signs in their natural order, as was the case for the planets, a reconstruction of these collective correspondences for the letters of the Greek alphabet can be given as follows:

A	Moon	☽	N	Virgo	♍
B	Aries	♈	Ξ	Libra	♎
Γ	Earth	⏚	O	Mars	♂
Δ	Water	▽	Π	Fire	△
E	Mercury	☿	P	Air	⏛
Z	Taurus	♉	Σ	Scorpio	♏
H	Venus	♀	T	Sagittarius	♐
Θ	Ether	⊛	Y	Jupiter	♃
I	Sun	☉	Φ	Capricorn	♑
K	Gemini	♊	X	Aquarius	♒
Λ	Cancer	♋	Ψ	Pisces	♓
M	Leo	♌	Ω	Saturn	♄

Thus it is apparent that, from the earliest times, there were several different methods of allocating the Greek alphabet to the heavens and the elements. These associations appear generally to have involved groups of letters based on grammatical or other considerations. Yet individual letters also attracted specific symbolism, particularly from their shape, numerical value, or because they appeared as the initial letter of a name or word. Examples of Greek Qabalistic exegesis (examination of a word according to the symbolism of each letter) that have survived from the ancient world usually analyze names and words in terms of a combination of techniques, such as isopsephy, *notarichon*, Pythagorean numerology, or individual letter symbolism (see chapter 13).

Notes to Chapter Five

1 P. Kingsley, *Ancient Philosophy, Mystery and Magic* (Oxford: Clarendon Press, 1995), pp. 15–35.

2 Homer, *Iliad*, XXI; 6. See also Plato, *Cratylus*, 404g; cited in P. Kingsley, *Ancient Philosophy, Mystery and Magic*, pp. 15–35.

3 Plato, *Timaeus*, 55–6.

4 G. Morrow (trans.), *Proclus—A Commentary on the First Book of Euclid's Elements*, foreword by I. Muller, 1992, ¶ 167, Copyright © 1970 by Princeton University Press, 1st printing. Reprinted by permission of Princeton University Press.

5 W. Waddell (trans.), *Manetho*, Fragment 83 (London: William Heinemann, Ltd., 1964).

6 R. Patai, *The Jewish Alchemists* (Princeton: Princeton University Press, 1994), p. 204.

7 Zosimus, *Upon the Letter Omega*, in M. Berthelot and C. Ruelle, *Collection des Anciens Alchimistes Grecs* (Paris, 1888), p. 224; from J. Doresse (trans.), *The Secret Books of the Egyptian Gnostics* (Rochester, VT: Inner Traditions International, 1986), p. 101.

8 M. Berthelot, *La Chimie Des Anciens et du Moyen Age* (Paris, 1893), pp. 83, 102.

9 Apocryphon of John, 16.

10 *Sibylline Oracles*, III; 24–6. This Greek acrostic also appears in 2 Enoch 30:13.

11 Cited in R. Patai, *The Jewish Alchemists*, ch. 4, fn. 14, p. 550.

12 F. Dornseiff, *Das Alphabet in Mystik und Magie* (Leipzig: Teubner, 1925), p. 83.

13 Homer, *Iliad*, XVIII; 483–9; *Odyssey*, V; 271–7.

14 Aristotle, *Metaphysics*, Book N, 1093a.

15 J. Mansfield, *The Pseudo-Hippocratic Tract ΠΕΡΙ ΕΒΔΟΜΑΔΩΝ Ch. 1–11 and Greek Philosophy* (Assen: Van Gorcum & Co., 1971), pp. 138–146.

16 F. Dornseiff, *Das Alphabet in Mystik und Magie* (Leipzig: Teubner, 1925), p. 44; J. Godwin, *The Mystery of the Seven Vowels* (Grand Rapids, MI: Phanes Press, 1991), p. 22.

17 *Catalogus Codicum Astrologicorum Graecorum*, IV [1903] 146 (Brussels: 1903).

18 F. Gettings, *The Arkana Dictionary of Astrology* (London: Penguin, 1985), p. 354.

19 F. Robbins (trans.), *Tetrabiblos*, I; 12 and II; 7 (London: William Heinemann, Ltd., 1940).

20 E. Uhlig (ed.), *Dionysii Thracis Ars Grammatica* (Leipzig: Teubner, 1884), pp. 9–16.

21 A. Bouche-Leclercq, *L'Astrologie Grecque* (Paris: E. Leroux, 1899), pp. 149–150; F. Dornseiff, *Das Alphabet in Mystik und Magie*, pp. 83–89.

22 F. Dornseiff, *Das Alphabet in Mystik und Magie*, p. 83.

chapter six

SYMBOLISM OF INDIVIDUAL LETTERS

s we have already seen, the letters of the Greek alphabet were used not only as symbols for sounds and numbers, but for many other things as well. This symbolism arose from many sources, some of which, in fact, predate the arrival of the alphabet in Greece in the eighth century B.C.E. Several of the simple geometric shapes had been used centuries before in the pictographic Mycenaean and Minoan scripts, Linear A and Linear B. These included symbols identical to the early forms of the alphabetic letters Δ, E, Z, H, N, O, Σ, and X.[1] Although the universal simplicity of these shapes cannot exclude cultural coincidence, the parent North Semitic alphabet may have drawn upon shapes in Mycenaean or Minoan script at the time of its formation, just as it drew on Mesopotamian cuneiform and Egyptian hieroglyphics. Many of the symbols of these early Greek pictographic scripts are as yet untranslated, but we do know that the early symbol for the letter *sigma* (Σ), for instance, was previously used by the Mycenaean Greeks to represent a snake, an image still suggested by our own cursive form of that letter (S).

As mentioned earlier, several letters of the original North Semitic parent alphabet are also derived from specific Egyptian hieroglyphics. The letter A was originally based on the picture of the head of an ox (∀), although the horns were later turned upside down by the Greeks. The simplified ox-head picture was chosen to represent the initial sound in the Phoenician word for ox, *aleph*, and so the letter was named. The shape of the letter *daleth* (Greek *delta*, Δ) was derived from the Egyptian symbol for a tent flap or door; *waw* (*upsilon*, Y), a prop; *cheth* (*eta*, H), a courtyard or fence; *mem* (*mu*, M), water; *resh* (*rho*, P), a head; *ayin* (*omicron*, O) was derived from the picture of an eye. This pictorial heritage is, in fact, easier to see in the Greek letter forms than in Semitic alphabets such as Hebrew and Arabic, which became more cursive in shape over time. As an aid to memorization, the Phoenicians also named each non-pictorial letter in their alphabet after a word beginning with the sound it represented.

The Greeks, who had a long history of trade with the Phoenicians, were aware of the names and symbolism attached to the letters they inherited. For instance, among the essays on science and philosophy written by the Greek historian Plutarch (45–125 C.E.) is a discussion on the question of why the letter *alpha* stands first in the alphabet. Plutarch's speaker suggests that Cadmus, the Phoenician who was reputed to have settled in Thebes and introduced the alphabet to Greece, "placed *alpha* first because it is the Phoenician name for an ox, which they, like Hesiod, reckoned not the second or third, but the first of necessities."[2] The reference is to a passage in *Works and Days* by Hesiod (circa 700 B.C.E.), a contemporary of Homer, who advised the early Greek farmers, "First get an ox, then a woman."[3]

In addition to the old pictorial symbolism inherited from the Egyptians, Mycenaeans, and Phoenicians, the letters of the alphabet were soon given new meanings and attributions by the Greeks. Almost from the moment they inherited the alphabet in the eighth century B.C.E., the Greeks used letters as symbols for various animate and inanimate objects, of which numbers were the most important. During the Classical, Hellenistic, and Roman Ages, the letters of the Greek alphabet were associated with planets, stars, signs of the zodiac, musical notes, deities, angels, elements, parts of the human body, and numerous other objects and ideas. By the use of isopsephy and the accumulated symbolism of these systems, it was possible to analyze each letter of a name or word in a search for hidden meaning. Examples of this type of exegesis have survived in ancient classical writings and are examined in chapter 13.

Symbolism and correspondences were attached to letters by the Greeks for a variety of reasons, particularly because of their value or shape, or because they formed the initial of a particular word or name. *Alpha* (A) derived most of its symbolism from the fact that it was the first letter of the alphabet and therefore the symbol for the number one. As seen earlier in Plutarch, the Greeks were also aware of its identification by the Phoenicians with the ox, through its hieroglyphic origin. Following Plutarch's suggested natural order of attribution of the vowels to the planets, *alpha* was connected with the first of the planets, the Moon. Oxen were also associated with the Moon in both early Sumerian and Egyptian religious symbolism due to the crescent shape of their horns. But, as the first letter and as symbol of the sacred monad, *alpha* was also equated with the Sun. Iamblichus' *Theology of Arithmetic* contains the following passage revealing the solar connection in the Pythagorean tradition:

The mark which signifies the monad is the source of all things. And it reveals its kinship with the Sun in the summation of its name: for the word "monad" when added up yields 361, which are the degrees of the zodiacal circle.[4]

The "mark" referred to is *alpha*, the initial letter of *arche* (ΑΡΧΗ, source). The Greek word for monad (ΜΟΝΑΣ) has an isopsephic value of 361, counted as equivalent to the 360 degrees of the circle, presumably because the first degree is counted twice to indicate a complete revolution of the zodiac. Plutarch noted that the Greek name for the god of the Sun, *Apollon,* signified a unity, since *pollon* meant "many," and the prefix *a-* was a negative. Thus, *Apollon,* to a Greek, could be read as meaning "deprived of multitude." Apollo was consequently associated with the monad.[5]

Because *alpha* generally represented the first principle, it was used in the symbolism of the Gnostics as a name for Jesus, as recorded by the early Church Fathers Irenaeus and Hippolytus.

Now Jesus possesses this ineffable generation. From the mother of all things, that is, the first Tetrad, there came forth a second Tetrad, after the manner of a daughter; and thus an Ogdoad was formed, from which, again, a Decad proceeded: thus was joined a Decad and an Ogdoad. The Decad then, being joined with the Ogdoad, and multiplying it ten times, gave rise to the number eighty; and again, multiplying eighty ten times, produced the number eight hundred. Thus then, the whole number of letters proceeding from the Ogdoad [multiplied] into the Decad, is eight hundred and eighty-eight. This is the name of Jesus; for this name, if you reckon up the numerical value of the letters, amounts to eight hundred and eighty-eight [*Jesus*, ΙΗΣΟΥΣ = 888]. . . . Wherefore also, the alphabet of the Greeks contains eight Monads, eight Decads, and eight Hecatads, which present

Figure 13. Egyptian gem with Harpocrates and letters *alpha* and *omega*. (Reprinted from David Fideler, *Jesus Christ, Sun of God*, Wheaton, IL: Quest Books, 1993, used by permission.)

the number eight hundred and eighty-eight, that is, *Jesus*, who is formed of all numbers; and on this account He is called *Alpha* (and *Omega*), indicating His origin from all.[6]

Irenaeus also recounts "a false legend about the boy Jesus," in which Jesus is credited by Gnostic legend with an awareness of the true mystic symbolism of the letter *alpha*.

When the Lord was a boy learning his alphabet, his teacher said to him, as is customary, "Say Alpha," and he replied, "Alpha." But when the teacher ordered him to say Beta, the Lord replied, "First you tell me what Alpha is and I will tell you what Beta is." They explain this reply as meaning that he alone knew the Unknowable, whom he showed forth in the figure of Alpha.[7]

Alpha appears frequently in Greek and Coptic magical papyri, not only in conjunction with the other vowels, but also by itself as having special power (see figure 13, page 67). In a Christian Coptic spell from about 600 C.E., it is set out in "wing" formation.[8]

A A A A A A A

A A A A A A

A A A A A

A A A A

A A A

A A

A

In Arabic script, the Phoenician letter *aleph* was written as a vertical line, and was thus compared with the phallus, an association

SYMBOLISM OF INDIVIDUAL LETTERS

that, in Greek, we can fairly safely assume fell to the letter *iota*. In his historical survey of the sexual culture of the East, Allen Edwardes tells of the words of the aged Mohammedan:

> Who among us, pray, can boast that his prickle be as straight as the letter *alif*? No man in our decrepit midst can now jog his comrade in the coffeeshop and utter, tormentingly: *I am the thick and thou are the thin*. Now, we are all of us El-Mugheffef (the Shrivelled).[9]

The first five letters of the alphabet appear as a *notarichon* in a romantic biography of Alexander the Great written some time before the third century C.E., by an unknown author who took the name of one of Alexander's actual contemporaries, Callisthenes. Writing of the foundation of the city of Alexandria on the Nile delta, this pseudo-Callisthenes alleged of Alexander that:

> When he had laid the foundation for most of the city, he wrote upon it the five letters: A, B, Γ, Δ, E; A, Alexander; B, the greatest king; Γ, of the greatest nations; Δ, in the place of Aramazd; E, descended and built a unique city [Αλεξανδρος Βασιλεος Γενος Διος Εκτιοε (πολιν αειμνηστον].[10]

The letter *beta* (B), like most of the first ten letters of the Greek alphabet, also took most of its symbolism from the number in the Pythagorean decad that it represented. As the number two, *beta* was therefore connected with the second principle, and duality in all its forms. The Hellenistic philosopher Eratosthenes was unkindly nicknamed "Beta" because he was second-best in so many fields.[11] As seen in the above example from the *Life of Alexander*, it was also the abbreviation of the Greek word for "king" (*basileos*, from whence the English name Basil), just us we still find the letter R in use on British Commonwealth coins as the abbreviation for the Latin "king" or "queen" (as in ER, *Elizabetha Regina*, and GR, *Georgius Rex*).

Gamma, the third letter and symbol for the number three, was connected with various triplicities in Greek mythology, such as the goddess of the Moon with her three phases or faces (full, dark, and waxing or waning), who was also the goddess of the crossroads. As indicated by the Greek word for "crossroads" (*trisodos*), such an intersection was not cruciform for the Greeks, but formed by a meeting of three paths. Hence, "the crossroads letter" of Pythagoras was the three-stemmed letter *upsilon* (Y). Pennick states that *gamma* was also connected with the three Moirai, or, as the Romans called them, the Fates (Clotho, Atropos, and Lachesis).[12]

The letter used for the number four, *delta* (Δ), appears as a symbol for the four elements (earth, air, fire, and water) defined by the early Greek philosopher Empedocles, as well as for other tetrads. Its triangular shape, and the fact that 1+2+3+4 = 10, led to its being identified with the sacred *tetraktys*, the triangular representation of the decad upon which the Pythagoreans swore oaths. Thus Lucian, in his parody of various ancient schools of thought titled *Philosophies for Sale*, has the following exchange:

Pythagorean:	"How do you count?"
Buyer:	"1, 2, 3, 4. . ."
Pythagorean:	"Lo! What you think is four is ten, and a perfect triangle, and our oath!"[13]

As we have seen, the Δ was also used in the sixth century B.C.E. as a symbol for the number ten in the Herodianic numerical system, being the initial letter of *deka*, ten. The *delta's* triangular shape also led to it being used as a symbol for the female pudenda. The great Athenian comedian Aristophanes (447–385 B.C.E.) provides us with such an example in his comic play, *Lysistrata*, in which the women of Athens and Sparta agree to conduct a "sex strike" to force their warring men to make peace with each other. The leader of the strike, Lysistrata, says to the gathered women:

> Well, just imagine: we're at home, beautifully made up, wearing our sheerest lawn negligees and nothing underneath, and with our—our triangles [*delta*] carefully plucked; and the men are all like ramrods and can't wait to leap into bed, and then we absolutely refuse—that'll make them make peace soon enough, you'll see.[14]

Purely for the sake of amusement, and providing a taste of classical Greek comedy, it is worthwhile to recount that the strike by Lysistrata and the other women soon had the predicted effect, and a Spartan envoy urgently arranges to meet an Athenian magistrate:

Herald:	Where are the leaders of the Athenian council, or the Executive Committee? I would have words with them.
Magistrate:	[guffawing] Ha! Ha! Ha! What are you—a man or a phallic symbol?
Herald:	My dear boy, I'm a herald, and I'm here to talk about peace.
Magistrate:	[pointing] Which is why you've got a spear under your tunic I suppose?
Herald:	[turning his back] No, I haven't.
Magistrate:	What have you turned around for then? Why are you holding your cloak in that funny way? Did you get a rupture on the way here?
Herald:	[to himself] By Castor, the man's senile.
Magistrate:	Why, you rascal, you've got prickitis!
Herald:	No, I haven't. Don't be stupid.
Magistrate:	Well, what's that then?
Herald:	It's a standard Spartan cipher rod.[15]

The last line refers to the Spartan practice of sending secret messages by writing them on wooden rods around which a narrow strip of parchment had first been wound. Once unwound, the letters on the strip could only be read by the intended recipient, who had previously been given a wooden rod of identical circumference.

Concerning the letter *epsilon* (E), Iamblichus noted, in his *Theology of Arithmetic,* the observation of Nicomachus of Gerasa that:

> Those who first formed the characters of letters in terms of shape—since θ signifies nine, and the mean of it as a square is ε, and the mean is in nearly every case seen as half—considered that ε formed half of the letter θ, as it were cut [vertically] into two.[16]

Because the shape of *epsilon* was "not implausibly likened to beam-scales," Nicomachus goes on to say that E is representative of the scales of justice, and therefore of justice itself. This accorded neatly with the Pythagorean interpretation of the number five as symbolic of justice. As discussed above, *epsilon* was also closely associated with Helios-Apollo and the Sun, due to its appearance as an inscription at the ancient temple of Apollo at Delphi, and as one of the seven vowels ascribed to the planets. As the number five, it was also representative of ether, the fifth element. Its numerical value also connects it to the five-pointed star, the Pythagorean pentagon or pentagram, containing the mathematical ratio known as the Golden Section.

In a passage from Proclus that appears later in this book (see chapter 11), the Neoplatonist Theodorus of Asine (fourth century C.E.) analyzes the "double-letter" *zeta* (Z) at length. He interprets it as, among other things, the initial letter of the word for Life, *zoe* (ΖΩΗ).[17] Zoe figures as a goddess in Gnosticism and Neoplatonism. It is also the name given to Eve in the *Septuagint,* the Greek translation of the Hebrew scriptures. The Greek letters

SYMBOLISM OF INDIVIDUAL LETTERS

for the numbers 7 through 10 (ZHΘΙ) spell the word *zethi*, meaning "live" or "live long." Accordingly, the sequential appearance of these Greek numerals on sundials gave rise to an ancient epigram: "Six hours are enough to give; the next four stand for ZHΘΙ, meaning live."[18]

The letter *theta* (Θ) was, in its archaic form, written as a cross within a circle (⊕ ,⊗), and later as a line or point within a circle (Θ, ⊙). According to Porphyry (232–305 C.E.), the Egyptians used an X within a circle as a symbol of the soul.[19] Having a value of nine, it was used as a symbol for the Ennead, the nine major deities of the ancient Egyptians. The earliest of these, the Great Ennead of Heliopolis, was comprised of the original creator god, Atum (often identified with Ra); his children, Shu and Tefnut; their children, Geb and Nut; and the fourth generation, the brothers, Osiris and Seth, and their sisters, Isis and Nephthys. Johannis Lydus noted that the Egyptians also used a symbol in the form of a *theta* for the Kosmos, with an airy fiery circle representing the world, and a snake, spanning the middle, representing the Good Spirit (*Agathos Daimon*).[20] The Egyptians also used the sign of a point within circle (⊙) to represent the Sun god Ra, the probable origin of its use as the astrological symbol for the Sun. Coincidentally, *theta* had the same value in isopsephy as Helios (ΘΗΤΑ = 318 = ΗΛΙΟΣ).[21] In classical Athens, *theta* was also known as the "letter of death" because it was the initial letter of *thanatos* (death). It survives on potsherds used by Athenians when voting for the death penalty.

Iota (I) means "jot" and is, in fact, the origin of that word, although we also still use the word "iota" with this meaning. This is because the single-lined letter is the smallest and simplest to form of all letters in the alphabet. As a simple stroke, it is also used to represent the number one in the Herodianic system, as it did in other numerical systems, including the Roman (I) and our own Arabic numerical system (1). In Pythagorean terms, it is, of course, the line, as *delta* is the triangle and *omicron* the circle.

Clement, bishop of Alexandria (circa 150–215 C.E.), notes that the letter *iota* signified the name of Jesus, of which it was the initial letter in Greek. He also makes reference to the passage in the ninth chapter of the *Epistle of Barnabas,* in which *iota* and *eta* together form the initial letters of Jesus' name (ΙΗΣΟΥΣ).[22] In later Christian times, the standard abbreviation for Jesus consisted of the first and last letters, ΙΣ; or, using the cursive form of *sigma,* IC— a system of abbreviation we use for the short form of our words "Mister" or "Saint." In Christian iconography and Renaissance art, one can often see the figure of Jesus Christ indicated by the abbreviation IC XC. Irenaeus (125–203 C.E.) records that the Gnostic followers of Marcus "assert that the ten Aeons are pointed out by the letter *Iota,* which begins his name," and that, for the same reason, Jesus said:

> For assuredly, I say to you, till heaven and earth pass away, not one jot (*iota*) or tittle will pass from the law till all is fulfilled.[23]

In his dissertation, *Refutation of All Heresies,* Hippolytus of Rome (d. 235 C.E.) recounts the teachings of the Gnostic, Monoimus, in which the value and shape of *iota* (I = 10) are variously seen as representing the Ten Commandments, the rod of Moses, the decad, and its root value (1), the monad as source of all.[24] Interestingly, the value of *iota,* when spelled in full, gives a recurring monad— ΙΩΤΑ = 10 + 800 + 300 + 1 = 1111.

Kappa (Κ) is the first letter in Kronos, an alternative spelling for Chronos, or Saturn, the god of time. In early Christian inscriptions and amulets, we find *kappa* in the abbreviated letters ΚΣ (or ΚC) used for the Lord (*kurios*). Similarly, the letter M appears frequently as an abbreviation for Mary (*Maria*); *theta* (Θ) is the initial used for God (*theos*); *upsilon* (Υ) for the Son (*[h]uios*); and *pi* (Π) as the initial of the Father (*pater*).[25]

The letter *lambda* (Λ) was connected by the philosopher Crantor in the fourth century B.C.E. with Plato's passage in the

Timaeus describing the primary sequence of numbers giving life to the universe.[26] These numbers—1, 2, 3, 4, 8, 9, 27—demonstrate the principles "twice" and "thrice," and were placed on a two-armed *lambda*-shaped diagram thus:

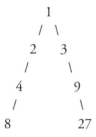

Each arm has three intervals. The left arm shows the progression from 2 into a plane of 4 and a cube of 8. The opposite arm shows 3 with its plane of 9 and its cube of 27. Because of the convention of triangular numbering among the Greeks, the *lambda* was readily comparable to the *tetraktys*. The *lambda* diagram is used by Nicomachus, and Proclus records its use among the ancients for the same purpose in his commentary on the *Timaeus*.[27]

As a means of representing mathematical progression, the letter *lambda* also became a symbol of the geometric ratio known as the Golden Section. This theorem requires dividing a line into two unequal parts, so that the lesser is in the same proportion to the greater as the greater is to the whole. The star-pentagon or pentagram, always associated with magic, requires the proportions of the Golden Section for its construction. It was one of the most important symbols of the Pythagoreans.[28] The famous drawing of Leonardo da Vinci, depicting the figure of a naked man imposed on a pentagram, his feet and legs forming the shape of the letter *lambda*, can be seen as an attempt to portray the Golden Section in dynamic form.

Hippolytus says that the Gnostics also attached specific allegorical symbolism to the letters *lambda* and *mu*.[29]

And with a similar reference to the dodecad [12], they speak of the piece of money which, on losing, a woman, having lit a candle, searched for diligently. And they make a similar application of the loss sustained in the case of one sheep out of the ninety and nine; and adding these one into the other, they give a fabulous account of numbers. And in this way, they affirm, when the eleven is multiplied into nine, that it produces the number ninety and nine; and on this account that it is said that the word Amen embraces the number ninety-nine [AMHN = 99]. And in regard of another number they express themselves in this manner: that the letter *Eta* along with the remarkable letter [*stigma*, or *episemon*, the obsolete sixth letter] constitutes the Ogdoad, as it is situated in the eighth place from *Alpha* [if the "remarkable letter" *stigma* is counted]. Then, again, computing the number of these elements without the remarkable letter, and adding them together up to *Eta*, they exhibit the number thirty. For anyone beginning from the *Alpha* to the *Eta* will, after subtracting the remarkable letter, discover the number of the elements to be the number thirty. Since, therefore, the number thirty is unified from the three powers; when multiplied thrice into itself it produced ninety, for thrice thirty is ninety (and this triad when multiplied into itself produced nine). In this way the Ogdoad brought forth the number ninety-nine from the first Ogdoad, and Decad, and Dodecad. . . . Since, however, the twelfth Aeon, having left the eleven (Aeons above), and departing downwards, withdrew, they allege that even this is correlative with the letters. For the figure of the letters teaches us as much. For Λ is placed eleventh of the letters, and this Λ is the number thirty [Λ = 30]. And they say that this is placed according to an image of the dispensation above; since from *Alpha*, irrespective of the remarkable letter, the number of the letters themselves, added together up to Λ, according to the augmentation of

76

the letters with the Λ itself, produces the number ninety-nine. But that the Λ, situated eleventh in the alphabet, came down to search after the number similar to itself, in order that it might fill up the twelfth number, and that when it was discovered it was filled up, is manifest from the shape itself of the letter. For *Lambda*, when it attained unto, as it were, the investigation of what is similar to itself, and when it found such and snatched it away, filled up the place of the twelfth, the letter **M**, which is composed of two *Lambdas* [in appearance, ΛΛ = **M**]. And for this reason it was that these adherents of Marcus, through their knowledge, avoid the place of the ninety-nine, that is, the Hysterema [υστερημα, *deficiency*], a type of the left hand, and follow after the one which, added to ninety-nine, they say was transferred to his own right hand.[29]

Hippolytus here refers to the custom of the ancients, probably derived from trade between people speaking different languages, of representing the numbers below 100 by various positions of the left hand and its fingers, while numbers of 100 and greater were shown by corresponding gestures of the right hand. Hebrew scripture placed evil-doers on the left hand, and therefore it also symbolized the evil principle of matter in Gnostic theory, an association here carried over to the "left hand" number, ninety-nine.

As seen earlier, the Greek letter *mu* was derived from the zigzag Egyptian hieroglyphic symbol for water, which had been simplified by the Phoenicians and named after their word for water, *mem*. The sound "M" is still connected with the sea in many languages, as in Hebrew *marah*, Latin *mare*, and French *mer*. It was used in the sixth century B.C.E. as a symbol for the number 10,000, being the initial of *myrioi*, many. The letter *mu* appears in conjunction with *alpha* and *omega* to signify the "beginning, middle (*meson*) and end," a phrase first found in an Orphic verse describing Zeus, and later adopted to describe both Jehovah and

Jesus.[30] In Aeschylus' *Eumenides*, the repeated moaning of the letter *mu* is the sound made by the sleeping Furies as the ghost of Clytemnestra begins to invoke them. It appears in a tenth-century-C.E. Coptic papyrus, containing a Christian curse against perjurers that invokes the angel, Temeluchos:

> I adjure you by the seven perfect letters, MMMMMMM. You must appear to him, you must appear to him. I adjure you by the seven angels around the throne of the father.[31]

The letter *xi* (Ξ) occurs in a very early example of individual letter symbolism found on the Greek island of Thera, where it was, by chance, suitable for the local pronunciation of Zeus. Thus the letter was actually used on rare occasions.[32]

The ancient symbolism of the cross as a protective emblem and phallic image was connected not only to the letter *chi* (X), but also to *tau* (T), the last letter in the Phoenician and Old Hebrew alphabets and originally cruciform in shape. The early Christians made much of the existing linguistic connection and physical similarity of the letter *tau* with the cross upon which the Romans had executed their founder. One such association can be seen in the ninth chapter of the Epistle of Barnabas, probably written during the first half of the second century C.E., that interprets the number 318 found in Genesis 4:14 according to the Greek letters for that number (318 = ΤΙΗ):

> For [Scripture] saith, "and Abraham circumcised out of his house men Eighteen and Three Hundred." What therefore is the knowledge [η γνωσις] given to him? Mark that it says the Eighteen first, then marking an interval, the Three Hundred. The Eighteen: I, ten; H, eight: you have ΙΗ(ΣΟΥΣ) [Jesus]. But because the Cross in the T was about to have the grace it has, Scripture saith, "and Three Hundred" [T = 300]. Wherefore by two letters he signified

Jesus, and by a third His cross. He knows this who has put the engrafted gift of his doctrine within us. No one has learned a more genuine word from me than this, but I know that ye are worthy of it.[33]

This Qabalistic analysis was also known and referred to by Clement (circa 150–215 C.E.), who, in his *Miscellanies,* confirms *tau* as being "as to shape the type of the Lord's sign," while the two letters *iota* and *eta* signify the Savior's name.[34]

Another such reference appears in an essay written around 160 C.E. attributed (probably in error) to Lucian, a mock legal prosecution called *The Consonants at Law—Sigma v. Tau in the Court of the Seven Vowels.* Sigma petitions the court to sentence Tau to death by crucifixion, saying:

> Men weep, and bewail their lot, and curse Cadmus with many curses for introducing *Tau* into the family of letters; they say it was his body that tyrants took for a model, his shape that they imitated, when they set up structures on which men are crucified. *Stauros* [cross] the vile engine is called, and it derives its vile name from him. Now, with all these crimes upon him, does he not deserve death, nay, many deaths? For my part I know none bad enough but that supplied by his own shape—that shape which he gave to the gibbet named *stauros* after him by men.[35]

Crucifixion was a cruel form of torture and capital punishment that was originally used by the Assyrians and later adopted as a good idea by the equally pitiless Romans, who encountered it after their empire extended to the east. It was considered one of the most severe and degrading methods of execution, reserved only for the poor and for slaves, and only then for crimes deserving of especially harsh treatment, such as spying and desertion. In fact, the particular stigma attached to death by crucifixion was so

Figure 14. Pythagoras' letter Y, representing moral choice. (Reprinted from Geofroy Tory, *Champfleury,* 1529.)

shameful that it was not until the third century C.E. that Jesus' cross became commonly used by the Christians as a symbol of their faith.[36]

One of the best-documented examples of letter symbolism occurs in one of the few fragments attributed to Pythagoras himself, in which the letter *upsilon* (Y) is interpreted as a symbol of human life, representing the crossroads of moral choice (see figure 14, page 80).[37] The lower stem represents the early part of life, when the character is unformed; the right-hand branch, which is narrower and more difficult, is the path of virtue; and the broader, easier, left-hand branch represents vice.

> The Pythagoric Letter two ways spread
> Shows the two paths in which Man's life is led.
> The right track to sacred Virtue tends,
> Though steep and rough at first, in rest it ends;
> The other broad and smooth, but from its Crown
> On rocks the Traveller is tumbled down.
> He who to Virtue by harsh toils aspires,
> Subduing pains, worth and reknown acquires:
> But who seeks slothful luxury, and flies,
> The labour of great acts, dishonoured dies.[38]

This idea of *upsilon* as the "crossroads letter" apparently received much attention in the ancient world. The Roman satirist Persius (34–62 C.E.) writes:

> Pythagoras' Y shows the moment of a young man's moral choice.
> Your eyes are set on the path which climbs steeply to the right.[39]

Other ancient writers who comment on this theme include Xenophon, Cicero, Servius, and Martianus Capella.[40] The same general idea is ascribed to Jesus of Nazareth, in the writings attributed to his apostle Matthew:

> Enter by the narrow gate: for wide is the gate, and broad is the way, that leads to destruction, and there are many who go in by it: Because narrow is the gate, and difficult is the way, which leads to life, and there are few who find it. (Matthew 7:13–14)

Another of the early Church Fathers who makes use of the association is the North African author, Lactantius, who lived in the early fourth century C.E. Lactantius was tutor to the Emperor Constantine's son, Crispus. The reference occurs in his *Divine Institutes*, an apology of Christianity aimed at the pagan Latin intelligentsia:

> Why is there the need of the letter Y in opposite and diverse things? That one road, the better one, is turned toward the rising sun; the other, the worse, towards its setting, since he who follows truth and justice will secure possession of the accepted reward of immortality, perennial light; but he who has preferred vice to virtue, falsehood to truth, ensnared by that evil guide, must be borne to the west and to eternal darkness.[41]

Even Shakespeare was familiar with this image, as is made clear in Ophelia's speech to her brother, Laertes, in *Hamlet*:

> Do not, as some ungracious pastors do,
> Show me the steep and thorny way to heaven;
> Whilst, like a puff'd and reckless libertine
> Himself the primrose path of dalliance treads,
> And recks not his own read.[42]

Dating from the sixth century B.C.E., Pythagoras' metaphorical interpretation of the letter Y is probably the earliest example, in any language, of a deliberately drawn correspondence between a letter of the alphabet and a philosophical concept. As seen from the other authors quoted above, the idea had a widespread influence, and other letters of the alphabet became the subject of similar conjecture by the Greeks. Besides being reputed as the founder of divination by isopsephy, therefore, we may also acknowledge Pythagoras as the founder of Qabalistic letter symbolism.

Even more famous in the ancient world was the use of the Greek letter *chi* (X) by Plato in his hugely influential work on the origin of the universe, the *Timaeus*, in which he refers to God creating the universe by joining two circular strips of soul-stuff in the form of a *chi*, with its ends extended to form circles.[43] This *Psychogonia* passage, as we will see later, was the source of much comment by the Neoplatonists and others. Justin Martyr (circa 100–165 C.E.), in his *Apologia* of Christianity, addressed to the Emperor Marcus Aurelius, connected this *chi* reference by Plato to the cross, an association echoed in the use of the cross or *stauros* by the Gnostics as the bridge between worlds.[44]

The letter *chi* was also used by the Greeks as a solar symbol and was connected to Saturn as the abbreviation of his name, *Chronos* (ΧΡΟΝΟΣ), as was the wheel-shaped sign formed by the first two letters combined, the so-called *chi-rho*.[45] Both abbreviations were adopted by the Christians as the initials of Christ (ΧΡΙΣΤΟΣ), and are still in use today, the *chi* appearing in our shorthand word for Christmas, Xmas. The bind-letters, or monogram, *chi-rho* (and occasionally *chi-iota*) became one of the most prominent of Christian symbols, and can still be seen in almost any Roman Catholic church (see figure 15 on page 84). As the initial of *chilioi*, the letter *chi* also appears as the sign for 1,000 in early Greek inscriptions using the Herodianic numerical system.

The letter *psi* (Ψ), together with the other letters in *psyche* (ΨΥΧΗ), is analyzed in terms of its shape and value by Theodorus of Asine in a passage from Proclus, set out later in this book in the chapter on the Neoplatonists. It also appears as a magical name

Figure 15. Early representations of the *chi-rho* from the catacombs. (Reprinted from David Fideler, *Jesus Christ, Sun of God*, Wheaton, IL: Quest Books, 1993, used by permission.)

"PSEE" in a long list of words and names of power in a Coptic ritual text produced sometime between the fourth and sixth centuries.[46] It is unlikely that the Gnostics and early Christians would have failed to notice that the value of the Holy Spirit (*Pneuma Hagion*) was, by isopsephy, identical to that of the letter *psi* spelled in full (ΠΝΕΥΜΑ ΑΓΙΟΝ = 710 = ΨΙ, a correlation preserved if *psi* is spelled ΨΕΕ as above).

On the evidence we have seen, it is plainly incorrect to state that there are only a few correspondences to the letters of the Greek alphabet along the lines of those found much later in the Hebrew Qabalah.[47] It is also anachronistic, as well as completely pointless, to attempt to project Hebrew Qabalistic symbolism onto the Greek alphabet, or to imagine anything so historically impossible as an "Alexandrian Tree of Life," as has been done.[48] It is hoped that the extensive Greek letter symbolism examined above is enough to put an end to any perceived need for this unnecessary practice by those with a background in Hebrew Qabalah.

Notes to Chapter Six

[1] M. Bernal, *Cadmean Letters* (Winona Lake, IN: Eisenbrauns, 1990), p. 108.

[2] Plutarch, *Moralia*, IX; 2, 737.

[3] Hesiod, *Works and Days*, 405.

[4] R. Waterfield (trans.), *The Theology of Arithmetic* (Grand Rapids, MI: Phanes Press, 1988), p. 39.

[5] Plutarch, *Moralia*, 270, 394.

[6] Irenaeus, *Against Heresies*, I; 15; Hippolytus, *Refutation of All Heresies*, VI; 45, in J. H. MacMahon (trans.), *Philosopheumena* (London: Society for the Promotion of Christian Knowledge, 1921).

[7] Irenaeus, *Against Heresies*, I; 20, in Robert M. Grant (trans.), *Irenaeus of Lyons* (London: Routledge, 1985), p. 84. See also Gospel of Thomas 6:3 and 14:2

[8] M. Meyer and R. Smith (ed.), *Ancient Christian Magic* (New York: HarperCollins, 1995), p. 285.

[9] A. Edwardes, *The Jewel in the Lotus* (London: Tandem, 1969), p. 70.

[10] Pseudo-Callisthenes, *Life of Alexander*, I:32, in A. M. Wolohojian (trans.), *The Romance of Alexander the Great by Pseudo-Callisthenes* (New York: Columbia University Press, 1969), p. 51.

[11] A. R. Burn, *The Pelican History of Greece* (London: Pelican Books, 1966), p. 358.

[12] N. Pennick, *The Secret Lore of Runes and Other Ancient Alphabets* (London: Rider Books, 1991), p. 50. Unfortunately, Pennick nowhere cites any ancient sources for the symbolism he alleges for the letters of the Greek alphabet, making it impossible to rely on his observations in the present context.

[13] Lucian, *Philosophies for Sale,* 3, A. M. Harmon (trans.), vol. II, p. 457.

[14] Aristophanes, *Lysistrata*, 151, in A. H. Sommersten (trans.) (London: Penguin, 1973), p. 185.

[15] Aristophanes, *Lysistrata*, 960 ff, p. 221.

[16] R. Waterfield (trans.), *The Theology of Arithmetic*, 40; p. 72.

[17] F. Dornseiff, *Das Alphabet in Mystik und Magie* (Leipzig: Teubner, 1925), p. 116.

[18] *Anthologica Palatina*, X; 43, in O. A. W. Dilke, *Mathematics and Measurement* (London: British Museum Press, 1987), p. 56.

[19] T. Taylor (trans.), *The Commentaries of Proclus on the Timaeus of Plato* (London: A. J. Valpy, 1820), p. 118.

[20] Johannis Lydus, *On the Months*, IV; 161.

[21] D. Fideler, *Jesus Christ, Sun of God* (Wheaton, IL: Quest Books, 1993), pp. 224, 359.

[22] Clemens Alexandrinus, *Miscellanies*, VI; 16, 11.

[23] Matthew 5:18.

[24] Hippolytus, *Refutation Of All Heresies*, VII; 5–6.

[25] M. Meyer and R. Smith (ed.), *Ancient Christian Magic*, pp. 144–145, 357, 364.

26 Plato, *Timaeus*, 35; J. James, *The Music of the Spheres* (London: Abacus, 1985), p. 46.

27 T. Taylor (trans.), *The Commentaries of Proclus on the Timaeus of Plato*, p. 73.

28 W. Rutherford, *Pythagoras—Lover of Wisdom* (London: Aquarian Press, 1984), pp. 58–59; W. Burkert, *Lore and Science in Ancient Pythagoreanism* (Cambridge: Harvard University Press, 1972), p. 452.

29 Hippolytus, *Refutation of All Heresies*, VI; 47, in J. H. MacMahon (trans.), *Philosopheumena*.

30 Plutarch, *Moralia*, V; 436; Isaiah 44:6; Revelation 1:8, 11 and 21:6.

31 M. Meyer and R. Smith (ed.), *Ancient Christian Magic*, p. 194.

32 L. Jeffrey, *The Local Scripts of Archaic Greece* (Oxford: Oxford University Press, 1961), p. 35.

33 Epistle of Barnabas, IX, in S. Lea and B. Bond, *The Apostolic Gnosis* (Orpington, Kent, Great Britain: RILKO, 1979), p. 40; see also Jerome, *Homilies*, 84.

34 Clemens Alexandrinus, *Miscellanies*, VI; 11.

35 Lucian, *The Consonants at Law*, 61, A. M. Harmen (trans.), vol. VI, p. 409.

36 J. Rohmer, *Testament—The Bible and History* (London: Michael O'Mara Books, Ltd., 1988), pp. 178–179.

37 F. Dornseiff, *Das Alphabet in Mystik und Magie*, p. 24.

38 Maximinus; cited in K. S. Guthrie (trans.), *The Pythagorean Sourcebook and Library*, p. 158.

39 Persius, *Satires*, III; 56–57, in N. Rudd (trans.) *The Satires of Horace and Persius* (London: Penguin, 1973), p. 128.

40 Xenophon, *Memorabilia*, II; 1, 20 ff; *The Education of Cyrus*, II; 2, 24; Servius, *On Virgil's Aeneid*, VI; 540; Cicero, *On Duties*, I; 32; Martianus Capella, *The Marriage of Philology and Mercury*, II; 101.

41 Lactantius, *The Divine Institutes*, VI; 3, in M. F. McDonald (trans.) (Washington: Catholic University of America Press, 1948), p. 398.

42 Shakespeare, *Hamlet*, I, iii.

43 Plato, *Timaeus*, 36.

44 Justin, *Apologia*, I; 60; B. Walker, *Gnosticism* (London: Aquarian Press, 1983), p. 35.

45 W. Moeller, *The Mithraic Origin and Meaning of the Rotas-Sator Square* (Leiden: Brill, 1973), p. 8.

46 M. Meyer and R. Smith (ed.), *Ancient Christian Magic*, pp. 302, 309.

47 See for example, D. Godwin, *Light in Extension—Greek Magic from Modern to Homeric Times* (St. Paul, MN: Llewellyn, 1992), pp. 197–198. Through historical error, Godwin also unfortunately alleges that the Milesian system "which seems to have originated around 400 B.C., more or less copies the Hebrew/Phoenician system"; all of which is quite wrong.

48 See for example, S. Flowers, *Hermetic Magic* (York Beach, ME: Samuel Weiser, 1995), a forgettable mixture of historical fact and personal fantasy.

chapter seven

ORACLES AND
INVOCATIONS

t was inherent in Pytha-
gorean doctrine that arith-
metical relationships were
a manifestation of the
divine, and it followed
from this that the voice of heaven could be revealed by the use of
isopsephy or, as it was later called, *gematria*. Accordingly, isopsephy became important in magic and divination, and as an aid to
the interpretation of dreams and oracles. Artemidorus Daldianus
(second century C.E.), for instance, uses isopsephy to associate
numerically equivalent words in his *Interpretation of Dreams*.[1] A
good example can be found in the *Life of Alexander,* Pseudo-
Callisthenes' biography of Alexander the Great, written some
time during the third century C.E. According to this influential
biography, on the occasion of his founding of the Egyptian city

89

of Alexandria, a god supposedly appeared to Alexander in a dream, and addressed him as follows:

> "The city of Alexandria, which you are building in the middle of the land, is to be coveted by the world; . . . And I shall be its protecting deity for all time to come . . . .You shall dwell there both when you are dead and when not yet dead; for this city you are building is to be your grave. And I shall quickly prove to you where you were meant to be. Take two hundred and add one; then one hundred and one; and four times twenty, and ten; and take the first number and make it the last; and learn for all time what god I am."
>
> And having given the oracle, the god departed from there. And when Alexander awoke and recalled the oracle which had been delivered to him by the gods, he recognized the great Sarapis, lord of all. And he built a great altar and ordered that fitting sacrifices be brought for the gods.[2]

Alexander allegedly recognizes that the values given in the passage are 200 + 1 + 100 + 1 + 80 (4 x 20) + 10 + 200, those of the letters in the name of the Graeco-Egyptian deity, Sarapis (ΣΑΡΑ–ΠΙΣ). The name of Sarapis, or Serapis, was probably derived from a compound of two Egyptian gods, Osiris and Apis. His attributes included various aspects of Greek gods such as Apollo and Zeus. The worship of Sarapis was actually introduced into Alexandria by Alexander's successor in Egypt, the Macedonian general Ptolemy (from Greek *ptolemaios*, warlike), as part of an attempt to unite the religious practice of the Greek ruling class and its Egyptian subjects.[3]

Further examples illustrative of the belief of the ancients that isopsephy was a method used by the gods to reveal secrets to humankind can be found in the so-called *Sibylline Oracles*, a collection of Jewish and Christian writings eventually numbering fifteen books, that came into being between the second century

B.C.E. and the fourth century C.E.[4] Sibyls were inspired prophet-esses who had a long history in the Graeco-Roman world, appear-ing, for instance, in the writings of the Greek comedian Aristophanes (circa 447–380 B.C.E.) and the greatest of all Roman poets, Virgil (70–19 B.C.E.).[5] The Romans had a collection of Sibylline books that were only consulted on the express order of the Senate in times of danger, or upon the occurrence of strange portents.[6] Unfortunately, the surviving Sibylline books retain no trace of the ritual injunctions that the Roman Quindecimvirs might have read, these having been removed by later Jewish and Christian editors. Book Five, probably written by an Egyptian Jew during the last quarter of the first century C.E., is an anti-Roman Apocalyptic work in the vein of the New Testament book of Revelation. It opens with fifty lines describing, allegedly prophet-ically, but obviously retrospectively, the Roman emperors down to Marcus Aurelius:

> After the babes who the wolf took for her nurslings, shall come a king first of all, the first letter of whose name shall sum twice ten; he shall prevail greatly in war: and for his first sign he shall have the number ten; so that after him shall rule one who shall have the first letter as his initial; before whom Thrace shall cower and Sicily, then Memphis, Memphis brought low by the fault of her leaders, and of a woman undaunted, who fell on the wave. He shall give laws to peo-ples and bring all into subjection, and after a long time shall hand on his kingship to one who shall have the number three hundred for his first letter, and a name well known from a river, whose sway shall reach from the Persians and Babylon: and he shall unite the Medes with the spear. Then shall rule one whose name-letter is the number three; then one whose initial is twenty: he shall reach the furthest ebb of Ocean's tide, swiftly travelling with his Ausonian company. Then one with the letter fifty shall be king, a fell dragon

breathing out grievous war, who shall lift his hand against his own people to slay them, and shall spread confusion, playing the athlete, charioteer, assassin, a man of many ill deeds; he shall cut through the mountain between two seas and stain it with blood; yet he shall vanish to destruction; then he shall return, making himself equal to God; but God shall reveal his nothingness. Three kings after him shall perish at each other's hand; then shall come a great destroyer of the godly, whom the number seventy plainly shows. His son, revealed by the number three hundred, shall take away his power. After him shall come a devouring tyrant, marked by the letter four, and then a venerable man, by number fifty: but after him one to whom falls the initial sign three hundred, a Celt, ranging the mountains, but hastening the clash of conflict he shall not escape an unseemly doom, but shall fall . . . .[7]

Roman legend recorded that the city of Rome was founded by twins suckled by a she-wolf—Romulus and Remus, "the babes who the wolf took for her nurslings." The letter having a value of twice ten is K, the initial of Caesar (*kaisar*), the first letter of whose given name, Julius (IVLIVS), in Latin is I, with a value of ten in Greek. In the next such cryptic reference, the "first letter" is of course A, indicating Julius Caesar's successor, Augustus or Octavian, later victor in the sea battle of Actium over Mark Antony and Cleopatra, "the woman undaunted, who fell on the wave." Then comes Tiberius, whose name is linked with the river Tiber and begins with the letter T, equal to three hundred. The letters indicated by the numerical values which follow are G (= 3) for Gaius, K (= 20) for Claudius, and N (= 50) for Nero. Reference is made to the then-popular legend of *Nero redivivus*, that Nero would rise again and lead an army into the empire from the east. This story is also alluded to in the roughly contemporaneous Revelation, in the allegorical description of the seven past Roman emperors as the seven-headed Beast, Nero being the head with the mortal wound that heals.[8] The "three kings" which follow are Galba, Otho, and Vitellius. Seventy is the value of O, indicating Vespasian (ΟΥΕΣΠΑΣΙΑΝΟΣ), followed by T as the initial of his son, Titus. The remaining emperors indicated by Greek letter values are Domitian (Δ = 4), Nerva (N = 50), and, finally, Trajan (T = 300), who, in actual fact, was not a Celt, but a Spaniard.

The authority of the *Sibylline Oracles* led the Christians to quote them in support of their claims to the divinity of Jesus, who had himself been regrettably silent on this point. So, in order to remove any doubt on the matter, the Christians wrote their own:

> Then from the east shall a star shine forth . . .
> Radiant and gleaming from heaven above,
> Proclaiming a great sign to mortal men.
> Yea, then shall the Son of great God come to men,
> Clothed in flesh, like unto mortal on earth.
> Four vowels he has, twofold the consonants in him,
> And now will I declare to thee also the whole number:
> Eight monads, and to these as many decads,
> And eight hundreds also his name will show . . .[9]

The oracle, plainly written in retrospect like the earlier example, refers to the name of Jesus (ΙΗΣΟΥΣ), which was the Greek transliteration of his given Aramaic name, Joshua. The writer notes that it has four vowels (I, H, O, and Y) and two consonants (Σ twice), and, when spelled in full, has the value of 888, being eight monads, eight decads, and eight hundreds. Thus, like Zeus, Hermes, Mithras, and Abraxas, the numerical aspects of the name of Jesus were calculated according to Greek Qabalah and became a known part of that god's perceived magical qualities.

It seems that it was not uncommon for oracles to be invented and attributed to Sibylline authority in an effort to give weight to the claim of a particular leader or religion. Another such oracle was reputedly invented by Alexander of Abonoteichus, the false priest of the healing god, Asclepius, whose religious activity lasted from around 150 to 170 C.E., and whose rather successful cult lasted for more than a century after his death. Playing on the credulity of his age, Alexander claimed to have a human-headed serpent which was the incarnation of the god Asclepius. He also claimed divine descent for himself. At the request of a friend, the satirist Lucian wrote an account of Alexander's activities around 180 C.E., after Alexander had been dead for ten years, entitled *Alexander the False Prophet.* Lucian tells how the following oracle turned up after Alexander's arrival, supposedly a prior prediction by the Sibyl:

> On the shores of the Euxine sea, in the vicinity of Sinope,
> A prophet shall be born, by a Tower, in Roman days;
> After the foremost unit and three times ten, he will
> shew forth
> Five more units besides, and a score told three times over,
> Matching, with places four, the name of a valiant
> defender![10]

This gives the values of 1 ("the foremost unit"), 30 ("three times ten"), 5 ("five more units"), and 60 (= 3 x 20, "a score told three times over"), being the letters ΑΛΕΞ (*Alex*), the first four letters of *Alexander,* the "valiant defender." To be even more specific, the first two Greek words of the last line (ανδρος αλεξητηρος) give the entire name (*andros-alex* = *Alexandros*). Lucian's verse may have been invented by him for the purpose of the satire, but, even if this is the case, it shows that isopsephy was in common use as a technique in the creation and interpretation of oracles.

As we have seen, a common form of Greek Qabalah, in addition to isopsephy, is the use of acrostic, or *notarichon,* in which the initial letters of a phrase or passage form a word. The appearance of acrostic in the *Sibylline Oracles* has already been noted earlier in relation to the interpretation there given to the name of Adam, being the initials of the four directions.[11] Dionysius of Halicarnassus in Asia Minor, writing around 30 B.C.E., said that the *Sibylline Oracles* had already suffered from interpolations that could be detected "by means of the so-called acrostics."[12] One of these was inserted toward the end of the second century C.E. by a Christian writer, obviously under the impression that the acrostical form was a sign of authenticity. Known in later Christian times simply as the "Sibylline acrostic," it occurs in Book Eight, and is described by Augustine of Hippo (354–430 C.E.) in *The City of God*:

> One day the distinguished proconsul, Flaccianus, who was a man of great eloquence and learning, was conversing with me about Christ, and he brought out a Greek manuscript containing, he said, the poems of the Sibyl of Erythrae. In the text he showed me how in a certain passage the initial letters of the verses fell in such a sequence that you could read the acrostic ΙΗΣΟΥΣ ΧΡΙΣΤΟΣ ΘΕΟΥ ΥΙΟΣ ΣΩΤΗΡ, which is Greek for *Jesus Christ, Son of God, Saviour* . . . . The verses are twenty-seven in number, which is the cube of three. If, moreover, you string along the initial letters of the five Greek words in question, you get the Greek word ΙΧΘΥΣ (*ichthys*) which means fish. This, by mystical application, is a name for Christ, because a fish can live in the depths of waters, as Christ was able to live in the abyss of our mortality without sin, which is truly to live.[13]

Augustine fails to mention that the acrostic was seven lines longer, and actually read ΙΗΣΟΥΣ ΧΡΙΣΤΟΣ ΘΕΟΥ ΥΙΟΣ ΣΩΤΗΡ ΣΤΑΥΡΟΣ; "Jesus Christ, Son of God, Redeemer, Cross."[14] It was this acrostic which suggested to the early Christians the use of a fish as a symbol of their faith, reinforced by the occurrence of fish in several of the stories concerning the life of Jesus. Christ-

Fish symbolism occurs, for example, in surviving inscriptions from the fourth century C.E. honoring two early Church Fathers, Abercius and Pectorius.[15] Like his contemporary, Jerome, Augustine also interpreted the New Testament in terms of number mysticism, going into a detailed analysis of the 153 fish caught by the apostles in John 21: 11, and showing that 153 was the sum of the numbers 1 to 17.[16] Despite this and other creative interpretations,[17] it is impossible for us to know now exactly why this number was chosen. It may even be that it was a good day's fishing and there actually were a memorable "153 big fish," and thus the number came down to posterity. We can be sure, however, in the knowledge that the early Christians enthusiastically fell upon specific numbers in biblical texts and tried to ascribe a retrospective secret meaning to the authors or the inspiring deity, like the analysis of the number 318 found in the Epistle of Barnabas.

Numerous examples of the use of Greek Qabalah appear in a body of papyri from Graeco-Roman Egypt known among schol-

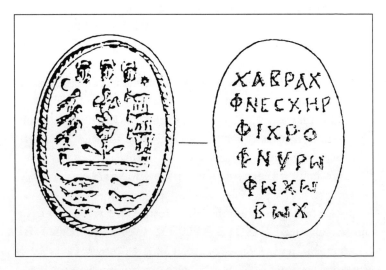

Figure 16. Egyptian gem with Harpocrates and 9999 formula. (Reprinted from David Fideler, *Jesus Christ, Sun of God*, Wheaton, IL: Quest Books, 1993, used by permission.)

OR A C L E S   A N D   I N V O C A T I O N S

ars simply as the *Greek Magical Papyri*. These contain a variety of hymns, rituals, and magical spells, dating mainly from the second century B.C.E. to the fifth century C.E.[18] These charms and invocations reflect the religious and cultural pluralism of Egypt under Greek and then Roman rule, often invoking long lists of gods without distinction, so that the name of the newcomer Jesus appears alongside those of Adonai, Apollo, and Abraxas. Among the lists of god names and magical words (*voces magicae*) written in Greek, Demotic, and Old Coptic are the names of Egyptian, Jewish, Greek, and Mesopotamian divinities. Other words, such as AKRAKANARBA and the like, from which our word "abracadabra" derives, seem to be gibberish.[19] According to these charms, the number of letters in a name could be important, as in those carefully constructed to have exactly 36, 49, or 100 letters, these numbers being the squares of 6, 7, and 10, respectively.[20] Isopsephy was also an ingredient, as seen, for instance, in the invocation to Helios-Apollo that refers to "knowledge of your most great name, of which the number is 9999" or the injunction to "clasp a pebble numbered 3663 to your breasts."[21] Also popular were palindromes ("running backward"), words that read the same in both directions, the most common of which is the celebrated and widespread magical charm ABLANATHANALBA (ΑΒΛΑΝΑΘΑΝΑΛΒΑ).[22] Other techniques include the repetition of magical words or groups of letters, particularly the name IAO or the seven vowels, in various permutations, or written in a shape such as a square or a triangle.

A particularly interesting example of this creativity with letters and words is the following fifth century C.E. love charm:

> I conjure you by the one who sits upon the pinnacles of the four winds. Do not disobey me, but do it quickly, because ordering you is AKRAMMACHAMARI BOULOMEN-TOREB GENIOMOUTHIG DEMOGENED ENKYKLIE ZENOBIOTHIZ ESKOTHORE THOTHOUTHOTH

97

IAEOUOI KORKOOUNOOK LOULOENEL MORO-
THOEPNAM NERXIARXIN XONOPHOENAX
ORNEOPHAO PYROBARYP REROUTOER SESEN-
MENOURES TAUROPOLIT YPEPHENOURY PHIME-
MAMEPH CHENNEOPHEOCH PSYCHOMPOIAPS
ORION, the true one. May I not be compelled to say the
same things again.[23]

Certainly, this mouthful is not an invocation one would want to
be compelled to repeat too often. What is interesting to note is
that the list appears to be the magical names of the twenty-four
letters of the Greek alphabet, in sequential order. Each name,
apart from the first and last, begins and ends with the relevant letter of the alphabet. While most of these *voces magicae* seem to be
nonsense-words, some show traces of their derivation. That associated with *theta,* for instance, (THOTHOUTHOTH), contains
a triple repetition of the name of the god Thouth or Thoth, the
ibis-headed Egyptian god whom the Greeks called "thrice-greatest
Hermes." The name of *iota,* IAEOUOI (ΙΑΕΟΥΩΙ), has been
created by inserting the remaining six of the magical seven vowels
between the repeated letter *iota*. We might guess that magical
names for *pi* and *phi*, PYROBARYP and PHIMEMAMEPH,
started out as palindromes, but error has crept in through subsequent copyists to remove this quality, though we can still see the
Greek word for "fire" (*pyr*) in the name for *pi*, which we have
already seen was associated with it by *notarichon*. Knowledge of
these secret names of the letters apparently empowers the speaker
to command the supreme deity, so plainly the Greek Qabalah had
become a most potent magical gnosis.

Other Greek magical papyri evidence the use of isopsephy in
various forms of divination, including for the purposes of medical
diagnosis, as in Democritus' Sphere for the prognosis of life and
death.

1	10	19
2	11	20
3	13	23
4	14	25
7	16	26
9	17	27
5	15	24
6	18	28
8	21	29
12	22	30

Find out what day of the month the sick one took to bed. Add the day of the month to the number of his name from birth and divide by thirty. Look up the answer on the Sphere: if the number is on the upper register, he will live, but if it is on the lower register, he will die.[24]

Democritus was a philosopher in Abdera in the fifth century B.C.E. who was reputed in antiquity to have been involved in magic. The authorship of numerous works of a magical nature were thus attributed to him, a fate he shared with Orpheus, Moses, and Zoroaster. According to the above "sphere," as such tables were known, if someone named Democritus had taken to bed sick on the 21st day of the month, he would no doubt have been extremely alarmed. For Democritus' "name from birth," or first name (ΔEMOKPITOΣ), adds up 819; "the day of the month" is 21, which, added to 819, equals 840; 840 divided by 30 gives 28, a number on the ominous lower register. Thorndike records that the same method of diagnosis persisted among physicians in Europe into the early Middle Ages.

Having calculated the value of a person's name by adding together the Greek numerals represented by its component letters, and having further added in the day of the moon, one divides the sum by some given divisor and looks for the quotient in the compartments [in the Sphere of Fortune].[25]

The Greek magical papyri also provide examples of divination by means of a bowl or cup filled with water, a technique popular in ancient Egypt and referred to in the Old Testament.[26] One example of bowl divination incorporates isopsephy purely as a magical embellishment, without any actual effect on the outcome, which is determined by the roll of a die.

> *A means to learn from a die whether a man is alive or dead:*
> Make the inquirer throw this die in the bowl. Let him fill this with water. Add to the cast of the die 612, which is the numerical value of the name of god, that is, Zeus, [ΖΕΥΣ] and subtract from the sum 353, which is the numerical value of Hermes [ΕΡΜΗΣ]. If the number remaining is divisible by two, he lives; if not, death has him.[27]

The net effect of this operation is to add 259 to the number of the throw, making an odd number even, and an even number odd. It would therefore have been simpler to say that an even-numbered throw meant the subject was dead. But that would not have visibly involved any divine connection, and thus would have been less "magical."

We can see from this last example that the numerical values of the names of the gods were particularly important in Greek isopsephy. Some deities had their names fit specific numbers of importance, such as the seven-lettered names for the solar gods Mithras/Meithras and Abrasax/Abraxas, both of which added to 365 (ΜΕΙΘΡΑΣ = 365; ΑΒΡΑΣΑΞ = 365). The observation that Mithras' name added up to 365 was made by Jerome (342–420

Figure 17. Gnostic gem with Abraxas and the name $IA\Omega$ (Reprinted from David Fideler, *Jesus Christ, Sun of God*, Wheaton, IL: Quest Books, 1993, used by permission.)

C.E.), the learned author of the Vulgate Bible. Irenaeus (125–203 C.E.) made the same observation with respect to the Gnostic deity, Abrasax.[28] Abrasax is depicted in amulets as a snake-footed (anguipede) figure clad in armor, with the head of a rooster. The rooster was identified with the Sun because its red comb was evocative of the Sun's rays (see figure 17, page 101). Abrasax was equated with the God of the Jews, Jehovah or Yahweh, and his name probably derives from the secret paraphrase of the name of Yahweh, the *tetragrammaton*, which was written in four (Hebrew *arba* = *abra*) consonants.[29] The magical papyri used by the magicians of ancient Alexandria include statements such as: "You are the number of the year, ABRASAX"; and "This is your name . . . with the exact number 365, corresponding to the days of the year. Truly: ABRASAX."[30] Heliodorus (circa 220–250 C.E.) echoed a similar sentiment when he observed that the river Nile was also "actually the year incarnate" (ΝΕΙΛΟΣ = 365).[31]

Actual examples supporting such deliberate manufacture of names or words to achieve a given numerical value are extremely rare. Indeed, much Qabalistic conjecture in both ancient and modern times is wishfully retrospective, since the driving forces behind the creation of language are generally far more mundane. Etymology and linguistics, in fact, usually indicate origins independent of esoteric considerations about alphabetic numerals. The same is true of the historical forces behind the evolution of philosophical, magical, and religious texts. Apart from a very few exceptions, the Greek Qabalah served not as a "Bible code" or technique behind the creation of sacred words or writings, but only as a tool for their subsequent analysis in the search for deeper meaning. However, as we can see from the *Sibylline Oracles* and other examples given above, whether isopsephy was intentional or coincidental in any given case, it was perceived by the ancients as evidence of the voice of heaven, the secret language of the gods.

Notes to Chapter Seven

1 Artemidorus, *Oneirocritica*, II; 70 and IV; 74; R. A. Pack (trans.) (Leipzig: Teubner, 1963), pp. 196–203.

2 Pseudo-Callisthenes, *Life of Alexander*, 93–94, in Albert M. Wolohojian (trans.), *The Romance of Alexander the Great by Pseudo-Callisthenes* (New York: Columbia University Press, 1969), p. 55.

3 Plutarch, *Isis and Osiris*, 28, in J. Gwynn Griffiths (trans.), *Plutarch—On Isis and Osiris* (Cardiff, Great Britain: University of Wales Press, 1970), p.171.

4 J. R. Bartlett, *Jews in the Hellenistic World* (Cambridge: Cambridge University Press, 1985), p. 35.

5 Aristophanes, *Peace*, 1074ff; *Birds*, 967ff; Virgil, *Aeneid*, VI; 45ff; *Fourth Eclogue*.

6 See for instance Livy, *History of Rome*, VII; 27–8.

7 *Sibylline Oracles*, V; 11–45.

8 Revelation 8:3.

9 E. Henneke and W. Schneemelcher (ed.), *New Testament Apocrypha* (Cambridge: James Clarke and Co. Ltd., 1992), p. 656.

10 Lucian, *Alexander the False Prophet*, 12, A. M. Harmon (trans.), vol. IV, p. 191.

11 *Sibylline Oracles*, III; 24–6.

12 *Sibylline Oracles*, IV; 62, in *The Roman Antiquities of Dionysius of Halicarnassus*, E. Cary (trans.) (London: William Heinemann, Ltd., 1978), p. 469.

13 Augustine, *The City of God*, XVIII; 23. *Sibylline Oracles*, VIII; 217–50. See also Acts 8:37.

14 E. Henneke and W. Schneemelcher (ed.), *New Testament Apocrypha*, pp. 673–674.

15 F. L. Cross, *The Early Christian Fathers* (London: Gerald Duckworth, Ltd., 1960), pp. 198–199.

16 Augustine, *Tractates on the Gospel of John*, 122.

17 D. Fideler, *Jesus Christ, Sun of God* (Wheaton, IL: Quest Books, 1993), p. 307, suggests that the number refers to the ratio 153:265 used by Archimedes (circa 287–212 B.C.E.) in his treatise *On the Measurement of the Circle* to approximate the square root of three; this is the controlling ratio behind the equilateral triangle, that in turn forms the rhombus, that supposedly resembles the stretched mesh of a fishing net and also underlies the fish–bladder shape of the *vesica piscis*. That sequence of associations seems overly tenuous, and no evidence is given to support the contention that 153 was known specifically as the so–called "measure of the fish."

18 K. Preisendanz (ed.), *Papyri Graecae Magicae*; republished by H. D. Betz (ed.), *The Greek Magical Papyri in Translation* (Chicago: University of Chicago Press, 1986). See also the additional texts in M. Meyer and R. Smith (ed.), *Ancient Christian Magic—Coptic Texts of Ritual Power* (New York: HarperCollins, 1995).

[19] *PGM*, II; 64.

[20] *PGM*, IV; 242, 1210–1226, 1380–9: XIII; 150, 184–5, 505–6, 522, 645.

[21] *PGM*, II; 129 and *PGM*, IV; 937. 3663 is the number for BAINCHOOOCH, "soul of Khukh," the god of darkness (BAINXΩΩΩX), a magical name that appears frequently in the Greek magical papryri. Different formulae totalling 9999 appear on a gem with the Egyptian deity Harpocrates (ΧΑΒΡΑΧ ΦΝΕΣΧΗΡ ΦΙΧΡΟ ΦΝΥΡΩ ΦΩΧΩ ΒΩΧ: see figure 16, page 96), and a papyrus invoking *Agathos Daimon*, "the Good Spirit," originally a god invoked at Greek banquets (ΦΡΗ ΑΝΩΙ ΦΩΡΧΩ ΦΥΥΥΥ ΡΟΡΨΙΣ ΟΡΟΧΩΩΙ); D. Fideler, *Jesus Christ, Sun of God*, pp. 262–263. The secret seems to be to use lots of *phis* (= 500) and *omegas* (= 800).

[22] *PGM*, III; 150, 341.

[23] *PGM*, CI; 23–29.

[24] *PGM*, XII; 351–64.

[25] *History of Magic*, I; 682–3, cited in V. F. Hopper, *Medieval Number Symbolism* (New York: Columbia University Press, 1938), p. 118.

[26] Genesis 44:5, where Joseph plants the Pharoah's divination cup in his brothers' sacks. See also *PGM*, IV; 164, 222–234.

[27] *PGM*, LXII; 47–51.

[28] Jerome, *On Amos*, I; 3. Irenaeus, *Against Heresies*, I; 24.

[29] K. Rudolph, *Gnosis—The Nature and History of Gnosticism* (San Francisco: HarperSanFrancisco, 1987), p. 311.

[30] *PGM*, XIII; 155–6; VIII; 49.

[31] Heliodorus, *An Ethiopian Story*, IX; 22.

chapter eight

THE GNOSTICS

nosticism is the name applied to the beliefs of the dualistic salvation sects that arose around the beginning of the Current Era. These sects represented a fusion of Hebrew mysticism, Greek philosophy, and the Hermetic traditions of Egypt and the Near East. Although Gnosticism's origins and philosophy are essentially pre-Christian, it became linked with Christian ideas at an early stage and, because of Christianity's influence, is still identified as an "heretical" doctrine. Starting out as a sect on the fringes of Hellenistic Judaism, the Gnostics believed that the Jewish creator-god of the material world, Yahweh or Jehovah, was in fact an evil demiurge. The real spiritual god resided elsewhere, beyond the Kosmos. The true soul, increasingly represented by the figure of

Jesus, could ascend above the material plane and journey through the heavenly realms controlled by various powers, angels, and planets to experience the nature of the higher god. The first century C.E. Jewish phase is generally known as Sethian Gnosticism, since its adherents believed they were descended from Seth, the third son of Adam. The later phase is known as Valentinian Gnosticism, after Valentinus of Alexandria (110–175 C.E.), who was responsible for a major synthesis of Gnostic theory in the second century C.E. Other prominent Gnostics of the second century included Basilides, Marcion, and Marcus. In the first century, Simon Magus, whose prominence is indicated by his appearance in the New Testament, played a major role.[1]

Gnosticism eventually entered the religious mainstream as Manicheism, achieving the status of Buddhism, Christianity, and Islam as a worldwide faith. Of these four world religions, however, Manicheism alone has not survived to the present day. Manicheism took its name from its founder, Mani (216–276 C.E.), an Iranian who was eventually killed by the magi due to the threat he posed to the incumbent religion, Zoroastrianism. As in the case of Jesus, Mani's martyrdom had a spectacular effect. Manicheism flourished in Mesopotamia and spread through Syria, Palestine, Asia Minor, Armenia, northern Arabia, Egypt, and Africa, where Augustine adopted it from 373–382 C.E.[2] The "teaching of light," as Manicheism was known, also spread rapidly in the West, surviving in Europe into the Middle Ages in the form of sects such as the Bogomils and the Cathars. These sects were ultimately suppressed by the Inquisition in the West and by the advent of Islam in the Middle East. Only one Gnostic sect survives to the present day—the Mandeans of southern Iraq.

All the surviving evidence shows that Greek Qabalah played a prominent role in the development of Gnostic doctrine through the teachings of Gnostic figures such as Marcus, Marsanes, and Monoimus. In turn, the extremely close relationship between Gnosticism and early Christianity indicates Gnostic influence in the introduction of Greek Qabalah into Christian thought. We have already seen, for example, how in the important second century C.E. Gnostic text known as the *Pistis Sophia,* authorship of which is usually attributed to Valentinus himself, Jesus uses Qabalistic exegesis to explain the symbolism of the name IAO to his disciples.[3] Another example found in the *Pistis Sophia* is the following mysterious cryptogram inserted at the end of the First Book, which also seems to refer to the symbolism of IAO in its first few sentences:

> But these are the names which I shall give from the Boundless One downwards. Write them with a sign, that the sons of God should be manifested from this place onwards. This is the name of the Deathless One AAA ΩΩΩ. And this is the name of the sound by which the Perfect Man was moved III. But these are the interpretations of the names of these Mysteries. The first is AAA. Its interpretation is ΦΦΦ. The second is MMM or ΩΩΩ. Its interpretation is AAA. The third is ΨΨΨ. Its interpretation is OOO. The fourth is ΦΦΦ. Its interpretation is NNN. The fifth is ΔΔΔ. Its interpretation is AAA. He who is upon the throne is AAA. This is the interpretation of the second AAAA AAAA AAAA. This is the interpretation of the whole name.[4]

Until the recent discovery of the Nag Hammadi codices in 1945, the only detailed information available on the Gnostic sects came from the early Fathers of the Christian church. During the heated religious debate with the Gnostics in the second and third centuries, Irenaeus, Hippolytus, Tertullian, Clement, and Origen wrote criticisms and refutations of teachings they considered heretical, in the process defining for the first time much of Christian doctrine. Their accounts of the Gnostics are naturally unsympathetic, but, because they were among the earliest Christian writers, their books survived later persecutions and today provide us with invaluable first-hand accounts of Gnostic philosophy. It is worth recounting at length a passage from Irenaeus describing the teachings of one particular sect known as the Marcosians, the followers of the famous magician, Marcus (d. 175 C.E.), who was a close personal disciple of Valentinus. Irenaeus (125–203 C.E.) was bishop of Lyons during the second century. He wrote a work in five volumes entitled *Against Heresies* in which his account of Marcosian theology preserves a complete system of Gnostic symbolism attached to the letters of the Greek alphabet, and connects them with the Aeons, the powers involved in the creation of the Kosmos:

> They affirm that these eighteen Aeons are strikingly indicated by the first two letters of Jesus' name [ΙΗΣΟΥΣ], namely *Iota* [= 10] and *Eta* [= 8]. And, in like manner, they assert that the ten Aeons are pointed out by the letter *Iota* [= 10], which begins His name; while, for the same reason, they tell us the Saviour said, "Not one *Iota*, or one tittle, shall pass away until all be fulfilled." [Mark 5:31]. . . This Marcus then . . . declares that the infinitely exalted Tetrad descended to him in the form of a woman . . . and expounded to him alone its own nature, and the origin of all things, which it had never before revealed to gods or men.
>
> Moreover, the Tetrad, explaining these things to him more fully, said:- I wish now to show thee Truth [*Aletheia*] herself; for I have brought her down from the dwellings above, that thou mayest see her without a veil, and understand her beauty—that thou mayest also hear her speaking, and admire her wisdom. Behold then, her head on high, *Alpha* and *Omega*; her neck, *Beta* and *Psi*; her shoulders with her hands, *Gamma* and *Chi*; her breast, *Delta* and *Phi*; her diaphragm, *Epsilon* and *Upsilon*; her back, *Zeta* and *Tau*; her belly, *Eta* and *Sigma*; her thighs, *Theta* and *Rho*; her knees, *Iota* and *Pi*; her legs, *Kappa* and *Omicron*; her ankles,

Lambda and *Xi*; her feet *Mu* and *Nu*. Such is the body of Truth, according to this magician, such the figure of the element, such the character of the letter. . . .

When the Tetrad had spoken these things, Truth looked at him, opened her mouth, and uttered a word. That word was a name, and the name is this one that we now speak of, viz. Christ Jesus. When she had uttered this name, she at once relapsed into silence. And as Marcus waited in the expectation that she would say something more, the Tetrad again came forward and said:- Thou hast reckoned as contemptible that word which thou hast heard from the mouth of Truth. This which thou knowest and seemest to possess, is not an ancient name. For thou possesseth the sound of it merely, whilst thou art ignorant of its power. For Jesus [ΙΗΣΟΥΣ] is a name arithmetically symbolical, consisting of six letters, and is known by all those that belong to the called.

Know then that the twenty-four letters which you possess are symbolical emanations of the three powers that contain the entire number of elements above. For you are to reckon thus—that the nine mute letters [Β, Γ, Δ, Θ, Κ, Π, Τ, Φ, Χ] are the images of [the Aeons] Pater and Aletheia [Father and Truth], because they are without voice, that is, of such a nature as cannot be uttered or pronounced. But the semi-vowels [Ζ, Λ, Μ, Ν, Ξ, Ρ, Σ, Ψ] represent [the Aeons] Logos and Zoe [Word and Life], because they are, as it were, midway between the consonants and the vowels, partaking of the nature of both. The vowels, again, are representative of [the Aeons] Anthropos and Ecclesia [Man and Church], inasmuch as a voice proceeding from Anthropos [Man] gave being to them all; for the sound of the voice imparted to them form. Thus, then, Logos and Zoe possessed eight [of these letters]; Anthropos and Ecclesia seven; and Pater and Aletheia nine. But since the number allotted to each was unequal, He who existed in the Father came down, having been specially sent by Him from whom He was separated, for the rectification of what had taken place . . . and the three sets were rendered alike in point of number, all becoming Ogdoads; which three, when brought together, constitute the number twenty-four [8 + 8 + 8]. . . . These [three elements or Ogdoads] were endowed by the three powers [Pater, Anthropos, and Logos] with a resemblance to Him who is invisible. And he says that those letters which we call double [Z, Ξ, Ψ = δς, κς, πς] are the images of these three elements.

He asserts that the fruit of this arrangement and analogy has been manifested in the likeness of an image, namely Him [Jesus] who, after six days, ascended into the mountain along with three others, and then became one of six (the sixth) [Moses and Elias being added to the company described in Mark 9:2 and Matthew 17:7, namely Peter, James and John], in which character He descended, and was contained in the Hebdomad, since He was the illustrious Ogdoad [because *Christ*, ΧΡΕΙΣΤΟΣ, has eight letters], and contained in Himself the entire number of the elements, which the descent of the dove (who is Alpha and Omega) made clearly manifest, when He became baptized; for the number of the dove is eight hundred and one [*dove*, ΠΕΡΙ–ΣΤΕΡΑ = 801 = 1 + 800 = A + Ω]. And for this reason did Moses declare that man was formed on the sixth day; and then again, according to this arrangement, it was on the sixth day, which is the preparation, that the last man appeared, for the regeneration of the first. Of this arrangement, both the beginning and the end were formed at the sixth hour, at which He was nailed to the tree. For that perfect being Nous [Mind], knowing that the number six had the power both of formation and regeneration, declared to the children of light, that regeneration which has been wrought out by Him who appeared as *Episemon* [ς = 6] in regard to that number. Whence he also declares it is that the double letters [Z, Ξ, Ψ = δς, κς, πς] contain the *Episemon* number; for this *Episemon*, when joined to the twenty-four elements, completed the name of thirty letters.

Consider this present *Episemon*, . . . Him who was formed after the original *Episemon* . . . who, by His own power and wisdom, through means of that which he had produced by Himself, gave life to this world, consisting of seven powers. . . . And the first heaven indeed pronounces *Alpha*, the next to this *Epsilon*, the third *Eta*, the fourth, which is also in the midst of the seven, utters the sound of *Iota*, the fifth *Omicron*, the sixth *Upsilon*, the seventh, which is also fourth from the middle, utters the element *Omega*. . . . Hence also it comes to pass, that when the soul is involved in difficulties and distress, for its own relief it calls out, "Oh" (Ω), in honour of the letter in question, so that its cognate soul above may recognise its distress, and send down to it relief.[5]

Irenaeus' account clearly shows that Greek Qabalah was already well advanced among the Gnostics in the second century. Since Christian doctrine and orthodoxy was, at this early stage in its development, still largely undefined, teachings such as those of Valentinus and Marcus, although later called "Gnostic" and labeled as heretical, were at the time an integral part of the variegated Christian phenomenon. Although other aspects of Gnostic thought, such as the existence of the Aeons, did not survive to become part of orthodox Christianity, aspects of the Greek Qabalistic treatment of Jesus's name demonstrated by the Gnostics remained part of Christian gnosis in the popular psyche.

This passage from Irenaeus provides us with perhaps the fullest surviving account of Gnostic numerology from the ancient world, and is notable for several specific aspects in relation to Greek Qabalah. The correlation of Christ, as *Alpha* and *Omega*, with the 801 of the Dove, is an illustration of the use of isopsephy to associate words or phrases of equal value. In addition to the attribution of the seven vowels to the seven heavens of the Gnostics, we also see here a complete set of correspondences for the whole of the Greek alphabet, in the allocation of pairs of letters to various parts of the human body. Although there is no proven connection between the two, there are also striking similarities between Marcus' mystical interpretation of the alphabet's role in the creation of the universe and the later earliest known work of the Hebrew Qabalah, the *Book of Formation* or *Sefer Yezirah.* In this work, which dates from about the third to the sixth century C.E., the letters of the Hebrew alphabet play a similar role. The teachings of Marcus also analyze the alphabet in terms of groups of letters, here divided grammatically into nine mutes, eight semi-vowels, and the seven vowels, in which groups they had also been allocated to the signs of the zodiac in Graeco-Roman astrology, as discussed earlier. The Gnostics' treatment of the three double letters as a special group had been observed, as we have also seen, as far back as the fourth century B.C.E. by Aristotle in his *Metaphysics.*

The division of the alphabet into grammatical groups, as well as its association with the powers of heaven, is also seen in the recently translated Nag Hammadi codices, a collection of thirteen Gnostic texts found in a clay jar near Nag Hammadi in Egypt in December 1945. We know from internal evidence that these goatskin-bound papyri were actually manufactured around 350 C.E., although the teachings contained in them are probably considerably older Coptic translations of Greek originals. The one that concerns us, Codex X, is known as *Marsanes,* from the name of its probable author, and has most unfortunately survived only in a frustratingly fragmentary condition. At least 60 percent of the text has been totally lost. What remains reveals a work of the Apocalyptic genre, in which Marsanes, referring to previous oral teachings on the subject matter, recounts a heavenly journey and various visions, and deals with Pythagorean arithmology and the relation of the letters of the alphabet to parts of the soul and to the angels.

But their powers, which are as angels, are in the form of beasts and animals. Some among them are polymorphous, and contrary to nature they have [...] for their names which [...]. They are divided and [...] according to the [... and ...] in form [...]. But these that are aspects of sound according to the third originate from being. And concerning these, all of these remarks are sufficient, since we have already spoken about them. For this division takes place again in these regions in the manner we have mentioned from the beginning. However, the soul, on the other hand, has different shapes. The shape of the soul exists in this form, i.e. the soul that came into existence of its own accord. The shape is the second spherical part while the first follows it, EHIOY, the self-begotten soul, AEHIOYΩ. The second shape, EHIOY, . . . by those having two sounds (diphthongs), the first being placed after them [...] and [...] the light. . . . But know that the oxytones exist among the vowels and the diphthongs which are next to them. But the short vowels are inferior, and the [...] are [...] by them. Those that [...] since they are intermediate [...]. The sounds of the semi-vowels are superior to the voiceless consonants. And those that are double are superior to the semi-vowels which do not change. But the aspirates are better than the inaspirates of the voiceless consonants. And those that are intermediate will accept their combination in which they are; they are ignorant of the things that are good. The vowels are combined with the intermediates which are less. Form by form, they constitute the nomenclature of the gods and the angels, not because they are mixed with each other according to every form, but only because they have a good function. It did not happen that their will was revealed. . . . But I am speaking to you concerning the three shapes of the soul. The third shape of the soul is [...] a spherical one, put after it, from the simple vowels: [AAA] EEE, [HHH], III, OOO, YYY, ΩΩΩ. The diphthongs were as follows: AI, AY, EI, EY, HY, OY, ΩY, OI, HI, YI, ΩI. . . . The third shape is spherical. The second shape, being put after it, has two sounds. The male soul's third shape consists of the simple vowels: AAA, EEE, HHH, III, OOO, YYY, ΩΩΩ, ΩΩΩ, ΩΩΩ. And this shape is different from the first, but they resemble each other and they make some ordinary sounds of this sort: AEHOΩ. And from these are made the diphthongs. So also the fourth and the fifth. With regard to them, they are not allowed to reveal the whole topic, but only those things which are apparent. You were taught about them, that you should receive them in order that they, too, might all seek and find who they are, either by themselves alone, or by each other, or to reveal destinies that have been determined from the beginning, either with reference to themselves alone or with reference to one another, just as they exist with each other in sound, whether partially and formally. They are commanded to submit or their part is generated and formal. Either they are commanded by the long vowels [H and Ω], or by those of dual time value [A, I, Y], or by the short vowels [E and O] which are small [...] or those that are high in tone [oxytones] or those in the middle [circumflex] or those that are low in tone [barytones]. And the consonants exist with the vowels, and individually they are commanded, and they submit. They constitute the nomenclature of the angels. And the consonants are self-existent, and as they are changed they submit to the hidden gods by means of beat and pitch and silence and impulse. They summon the semi-vowels, all of which submit to them with one accord; since it is only the unchanging double consonants that co-exist with the semi-vowels. But the aspirates and the inaspirates and the intermediates constitute the voiceless consonants. Again, they are combined with each other, and they are separate from one another. They are commanded and they submit, and they constitute an ignorant nomenclature. And they become one or two or three or four or five or six up to seven having a simple sound, together with these which have two sounds, . . . the place of the seventeen consonants. Among the first names some are less. And since these do not have being, either they are an aspect of being or they are divided from the nature of the mind, which is masculine and which is intermediate. And you put in those that resemble each other with the vowels and the consonants. Some are: ΒΑΓΑΔΑΖΑΘΑ, ΒΕΓΕΔΕΖΕΘΕ, ΒΗΓΗΔΗΖΗΘΗ, ΒΙΓΙΔΙΖΙΘΙ, ΒΟΓΟΔΟΖΟΘΟ, ΒΥΓΥΔΥΖΥΘΥ, ΒΩΓ–ΩΔΩΖΩΘΩ. And the rest ΒΑΒΕΒΗΒΙΒΟΒΥΒΩ. But the rest are different: ΒΑΒΕΒΗΒΙΒΟΒΥΒΩ, in order that you might collect them, and be separated from the angels.[6]

In the above passage, Marsanes commences by making reference to Graeco-Roman astrological speculation referred to earlier, in which the signs of the zodiac were classified as animal-shaped, human-shaped, or anthropomorphic, and associated with groups of letters according to grammatical divisions. From the shapes of these zodiacal signs, Marsanes then goes on to discuss the shapes of the various parts of the soul. Based upon the discussion on the construction of the World-Soul appearing in Plato's *Timaeus*, the human soul is seen as divided into three parts, a doctrine reputedly derived from the Pythagoreans. Marsanes here attributes various combinations of the vowels to these parts of the soul: the "self-begotten soul" is ascribed to ΑΕΗΙΟΥΩ, while the soul's "second shape" is connected with the reduced combination, ΕΗΙΟΥ. The repetition of the vowels in the above passage is an indication that they were probably meant to be chanted.

Marsanes goes on to show considerable familiarity with the work of the ancient Greek grammarians, like Marcus, dividing the alphabet into groups of seven vowels, eight semi-vowels (Ζ, Λ, Μ, Ν, Ξ, Ρ, Σ, Ψ), and nine voiceless consonants, or mutes (Β, Γ, Δ, Θ, Κ, Π, Τ, Φ, Χ). These are then further divided according to their various grammatical subgroups, and each subgroup is ranked according to its perceived qualities. For instance, the aspirates, the name given to consonants blended with the "*h*" sound (in Greek, these are Θ, Φ and X, giving the sounds *th*, *ph*, and *ch*), were seen as better than inaspirates. One ancient commentator on the *Ars Grammatica* informs us that this is because they have more spirit or breath (*pneuma*).[7] Both the aspirates and the double letters (consonant + Σ) are formed from three subgroups of mutes; labials (B, Π, Φ), gutturals (Γ, K, X), and dentals (Δ, T, Θ), which can also be classified into smooth (Π, K, T), middle (B, Γ, Δ), and rough (Φ, X, Θ).

The teachings of Marsanes and Marcus prove that, by the second century C.E., the work of the Greek grammarians in grouping the letters of the alphabet according to their sound qualities had been a major influence in the continuing extension of the Greek Qabalah. Philo also likened the vowels to the mind, the semi-vowels to the senses, and the consonants to the body.[8] The various groups of letters are ranked by Marsanes according to their perceived place in a hierarchy of power, in the order set out below:

Vowels	Long	H Ω
	Intermediate	A I Y
	Short	E O
Semi-vowels	Double	Z Ξ Ψ
	Single	Λ M N P Σ
Voiceless	Aspirate	Θ Φ X
	Intermediate	B Γ Δ
	Inaspirate	K Π T

Although much of the meaning of the fragmentary Nag Hammadi codex can now only be guessed at, it is clear that both Marsanes and Marcus taught that the letters of the Greek alphabet were connected with the creative powers of the Kosmos, and that a knowledge of the various combinations of vowels and consonants could bring about control of these powers. The Greek letters are "the nomenclature of the gods and the angels"; "and as they are changed they submit to the hidden gods by means of beat and pitch and silence and impulse." This concept was central to much of Hellenistic magic, and can be seen throughout the Greek magical papyri in the combinations of vowels, letter permutations, and long lists of "barbarous names," or *voces magicae,* that were contained in various charms and divine invocations.

Hippolytus also gives us an account of the teachings of Marcus and various other Gnostics, drawing most of his material from Irenaeus. One of these is an Arabian Gnostic named Monoimus, who made extensive use in his teaching of the letter *iota.* We can see in his reasoning a vivid illustration of how mystical symbolism came to be attached to various letters by virtue of their geometrical shape and numerical value.

> Monoimus the Arabian . . . says that man is the universe. . . . And this man constitutes a single monad, which is uncompounded and indivisible, and yet at the same time compounded and divisible. . . . This monad is likewise, as it were, a certain musical harmony, which comprises all things in itself. . . . As an illustration, however, consider, he says, as a greatest image of the perfect man, the one jot—that one tittle. And this one tittle is an uncompounded, simple, and pure monad, which derives its composition from nothing at all. And yet this tittle is likewise compounded, multiform, branching into many sections, and consisting of many parts. That one indivisible tittle is, he says, one tittle of the letter *iota*, with many faces, and innumerable eyes, and countless

names, and this tittle is an image of that perfect invisible man. The monad, that is, the one tittle, is therefore, he says, also a decad. For by the actual power of this one tittle, are produced duad, and triad, and tetrad, and pentad, and hexad, and heptad, and ogdoad, and ennead, up to ten.... For cubes, and octahedrons, and pyramids, and all figures similar to these, out of which consist fire, air, water, and earth, have arisen from numbers which are comprehended in that simple tittle of the *iota*. And this tittle constitutes a perfect son of a perfect man. When, therefore, he says, Moses mentions that the rod was changeably brandished for the introduction of the plagues throughout Egypt—now these plagues, he says, are allegorically expressed symbols of the creation—he did not (as a symbol) for more plagues than ten shape the rod. Now this rod constitutes one tittle of the *iota*, and is both twofold and various. . . . Conformably with that one tittle, the law of Moses constitutes the series of the ten commandments which expresses allegorically the divine mysteries of those precepts. For, he says, all knowledge of the universe is contained in what relates to the succession of the ten plagues and the series of the ten commandments.[9]

Thus Monoimus takes the meaning of the word *iota*, a jot or tittle, and connects it with its root value, for 10 reduces to 1, the monad and the smallest unit, from which all other numbers and shapes are derived. Its full value of 10 is representative of the perfection of the Pythagorean decad, and therefore "a perfect son of a perfect man," as well as connecting it with various other decads such as the Ten Commandments. Its linear shape is also seen as symbolizing the rod of Moses, which was "changeably brandished" into a serpent in the Exodus account of Moses' confrontation with the Pharaoh and the introduction of the ten plagues of Egypt.[10]

As seen earlier in the discussion by Hippolytus on the symbolism of the letters *lambda* and *mu*, the ancient convention was to use the left hand in sign-language to represent numbers of less than a hundred, which led to the attribution of a negative connotation to words with an isopsephy of 99 or less.[11] Irenaeus refers to this practice in arguing against the follies of the Gnostics' use of Greek Qabalah:

> They endeavour to bring forward proofs of their system . . . through those numbers which are, according to the practice followed by the Greeks, contained in different letters; this, I say, demonstrates in the clearest manner their confusion . . . . For, transferring the name Jesus, which belongs to another language, to the numeration of the Greeks, they sometimes call it "Episemon," as having six letters, and at other times "the Plenitude of the Ogdoads," as containing the number eight hundred and eighty-eight. But his corresponding Greek name, which is "Soter," that is, *Saviour*, because it does not fit in with their system, either with respect to numerical value or as regards its letters, they pass over in silence . . . because it is a word of five letters, and its numerical value is one thousand four hundred and eight [ΣΩΤΗΡ = 1408]. . . . Moreover, *Jesus*, which is a word belonging to the proper tongue of the Hebrews, contains, as the learned among them declare, two letters and a half [Hebrew ישׁו, *IShU*; counting ׳ or *yod* as half a letter]. . . . From this fact, therefore, that the more important names, both in Hebrew and in Greek languages, do not conform to their system, either as respects the number of letters or the reckoning brought out of them, the forced character of their calculations respecting the rest becomes clearly manifest. . . .

> But further, as to their calling material substances "on the left hand," and maintaining that those things which [add to less than 100 and] are thus on the left hand fall into corruption . . . . This Greek word *Agape* (love), then, according to the letters of the Greeks, by means of which reckoning is car-

ried on among them, having a numerical value of ninety-three [ΑΓΑΠΗ = 93], is in like manner assigned to the place of the rest on the left hand. *Aletheia* (truth) too, having in like manner, according to the principle indicated above, a numerical value of sixty-four [ΑΛΗΘΕΙΑ = 64], exists among the material substances. And thus, in fine, they will be compelled to acknowledge that all those sacred names which do not reach a numerical value of one hundred, but only contain numbers summed by the left hand, are corruptible and material.[12]

Hippolytus also provides us with a description of a technique used in Gnostic numerology known as *pythmenes* (thrones, or roots).

Those, then, who suppose that they prophesy by means of calculations and numbers, and elements and names, constitute the origin of their attempted system to be as follows. They affirm that there is a root of each of the numbers; in the case of the thousands, so many monads as there are thousands; for example, the root of six thousand, six monads . . . . And in the case of hundreds . . . . And it is similar respecting decads. . . . And in the case of monads, the monads themselves are a root . . . . In this way, also, ought we therefore to act in the case of the elements [of words], for each letter has been arranged according to a certain number: for instance, the letter N according to fifty monads; but of fifty monads five is the root, and the root of the letter N is therefore five. Grant that from some name we take certain roots of it. For instance, ... The name Hector [ΕΚΤΩΡ] has five letters—E, and K, and T, and O, and R. The roots of these are 5, 2, 3, 8, 1; and these added together make 19 monads [10 + 9]. Again, of the ten the root is one [10 = 1 + 0 = 1]; and of the nine, nine; which added together make up ten: the root of ten is a monad. The name Hector, therefore, when made the subject of computation, has formed a root, namely a monad.

It would, however, be easier to conduct the calculation thus: Divide the ascertained roots from the letters—as now in the case of Hector we have nineteen monads—into nine, and treat what remains over as roots. For example, if I divide 19 into 9, the remainder is 1, for 9 times 2 are 18, and there is a remaining monad: for if I subtract 18 from 19, there is a remaining monad; so that the root of the name Hector will again be a monad. . . . But when one computes names, and finds the letter occurring twice, he calculates it once; as, for instance, the name Patroclus [ΠΑΤΡΟΚΛΟΣ] has the letter O occurring twice in it, they therefore take it into calculation only once. . . .

In like manner, the name Sarpedon [ΣΑΡΠΗΔΩΝ], when made the subject of calculation, produces as a root, according to the rule of nine, two monads. Patroclus, however, produces nine monads; therefore Patroclus gains the victory. For when one number is uneven, but the other even, the uneven number, if it is larger, prevails. But again, when there is an even number, eight, and five an uneven number, the eight prevails, for it is larger. If, however, there were two numbers, for example, both of them even, or both of them odd, the smaller prevails. But how does the name Sarpedon, according to the rule of nine, make two monads, since the letter long *o* [*omega*] is omitted? Because when there may be in a name both the letter long *o* [Ω], and long *e* [H], they leave out the long *o*, using only one [long] letter, for they say both are equipollent; and the same must not be computed twice over, as has been above declared.[13]

The method of computation referred to above by Hippolytus was known to classical mathematicians as the "rule of nine." When any number is divided by nine, the remainder is the same as that left if the sum of the digits in the original number is divided by nine. The results of this method are the same as if the value for each letter in a word is reduced to a single unit, and then further reduced by addition of these root values to a final single digit. Hippolytus also records other variations used by the Gnostics. Some used a "rule of seven" rather than a "rule of nine," while others first divided each word into mutes, vowels, and semi-vowels, and then analyzed each group of letters separately. The *pythmenes* method described by Hippolytus would use the following root values for the relevant groups of letters:

1 A I P	2 B K Σ	3 Γ Λ T
4 Δ M Y	5 E N Φ	6 Ξ X
7 Z O Ψ	8 H Π Ω	9 Θ

The Hebrew Qabalists later adopted and employed the *pythmenes* technique under the name of *aiq beker* (אי״ק בכ״ר), so called after the first two groups of letters in the Hebrew alphabet that were reduced by this method to the root values of one and two, respectively (*AIQ BKR*). It is also sometimes referred to as the Qabalah of Nine Chambers. *Pythmenes* was also used by Nicomachus of Gerasa in ascribing the hexad and its Pythagorean qualities of peace and harmony to the universe, because the word *kosmos* reduces to a value of six (ΚΟΣΜΟΣ = 600 = 6+0+0 = 6; or else 20 + 70 + 200 + 40 + 70 + 200 = 2 + 7 + 2 + 4 + 7 + 2 = 24 = 2 + 4 = 6).[14] Hippolytus also mentions the "rule of nine" in a numerological system used by the Egyptians.

For the monad, therefore, as being beneficent, they assert that there are consequently names ascending, and beneficent, and masculine, and carefully observed, terminating in an uneven number; whereas that those terminating in the even number have been supposed to be both descending, and feminine and malicious. For they affirm that nature is made up of contraries, namely bad and good, as right and left, light and darkness, night and day, life and death. And moreover they make this assertion, that they have calculated the word "Deity," (and found that it reverts into a pentad with an ennead subtracted). Now this name is an even number, and when it is written down (on some material) they attach it to the body, and accomplish cures by it. In this manner, likewise, a certain herb, terminating in this number, being similarly fastened around (the frame), operates by reason of a similar calculation of the number. Nay, even a doctor cures sickly people by a similar calculation. If, however, the calculation is contrary, it does not heal with facility. Persons attending to these numbers reckon as many as are homogeneous according to this principle; some, however, according to vowels alone; whereas others according to the entire number. Such also is the wisdom of the Egyptians, by which, as they boast, they suppose that they cognise the divine nature.[15]

The word for divinity in Greek and Coptic is *theos*, the letters of which add to 284 (ΘΕΟΣ = 9 + 5 + 70 + 200 = 284), an even number which by the rule of nine "reverts into a pentad with an ennead subtracted"; since 284 becomes 2 + 8 + 4 = 14 = 9 + 5; or alternatively, 284 divided by 9 is 31, with a remainder of 5. The Egyptian belief in the qualities of odd and even numbers recounted here can be traced as directly descended from the Pythagoreans' columns of cognates or dualities listed by Aristotle in his *Metaphysics*, from which it was alleged that all numbers and the universe were constructed. And again we see here that the Gnostics would often divide words into grammatical groups, such as vowels and consonants, before the application of techniques of purely numerical analysis.

To summarize, the surviving information we have about the teachings of the Gnostics provides us with a glimpse of the most developed form and systematic application of Greek Qabalah in the ancient world at that time. In the Gnostic teachings we have seen, the letters of the alphabet are written of as spiritual entities capable of feeling and action, divine agents involved in the creation of the universe, so that a knowledge of their proper combinations and annunciation would allow control of the powers of the universe. We know that, by the second century C.E., the Gnostics had developed a system of Greek Qabalah in which each letter of the alphabet had its own specific religious and symbolic associations, including aeons, angels, heavens, and parts of the human soul and physical body. Different qualities of letters arising from considerations of grammar and phonetics had also resulted in the letters being ranked according to their perceived relative power, from long vowels down to inaspirate mutes. In addition to this, the isopsephy used by the Pythagoreans had developed by Gnostic times into several different techniques that were used for a wide range of purposes, including divination, doctrinal allegory, and medical prognosis and treatment. Although some of these ideas or techniques already existed in the Greek Qabalah of the Hellenistic Age that they inherited, there can be little room for doubt that the Gnostics were a major force in its development.

Notes to Chapter Eight

1 Acts 7:9–25.

2 K. Rudolph, *Gnosis—The Nature and History of Gnosticism* (San Francisco: HarperSanFrancisco, 1987), pp. 329–331.

3 G. Horner (trans.), *Pistis Sophia* (London: Macmillan Co., 1924), p. 180.

4 G. Horner (trans.), *Pistis Sophia,* p. 62

5 Irenaeus, *Against Heresies*, I; 14–16, in F. R. M. Hitchcock (trans.) (London: Society for the Promotion of Christian Knowledge, 1916).

6 B. Pearson (ed.), *Nag Hammadi Codices IX and X* (Leiden: Brill, 1981), pp. 229–347.

7 Melampus, *Scholia in Dionysii Thracis Artem Grammaticam*, 6(7b), in A. Hilgard (trans.) (Leipzig: Teubner, 1901), pp. 10–58.

8 Philo, *Questions and Answers on Genesis*, IV; 117.

9 Hippolytus, *Refutation of All Heresies*, VII; 5–6 in J. H. MacMahon (trans.), *Philosopheumena* (London: Society for the Promotion of Christian Knowledge, 1921).

10 Exodus 7:9.

11 Hippolytus, *Refutation of All Heresies*, VI; 47.

12 Irenaeus, *Against Heresies*, II; 24, in F. R. M. Hitchcock (trans.).

13 Hippolytus, *Refutation of All Heresies*, IV; 14.

14 R. Waterfield (trans.), *The Theology of Arithmetic* (Grand Rapids, MI: Phanes Press, 1988), p. 80.

15 Hippolytus, *Refutation of All Heresies*, IV; 44.

chapter nine

THE ROMANS

t is worth briefly consider-
ing those few examples we
have of the use of Greek
Qabalah by the Romans.
The Romans dominated
Greece from the beginning of the second century B.C.E., although
they refrained from annexing it outright. Although considering
themselves superior in the arts of war, law, and statecraft, the
Romans were impressed by other aspects of Greek civilization,
such as art, architecture, religion, and philosophy, much of which
they adopted. This reverse influence grew along with Roman
dominance over its more ancient neighbor, and the Roman upper
class became increasingly Hellenized, particularly from the first
century B.C.E. on. Most educated Romans spoke Greek, and were
often sent to Greece in their youth to study philosophy and

rhetoric from Greek tutors, usually at Athens or Rhodes. Common Greek (*koine*) was also frequently used among traders, it having become widespread in the ancient world following the conquests of Alexander centuries earlier. In addition, Rome was increasingly a rival to Alexandria as the destination of Greek artists and intellectuals.

That the Romans should use Greek isopsephy is thus not surprising, because of the subsequent close fusion of the two cultures. Latin could not be used for isopsephy, since only a few of its letters were used as numerals. We know that knowledge of Greek isopsephy however, was sufficiently widespread among the Romans in the first century for it to be used in common graffiti, since instances have been found at Pergamum and at Pompeii. One such example, preserved under the layers of volcanic ash that buried Pompeii during the eruption of Mt. Vesuvius in 79 C.E., is a shy declaration that reads, "I love her whose number is 545" (φιλω ης αριθμος φμε). Another states "Amerimnus thought upon his lady Harmonia for good. The number of her honorable name is 45" (Αμεριμνος εμνησθη Αρμονιας της ειδιας κυριας επ αγαθω, ης ο αριθμος με [?]).[1]

An earlier and particularly interesting example is recorded in the writings of the Roman lawyer and historian Suetonius, born in 69 C.E., who eventually became chief secretary to the Emperor Hadrian during his reign from 117–138 C.E. Suetonius was author of many works, among them one of the most fascinating and richest of all Latin histories, *The Twelve Caesars*. In his brief account of the reign of the notorious Nero, Emperor of Rome from 54–68 C.E., Suetonius records that this piece of graffiti was posted on the city walls:

> Count the numerical values
> Of the letters in Nero's name,
> And in "murdered his own mother":
> You'll find their sum is the same.[2]

The allusion, of course, is to the well-known fact that Nero had arranged the assassination of his mother, Agrippina, in 59 C.E., a botched job colorfully recorded by the historian Tacitus.[3] In Greek, both Nero (Νερων) and "killed his own mother" (ιδιαν μητερα απεκτεινε) add to 1005 when their letters are counted as numbers. It is interesting to reflect upon why the author bothered to use isopsephy at all to make his point. A relatively well-educated Roman had clearly gone to some trouble to come up with this calculation, as well as risking horrendous punishment for writing it on the walls of Rome. Perhaps, as in the case of its use in oracles, the purpose of using isopsephy was to give the allegation the force of divine truth and predestination.

The above examples of the use of Greek isopsephy as common graffiti by the Romans are interesting in that they provide clear proof that isopsephy in the ancient world was not an esoteric science or inner gnosis. It was in common use and knowledge of it was widespread among ordinary people, even though Greek was not their first language. This is natural enough when one remembers that alphabetic numerals were also in widespread use throughout the Roman Empire, embracing as it did so many Mediterranean lands previously under Greek domination prior to the Roman ascendancy. In a large part of the Empire, it would have been only after Greek numerals were replaced with Roman or Arabic numerals that isopsephy would have become anything less than second nature.

Notes to Chapter Nine

[1] M. Farbridge, *Studies in Biblical and Semitic Symbolism* (Hoboken, NJ: Ktav Publishing House, 1970), p. 95; F. Dornseiff, *Das Alphabet in Mystik und Magie* (Liepzig: Teubner, 1925), p. 113.

[2] Suetonius, *Nero*, XXXIX; 2, in R. Graves (trans.), *The Twelve Caesars* (London: Penguin, 1957), p. 236.

[3] Tacitus, *Annals*, XIV.

chapter ten

THE CHRISTIANS

n one of the very few surviving independent con-
temporaneous sources
available to us on the
early Christian move-
ment, Pliny the Younger (61–113 C.E.), then Governor of
Bithnyia, wrote to the Emperor Trajan that, on investigating the
religion of the Christians of his day, he found only "a degenerate
sort of cult carried to extravagant lengths" (*superstitionem pravam
et immodicam*).[1] But, by the fourth century C.E., this divergent
cult of Judaism, based on the teachings of Jesus of Nazareth (circa
6 B.C.E.–30 C.E.), a carpenter and preacher from Roman
Palestine, had become sufficiently widespread for it to be adopted by the Emperor Constantine. From that point on, the stage
was set for it to become the official religion of the Empire. How

did this happen? For those interested in the topic, there is probably still no better study on the rise, establishment, and sects of Christianity than the incomparable work of Edward Gibbon (1737–1794), almost deceptively entitled *The Decline and Fall of the Roman Empire*. As Christianity is a subject upon which an exhaustive amount has been written by innumerable scholars, we may here confine ourselves to a brief summary of its early development while introducing a few apposite points.

Christian teaching states that Jesus was the one anointed (*Christos*) as the expected Redeemer by Jehovah, and that he was even the son of Jehovah himself. We must remember that this claim was not particularly unusual for the period. Indeed, it followed a long line of precedents. The elevation of revered human figures to godhead is a phenomenon of which examples can be found in most Mediterranean cultures in ancient times. In the third century B.C.E., the Sicilian skeptic philosopher Euhemeros published the theory that even the gods of Olympus were deified culture-heroes of earlier generations. Alexander the Great demanded to be honored as a god in his lifetime, as did several Roman emperors. Religious leaders also claimed divine descent, as Lucian recorded of Alexander of Abonoteichus, or else had this status ascribed to them by their followers. This latter tendency was encouraged by the widely-held expectation of a redeemer figure in several contemporary religions, including Persian Zoroastrianism, Judaism, and Gnosticism. It was because of this Zoroastrian belief that the early Christians later alleged that several Zoroastrian priests, who were known as the magi, had recognized and worshipped the infant Jesus as their own expected Redeemer (Matthew 2:1–12). The "star in the east" followed by the three magi is both an oblique reference to the Persians' widely acknowledged expertise in astrology and astronomy in the ancient world, and also to the "star prophecy" in the book of Numbers that predicted the advent of a Jewish Messiah: "A star from Jacob takes the leadership, a sceptre arises from Israel."[2]

Early Christians and contemporary Jewish and pagan philosophers were all in agreement that Joseph was not the real father of Jesus. The only historically and biologically possible account of Jesus' parenthood, which is recorded by both Celsus and contemporary Jewish sources, states that Jesus was the illegitimate son of Miriam and a Roman soldier named Panthera or Pandira; an allegation which the Gospel accounts of Luke and Matthew attempted to overcome with the less plausible but more memorable story of a virgin birth.[3]

Two early followers of Jesus, Paul and Barnabas, narrowly avoided deification by the same process that was to elevate their founder when they preached at Lystra, as is recounted in Acts:

> The people raised their voices, saying in the Lycaonian language, "The gods have come down to us in the likeness of men!" And Barnabas they called Zeus, and Paul, Hermes, because he was the chief speaker . . . . And they could scarcely restrain the multitudes from sacrificing to them. (Acts 14:11–12,18)[4]

If this was the experience of Paul and Barnabas, we cannot be surprised by Jesus' similar acclamation, which, predictably, was ultimately fatal, alarming both the secular Roman and religious Jewish authorities sufficiently for them to cooperate in his arrest and execution. Despite this setback, Jesus' following was taken over by his brother, James, whose subsequent execution by the jealous high priest, Annas, in 62 C.E. was recorded by the contemporary Jewish historian, Flavius Josephus (circa 37–100 C.E.).[5] Nor did Jesus' execution do anything to mitigate the simmering religious and political tensions in the region that shortly afterward exploded into the disastrous Jewish revolt of 66–70 C.E.

There are numerous examples of Jesus himself using Greek alphabetic symbolism, preserved in the many biographies and stories of Jesus which appeared in the early centuries of the Christian

Era. We have already seen examples from Gnostic papyri and Valentinus' *Pistis Sophia*. The following is to be found in the apocryphal Gospel of Thomas:

> Now a certain teacher, Zaccheus by name, stood there, and he heard in part when Jesus said these things to his father, and he marvelled greatly that being a young child he spake such matters. And after a few days he came near to Joseph and said unto him: Thou hast a wise child, and he hath understanding. Come, deliver him unto me that he may learn letters. And I will teach him with the letters all knowledge . . . . And he told him all the letters from Alpha to Omega clearly, with much questioning. But Jesus looked upon Zaccheus the teacher and saith unto him: Thou that knowest not the Alpha according to its nature, how canst thou teach others the Beta? Thou hypocrite first, if thou knowest it, teach the Alpha, and then we will believe thee concerning the Beta. Then began he to confound the mouth of the teacher concerning the first letter, and he could not prevail to answer him. And in the hearing of many the young child said to Zaccheus: Hear, O teacher, the ordinance of the first letter and pay heed to this, how it hath [*what follows is really unintelligible in this and in all the parallel texts: a literal version would run somewhat thus:* how that it hath lines, and a middle mark, which thou seest, common to both, going apart; coming together, raised up on high, dancing *(a corrupt word)*, of three signs, like in kind *(a corrupt word)*, balanced, equal in measure]: thou hast the rules of the Alpha. Now when Zaccheus the teacher heard such and so many allegories of the first letter spoken by the young child, he was perplexed at his answer and his instruction being so great, and said to them that were there: Woe is me, wretch that I am, I am confounded.[6]

Instances also appear in those writings eventually selected for the New Testament, for example:

> For assuredly, I say to you, till heaven and earth pass away, not one jot (*iota*) or tittle will pass from the Law till all is fulfilled. (Matthew 5:18)

The "Law" referred to is Mosaic law, and these words are cited by biblical scholars as evidence that Jesus insisted upon continued observance of Mosaic law by his followers. Not suprisingly, strict compliance with the Torah was also insisted on by his brother, James, a practice that aroused Annas' murderous jealousy. This highlights the later radical reinterpretation of Jesus' teaching by Paul, who, never having met Jesus during his lifetime, controversially advocated that his message should also be taught to the "uncircumcised," the gentiles (Acts 15).[7] Paul's conviction that righteousness came from faith in Jesus as the Messiah, and not from observance of Jewish religious laws, caused him to fall out seriously with James and the other apostles based in Jerusalem who, unlike Paul, had known Jesus personally. This led to the first major split in the early Christian movement. Assisted by the turmoil following the Roman destruction of Jerusalem in 70 C.E., however, the non-Jewish sect of Pauline Christianity eventually succeeded in ousting other rivals to become the basis of the religion's subsequent development. No less than fourteen of the twenty-seven books eventually collated as the New Testament, just over half, belong to the Pauline corpus.[8] Instead of the teachings of Jesus, Christianity became a religion *about* Jesus.

According to the sayings ascribed to him in the New Testament, Jesus himself made no clear claim to divinity. As we might expect in these circumstances, his identification as the Son of Jehovah apparently begins only after his death, at the insistence of his disciples. It was the formal adoption by the Christians of this relationship between Jesus and Jehovah that was later to be held against them by pagan critics such as Celsus, Porphyry, and Julian, since it involved breaking God's edict to Abraham, "Thou shalt worship no other god but me." Islam, on the other hand, resisted ascribing divine status to Jesus or Mohammed (circa 570–632 C.E.), instead maintaining more reasonably that both were prophets of the one God. Indeed, the consequent tension between Jesus as a historical person and Jesus as Son of Jehovah was to create enormous controversy and schism in the early Christian church. This was eventually settled at the Council of Nicaea in 325 C.E. by formal adoption of Eusebius' suggestion of a consubstantial Trinity (Father, Son, and Holy Spirit) as the orthodox view; the "Nicene Creed."

We may conclude this brief historical background with an excerpt from a lecture given early this century by Gilbert Murray, then Regius Professor of Greek at Oxford, on what he called the "failure of nerve" in the eventual triumph of Christian religion over Greek philosophy:

> It is a strange experience, and it shows what queer stuff we humans are made of, to study these obscure congregations, drawn from the proletariate of the Levant, superstitious, charlatan-ridden, and helplessly ignorant, who still believed in Gods begetting children of mortal mothers, who took the "Word," the "Spirit," and the "Divine Wisdom" to be persons called by those names, and turned the Immortality of the Soul into "the standing up of corpses"; [η αναστασις των νεκρων. Cf. Acts 17:32] and to reflect that it was these who held the main road of advance towards the greatest religion of the western world.[9]

There is no doubt that the early Christians made extensive use of the Greek Qabalah in all its forms, and that they were in large part responsible for its refinement and development in the opening centuries of the Current Era. A great number of the surviving examples of isopsephy, *notarichon*, and letter symbolism are from Greek and Coptic Christian writings, charms, amulets, and spells. It has even been suggested by the Reverends Simcox Lea and Bligh Bond that the New Testament incorporates extensive and deliberate use of isopsephy and sacred geometry, and that isopsephy forms part of the inner teachings of Christianity.

> With the Greek, this association of letter and number was of the most intimate nature. The coining of words for the representation of preferences in number commenced very early and much of the tradition is associated with the Pythagorean schools, in which the numbers are often recognisable as conventional symbols of ratio. Terms used in music, and in astronomy and chronometry betray a like influence, and those names of divinities which are symbols of planetary times and seasons can often be identified by their *gematria* or number. Thus, for example, the solar divinity, Lord of the year of 365 days is variously known as Abraxas (ΑΒΡΑΞΑΣ), or, with the same numeration, ΜΕΙΘΡΑΣ, ΝΕΙΛΟΣ, ΒΕΛΗΝΟΣ, ΣΑΡΔΙΝ, etc. More than all else, the notion of number-symbolism enters into, and colours, religious nomenclature. And we have ample proof from the Fathers of the Church that the earliest symbolism of God the Father was of a geometrical nature.[10]

Lea and Bond list some 500 phrases having the value of 2368, that of the name of Jesus Christ (ΙΗΣΟΥΣ ΧΡΙΣΤΟΣ), in an endeavor to show that the books of the New Testament were written to include an inner gnosis hidden in the original Greek.[11] Unfortunately, in spite of the elaborate geometry and isopsephy set out by Lea and Bond in their books *Gematria* and *The Apostolic Gnosis*, the basic theory of which has been expanded by John Michell in *City of Revelation* and, more recently, by the learned David Fideler in *Jesus Christ, Sun of God*, there is nowhere any evidence that this "reconstructed Greek canon" was in the slightest degree known to the ancient authors to whom they wish to impute its use, or is anything more than a selective series of mathematical coincidences.[12] As a subjective tool, the Greek Qabalah undoubtedly has value for these writers as a technique of scriptural analysis that helps them become closer to their God or understand the Kosmos, just as it served in antiquity. History is ill-served, however, by confusing subjectively impressive coincidences with the more limited objective evidence of the deliberate use of Greek Qabalah by ancient authors.

It is, however, clear from the evidence that there was an inner Christian gnosis of Greek Qabalah and isopsephy, and that this was heavily indebted to the Gnostics. We have already seen that the early Church Fathers, Irenaeus and Hippolytus, had noted the Gnostic Marcus' observation that Jesus (ΙΗΣΟΥΣ) added to 888 and was therefore the "plenitude of the Ogdoad," as well as his numerical correlation of the *Alpha* and *Omega*, the First and Last, to that of the Dove (A and Ω = 1 + 800 = 801 = ΠΕΡΙ–ΣΤΕΡΑ). The writings of Irenaeus and Hippolytus were preserved and studied by generations of later Christians, and thus, by a strange paradox, ensured that Gnostic numerology has survived, in spite of the fact that its sects were persecuted out of existence.

Several other Church Fathers also make use of Greek Qabalah, revealing that scriptural analysis using these techniques was not in itself necessarily seen as heretical. It was in fact, the religious view of the user and the point being illustrated that was decisive of whether or not the technique was acceptable. One example occurs in the writings of Justin (circa 100–165 C.E.), traditionally known as "the Martyr," who was interested in Pythagoreanism and Platonism before his conversion to Christianity. Justin was the author of two early Christian works: the *Apologia*, which he addressed to the Roman Emperor, Marcus Aurelius; and the *Dialogue with Trypho*, a defense of Christianity against its parent, Judaism. While arguing in the *Apologia* that the purpose of the Hebrew Old Testament was to point to the coming of Christ, Justin refers to the letter *chi* (X) in the *Psychogonia* of Plato's *Timaeus*:

> Plato likewise borrowed from Moses when, inquiring into the nature of the Son of God in his *Timaeus*, he states, "He placed him in the universe in the manner of the letter **X**." For, in the writings of Moses, it is stated that, at the time when the Israelites left Egypt and were living in the desert, they encountered poisonous beasts, vipers, asps, and every sort of serpent which brought death to the people, and that Moses, through the inspiration and the impulse of God, took some brass, shaped it into the figure of a cross, placed it over the holy tabernacle, and announced to the people, "If you gaze upon this figure and believe, you shall be saved thereby." He related that, after this was done, the serpents perished, and tradition has it that the people of Israel were thus saved from death. When Plato read this, he did not clearly understand it, for, not perceiving that the figure of the cross was spoken of, he took it for the form of the letter X, and said that the power next to the first God was placed in the universe in the form of the letter X.[13]

The Old Testament passage Justin is referring to (Numbers 21:8) actually makes no mention of a tabernacle or a cross at all, but says: "Moses therefore made a brazen serpent, and set it up for a sign." (Numbers 21:9). When translated into Greek for the Septuagint version of the Old Testament, the word used for "sign" was *semeion*, which Justin and other writers interpreted as the figure of the cross.[14]

Jerome (342–420 C.E.) also interprets the book of Genesis with the aid of letter symbolism in the eighty-fourth of his *Homilies*. He, however, makes the more usual connection of the cross with the letter *tau* (T) rather than *chi*, and uses isopsephy as well:

We read in Genesis that the ark that Noah built was three hundred cubits long, fifty cubits wide, and thirty cubits high. [Genesis 6:15–16] Notice the mystical significance of the numbers. In the number fifty, penance is symbolized because the fiftieth psalm of King David is the prayer of his repentance. Three hundred contains the symbol of crucifixion. The letter T is the sign for three hundred, whence Ezekiel says: "Mark TAU on the foreheads of those who moan; and do not kill any marked with TAU." No one marked with the sign of the cross on his forehead can be struck by the devil; he is not able to efface this sign, only sin can.[15]

Among the magical formulae appearing in early Christian texts and inscriptions, the initials ΧΜΓ (*ChMG*) occur frequently, an abbreviation for "Christ born of Mary" (*Christos [o ek] Marias Genetheis*), or perhaps "Mary gives birth to Christ" (*Christon Maria Genna*).[16] It has also been suggested that the letters are, in fact, a reference to isopsephy, having the value of 643 (ΧΜΓ = 643), for which two possible solutions have been offered. These are Αγειος ο Θεος (Holy God), which occurs frequently in Greek liturgies; and Η Αγια Τριας Θ[εος] (God is the Holy Trinity), both of which add to 643.[17] The archaeologist William Prentice found the following inscription on a Syrian house-lintel dating from the fifth or sixth century C.E.

ΧΜΓΟ ΘΙΧΘΥΣ [disc with *chi-rho*]
ΑΚΟΗΚΥΡΙΒΤΩΔΠΑΥ[18]

In the first group of letters, the meanings of the *notarichon* ΧΜΓ and the Sibylline acrostic ΙΧΘΥΣ have already been explained. In the center of these, the archaic letter *qoppa* (Ϙ) and *theta* (Θ) together signify the number ninety-nine, a common Coptic convention, being the value of the word *Amen* (ΑΜΗΝ), as Hippolytus noted.[19] In the center comes a disk containing one of the most frequent Christian symbols, the *chi-rho*, the stylized monogram representing the first two letters of the name of Christ. The next group of letters, AKOH, as well as being the Greek word for *hearing*, has the value of ninety-nine as before, the same as AMHN. Prentice suggests the remainder of the inscription is an abbreviation for Κυρι(ε), Β(οηθει) Τωι Δ(ουλω) (σου) Παυ(λω), or *Lord, help thy servant Paul*, which also has a value in isopsephy of 2127, equal to that of *Jesus of Nazareth* (Ιησους (ο) Ναζωραιος). This interpretation is assisted by the fact that Prentice found the word for *help* (βοηθει or βοηθησον) in fuller inscriptions some twenty times in his first Syrian expedition, almost always on lintels, generally of houses. Such phrases are also common on seals from the Byzantine period.

Another common protective and decorative inscription found by Prentice on Christian lintels in the Syrian region is the following form of the text of Psalms 120:8:

Κυριος φυλαξη την εισοδον σου και την εξοδον σου, απο νυν και εως αιωνων, αμην.
The Lord shall preserve thy coming in and thy going out, from now even for evermore, Amen.

This psalm apparently had strong appeal to the early Christians as a protective blessing suitable for doorways. At Serdjilla, over the outer doorway of a passage between the church and dwellings probably used by the clergy, Prentice found a large block lintel bearing only the carved letters HNA, which is the numerical representation of 8051, the isopsephy value of the text of the whole psalm given above. In a tomb at Shnan, the refrain Ιησους ο Χρειστος, or *Jesus the Christ*, is written out in full and then also expressed in the form ΒΥΜΓ, or 2443, the numerical value of the phrase in full. Plainly, these correlations could not have been observed except as a result of extensive isopsephical analysis of the New Testament by the earliest Christians.

In addition to the *chi-rho* monogram as an abbreviation for Christ, the early Christians also used the first three Greek letters in the name of Jesus, ΙΗΣ. In later Christian times, the Greek letter *eta* (H), with a phonetic value of "E," was mistakenly identified with the Roman letter H, which was aspirated in Latin as it is in English. The equivalent Latin letters, IHS, thus came to be interpreted as an abbreviation of the phrase *In Hoc Signo* (In This Sign), recalling the famous legend of the vision of Constantine, in which the *chi-rho* monogram was allegedly revealed to that Emperor with a voice that said, "In this sign thou shalt conquer."[20] In its Roman misinterpretation, the letters IHS also came to represent another *notarichon*, namely *Iesus Hominem Salvator*, or Jesus, Mankind's Redeemer.[21]

The best-known example of Christian isopsephy, and the subject of relentless uninformed comment, is the "number of the Beast," 666, that appears in Revelation 13:18. This was the title given to a work of the Apocalyptic genre incorporated in the New Testament in the fourth century C.E. Though not widely known, apocalypses or revelations (Greek *apokalypsis*, "revelation") are in fact the names given to a large number of works of religious literature that were produced by the Jews in reaction to the Hellenization, and later Romanization, of Jewish culture and religion by their conquerors. At least fifteen such works survive from the period 250 B.C.E. to 150 C.E.[22] The Apocalyptic view of the kingdom of God has sufficient points in common with the Gnostic view to suggest some form of connection: for instance, various angelic beings, a messianic savior figure, heavenly journeys, and rewards for those in possession of the correct wisdom.[23] Apocalyptic literature is generally eschatological, or concerned with the end of the world, prophesying a time when the forces of evil oppressing Judaism, being in fact the Greeks or the Romans, would be repelled by the righteous forces of Jehovah. It was the anticipation by pious Jews of a military Messiah who would lead such a holy war that inspired some to their fatal acclamation of

Jesus and erupted soon afterward in the disastrous Jewish Rebellion, ending in the destruction of Jerusalem and the Temple by the Roman legions in 70 C.E. It was, therefore, against the background of Apocalyptic literature and symbolism that the early Jewish Christians understood Jesus, with the effect that, as Ernst Kasemann remarked, "Apocalyptic . . . was the mother of all Christian theology."[24]

The author of the work titled Revelation in the New Testament was John of Patmos, who lived on the far side of the Roman empire in Asia Minor (modern Turkey) during the first century C.E. John was closely associated with the Christian Church at Ephesus. Although he wrote in Greek and his reference to the number of the Beast, "666," is in Greek letters (χξς), he also knew at least some Hebrew, as is evidenced by his use of terms such as Armageddon and Abaddon. Revelation, sometimes referred to as the Johannine Apocalypse, was probably written some time between 90 and 100 C.E., and is basically an anti-Roman polemic designed to encourage Christian opposition to the Empire. Rome is equated with Jerusalem's earlier conqueror (in 587 B.C.E.), Babylon, and the Roman Emperor is identified with the Antichrist. The seven heads of the Beast refer to the seven past emperors of Rome, and the seventh head with the mortal wound that heals is a reference to the legend of Nero Arisen (*Nero redivivus*), also referred to in other Apocalyptic works, such as the *Sibylline Oracles* (see figure 18, page 144).[25]

Today, it is widely accepted by academic scholars of Apocalyptic literature—although there are numerous other interpretations—that the 666 reference in the Apocalypse of John is to the Roman Emperor, Nero. Among other considerations, this is modeled on previous literature of the genre, such as the earlier Apocalypse of Daniel found in the Old Testament, in which the Beast is undoubtedly the Greek ruler of Syria, Antiochus IV Epiphanes, who began a persecution of the Jews in 167 B.C.E. that prompted the Maccabean revolt.[26] A further analogy is to

Figure 18. The Beast 666 of Revelation by Albrecht Dürer from *Images of the Apocalypse*, 1510.(Reprinted from *The Complete Woodcuts of Albrecht Dürer*, New York: Dover, 1963.)

Alexander the Great, who to this day throughout the lands of the old Persian Empire, appears in popular folklore as a supernatural devil-figure with two horns. It is not surprising, therefore, to see the oppressive rulers, Antiochus and Nero, similarly portrayed as horned devil-figures in the legends of the conquered Jews.

The isopsephy of 666 is based on the Hebrew version of Nero's name, and uses Hebrew, rather than Greek letter values. Because Hebrew has no vowel letters, the name Nero Caesar becomes *NRUN QSR*, totaling 666. Also persuasive is an early variant codex of Revelation that gives this figure as 616, which number is achieved when the final *nun* (N = 50) is dropped to give *NRU QSR*.[27] It was unlikely, moreover, to have gone unnoticed that the Greek equivalent, ΝΕΡΩΝ ΚΑΕΣΑΡ, added to 1332 (666 + 666). Robert Graves points out that John's transliteration into Hebrew is less than perfect, as the initial letter of Caesar should become *kaph* (K) rather than *qoph* (Q).[28] However, perhaps this is because exact transliteration was not as important as the need to identify Nero with a number that was clearly *mathematically* opposed to the already known value of 888 for Jesus Christ.[29] The whole of Revelation, and all of Apocalyptic literature generally, is based upon ethical and cosmological dualism: good and evil; heaven and earth; Jerusalem and Babylon; East and West; the Lamb and the Beast; Christ and Antichrist; 888 and 666. This dualism, played out in the battle between the forces of light and darkness, in which good ultimately triumphs, occurs not only in Apocalyptic, but also plays a major role in Mithraism and Gnosticism, and can ultimately be traced to the teachings of Persian Zoroastrianism. The popular appeal and corresponding influence of dualism on early Christianity also led to the elevation of Satan, from the subservient persecuting angel appearing in Job, to the figure of the Devil in open competition with Jehovah, an idea that remains widespread in grassroots Christianity even today, although still officially heretical.

John of Patmos was probably writing after Nero's death and
therefore after the graffiti recorded by Suetonius appeared on the
walls of Rome. Thus the best-known example of isopsephy in history, the famous 666 in Revelation, can be seen against a persuasive background of contemporaneous Qabalistic analysis of Nero's
name elsewhere in the Empire, as seen earlier in both Suetonius
and Book Five of the *Sibylline Oracles*. In both Revelation and
Suetonius' example, isopsephy is used as a tool by opponents of
the Roman Emperor, a coded political criticism to those in the
know. Nevertheless, with the passage of time and the decline of
the myth of *Nero redivivus*, the obscurity of John's isopsephial reference increased. Within a century, Irenaeus had begun the guess-
ing games that still plague the famous 666 passage from
Revelation:

> If . . . this number is placed in all the genuine and ancient
> copies, and those who saw John face to face provide attesta-
> tion, and reason teaches us that the name of the Beast
> according to the Greek way of counting by the letters in it is
> 666, that is, with tens equal to hundreds and hundreds equal
> to units (for the number six preserved the same through all
> indicates the recapitulation of all the apostasy at the begin-
> ning and in the middle and at the end)—I do not know how
> certain people went wrong following a special opinion and
> giving up the middle number of the name, deducting fifty
> and wanting only one ten in place of six [616 rather than
> 666]. I am sure this was by scribal error, common enough
> when numbers are written by letters, for the letter Xi (60) is
> easily spread out as Iota (10) in Greek[!] . . .
>
> If one finds many names with this number, which one
> will the man to come bear? We speak in this way not
> because we lack names with the number of the Antichrist
> but because of fear of God and zeal for truth. For the word
> EUANTHAS [ΕΥΑΝΘΑΣ] has the required number but
> we cannot say anything about it. Also LATEINOS

[ΛΑΤΕΙΝΟΣ] has the number 666, and it is very likely because the last kingdom has this name: the Latins are ruling at this time, but we make no boast about this. Also TEITAN, with the two vowels Epsilon and Iota in the first syllable, is of all those found among us, the most worthy of credit. It contains the number mentioned and consists of six letters, each syllable with three letters. It is an ancient and exceptional name, for none of our kings is called Titan, and none of the idols worshipped in public among Greeks and barbarians has this name. It is considered divine by many, so that the Sun is called Titan by our present rulers [the Romans]. This name also evokes vengeance and an avenger, because Antichrist will pretend to avenge the victims of oppression. Moreover it is royal and even tyrannical. Thus the name Titan has enough persuasiveness and probability for us to conclude out of many names that it could well be that of the man who is to come. However, we will not risk a pronouncement on this or assert positively that he will have this name, for we know that if his name had to be proclaimed openly at present, it would have been spoken by the one who saw the Apocalypse. It was seen not long ago but nearly in our generation, toward the end of the reign of Domitian.[30]

More evidence of Greek Qabalah appears elsewhere in Revelation. Jesus is given to say, no less than three times:

> I am the Alpha and the Omega, the Beginning and the End. (Revelation 1:8 and 21: 6; Isaiah 44 :6)

This passage gave the early Christians the ultimate authority for their use of Greek Qabalah in the interpretation of their faith, endowing it with the sanction of none other than Jesus Christ himself. It is the origin of the frequent appearance of the Greek letters *alpha* and *omega* together in Christian symbolism, from ancient times to the present (see figure 19, below). In addition to the repeated alphabetical symbolism of the famous *alpha* and *omega*, Revelation 4:1–8 is also worthy of note:

> Behold, a throne set in heaven, and One sat on the throne. And He who sat there was like jasper and a sardius stone in appearance; and there was a rainbow around the throne, in appearance like an emerald. Around the throne were twenty-four thrones, and on the thrones I saw twenty-four elders sitting, clothed in white robes; and they had crowns of gold upon their heads. And from the throne proceeded lightnings, thunderings, and voices. Seven lamps of fire were burning before the throne, which are the seven Spirits of God. Before the throne there was a sea of glass, like crystal.

Figure 19. Christian gem with *alpha* and *omega* and ΙΧΘΥΣ inscription. (Reprinted from David Fideler, *Jesus Christ, Sun of God*, Wheaton, IL: Quest Books, 1993, used by permission.)

And in the midst of the throne, and around the throne, were four living creatures full of eyes in front and in back. The first living creature was like a lion, the second living creature like a calf, the third living creature had a face like a man, and the fourth living creature was like a flying eagle. The four living creatures, each having six wings, were full of eyes around and within. And they do not rest day or night, saying: "Holy, Holy, Holy, Lord God Almighty, who was and is and is to come!"

The "seven Spirits" and all the other sevens that appear in John's vision have their origin in the seven planets or powers, also symbolized in the Jewish seven-branched candlestick or *menorah*. The thrice-repeated Greek word, *hagios* (holy), a formula known as the *trisagion* or *sanctus*, appears frequently in later Christian writings, and survives in the liturgies of both the modern Catholic and Greek Orthodox churches.[31] The other figures in this passage also came to be of great importance in the prayers and invocations of early Egyptian Christians, and numerous magic amulets and papyri spells have survived with invocations such as:

O twenty-four elders and the four creatures who support the throne of the father, perform my judgment.[32]

The twenty-four elders of Revelation (see figure 20, page 150) were seen as the letters of the Greek alphabet, as is made clear in a Coptic manuscript of spells from the tenth century, entitled *The Praise of Michael the Archangel*, that includes the following invocation:

I adjure you today by the twenty-four elders who are under your supervision, whom you established on the day when you created them from Alpha to Omega. I adjure you today by the great hand which you laid upon them. I adjure you

Figure 20. The 24 elders, the 7 lamps, and the 4 living creatures, from Albrecht Dürer, *Images of the Apocalypse*, 1510. (Reprinted from *The Complete Woodcuts of Albrecht Dürer*, New York: Dover, 1963.)

today by the twenty-four thrones upon which they sit, and their golden diadems upon their heads . . . .[33]

Another early Coptic Christian or Gnostic text refers to "the twenty-four angels who stand by the twenty-four elders."[34] In Coptic folklore, the twenty-four elders of Revelation came to be regarded as individual heavenly powers, whose names began with each of the letters of the Greek alphabet with which they were identified:

> You must send me your twenty-four elders, whose names are Achael, Banuel, Ganuel, Dedael, Eptiel, Zartiel, Ethael, Thathiel, Iochael, Kardiel, Labtiel, Merael, Nerael, Xiphiel, Oupiel, Pirael, Rael, Seroael, Tauriel, Umnuel, Philopael, Christuel, Psilaphael, Olithiel, who sit upon the twenty-four thrones, with twenty-four crowns upon their heads, and twenty-four censers in their hands, that they may stretch out their right ones, each of them by name.
>
> You must send me today your four incorporeal creatures, with four faces and six wings, Alpha Leon Phone Aner, Paramara Zorothion Perion Akramata, that they may stretch out their four spiritual fingers and seal the oil that is in my hand, in the name of the Father and the Son and the Holy Spirit.
>
> You must send today your seven holy archangels, Michael, Gabriel, Raphiel, Suriel, Zetekiel, Solothiel, Anael, that they may stretch out their seven fingers by name, and seal the oil that is in my hands, in the name of the Father and the Son and the Holy Spirit.[35]

The names given to the four living creatures, or *cherubim*, appearing in Revelation and Ezekiel, comprise another formula that is often repeated in early Christian charms and amulets. It has been referred to as the *Alpha* formula, since the first letter of each name makes a *notarichon* of the first letter in the Greek alphabet (Alpha,

Leon, Phone, Aner).[36] *Alpha* is the bull, derived, as we have seen, from the Phoenician *aleph*; *leon* is the Greek word for "lion"; the eagle's name *phone* is the Greek word for "voice"; and *aner* is Greek for "man."

It will be apparent from the foregoing that John of Patmos' Revelation treatise was widely influential, both as a source and an inspiration for the use of Greek Qabalah by the early Christians. Interestingly, Eusebius records that the status of Revelation in his day was considered spurious, but, despite argument, it was later included in the corpus of the "New" Testament—a phrase coined by Irenaeus, to stand beside the "Old"—when its contents were finalized in the fourth century C.E.[37] In retrospect, this decision was a terrible mistake. Not only did the adoption of Christianity as the religion of the Roman state soon afterward make the anti-Roman polemical in Revelation redundant, but later contortions of the many allegories of John's "vision," particularly by Puritans and millenarians, led to massive distortions of the original Christian message. Despite some passages of beautiful imagery, Christianity would probably have been much better off if Revelation had not been included in the books selected for the New Testament.

It is plainly evident that Christianity, under the influence of Gnosticism and contemporary Hellenistic philosophy and theurgy, absorbed and adapted the techniques of Greek Qabalah, as did its parent, Judaism. It would be fanciful to suggest that the Bible contains an inner code of numerology on the basis of the evidence we have, though recent evidence suggests a contrary conclusion would have made this book a best-seller. The Old Testament cannot do so, because its Hebrew writings predate the Jewish use of alphabetical numerals. Likewise, examples of Greek isopsephy extracted from the New Testament by recent authors cannot be safely or objectively regarded as any more than coincidence. However, we have seen that there are a few examples of the use of Greek Qabalah to be found in those texts included in the New

Testament (in Revelation), and in contemporaneous Christian writings that were rejected (such as the Gospel of Thomas and the Epistle of Barnabas).

The writings of the early Church Fathers are even more fruitful, and reveal numerous instances of letter symbolism, number mysticism, *notarichon,* and isopsephy. We also know from the archaeological evidence of Christian charms, magical amulets, and inscriptions, that all these Qabalistic techniques were used by the earliest Christians as part of the expression of their faith. Traces survive, even to the present day, in symbolism such as that of the Christ-fish, the *chi-rho*, and the *alpha-omega*. We can therefore conclude that the Greek Qabalah is, and always has been, part of the inner Christian gnosis.

Notes to Chapter Ten

1 B. Radice (trans.), *The Letters of the Younger Pliny*, X; 96 (London: Penguin, 1962), p. 294.

2 The "Star prophecy" also occurs in several places in the Dead Sea Scrolls, indicative of its importance in Judaism and early Christianity during the first century C.E.

3 Celsus, *True Doctrine,* I; 28–32, cited in Robert L. Wilken, *The Christians As The Romans Saw Them* (New Haven and London: Yale University Press, 1984), pp. 109–110; *Shabbath* 104, cited in R. Joseph Hoffman, *Jesus Outside the Gospels* (New York: Prometheus Books, 1984), p. 40.

4 This scene is evocative of the comical satire in the Monty Python film *Life of Brian*, where, in spite of his denials, a bewildered Brian is hailed by the superstitious masses as the expected Messiah.

5 Josephus, *Antiquities*, XX; 200–201. James' status as the brother of Jesus is mentioned by Josephus, and also confirmed in Galatians 1:19. According to Mark 6:3, Jesus had other brothers and sisters who were of lesser historical importance than James, and were therefore not mentioned in independent historical records.

6 Gospel of Thomas (Greek Text A), VI–VII; in M. R. James (trans.), *The Apocryphal New Testament* (Oxford: Oxford University Press, 1924); quoted in R. Joseph Hoffman, *Jesus Outside the Gospels,* pp. 118–119.

7 Compare Jesus's teaching in the passage from Matthew with Paul's in Galatians 1.

8 On the subject of Paul and Jesus generally, see S. Brown, *The Origins of Christianity—*

A Historical Introduction to the New Testament (New York: Oxford University Press, 1993).

9 G. Murray, *Five Stages of Greek Religion* (London: Watts and Co., 1925), p. 165. Compare the story of Mary and the Dove with that of Leda and the Swan, or Semele and the Thunderbolt.

10 S. Lea and B. Bond, *The Apostolic Gnosis* (Orpington, Kent, Great Britain: RILKO, 1979), p. 23.

11 S. Lea and B. Bond, *The Apostolic Gnosis*, p. 65; see also E. Bullinger, *Number In Scripture* (London: Lamp Press, 1952).

12 It is also overly straining serious academic credibility to suggest (D. Fideler, *Jesus Christ, Sun of God,* Wheaton, IL: Quest Books, 1993, pp. 72–80) that the names of Olympian deities such as Zeus, Hermes, and Apollo, that were known to Homer in the eighth century B.C.E. when alphabetic numerology was not in existence (unlike later Hellenistic deities such as Abraxas or Mithras), had their spelling based upon isopsephical or geometric considerations, or that such factors influenced the introduction of the long vowels into the alphabet.

13 Justin, *Apologia*, I; 60.

14 T. B. Falls (trans.), *Writings of St. Justin Martyr* (Washington: Catholic University of America Press, 1948), p. 98.

15 M. L. Ewald (trans.), *The Homilies of St. Jerome* (Washington: Catholic University of America Press, 1966), p. 190.

16 M. Meyer and R. Smith (ed.), *Ancient Christian Magic* (New York: HarperCollins, 1995), p. 388; W. K. Prentice, *American Journal of Archaeology*, Vol. X (1906), 147.

17 W. K. Prentice, *American Journal of Archaeology*, Vol. X (1906), 145.

18 W. K. Prentice, *American Journal of Archaeology*, Vol. X (1906), 145.

19 M. Meyer and R. Smith (ed.), *Ancient Christian Magic*, p. 361; Hippolytus, *Refutation of All Heresies*, VI; 47.

20 E. Gibbon, *The Decline and Fall of the Roman Empire* (London: Chatto and Windus Limited, 1960), ch. 20.

21 N. Pennick, *The Secret Lore of Runes and other Ancient Alphabets* (London: Rider Books, 1991), p. 65.

22 B. McGinn, *Antichrist* (New York: HarperCollins, 1994), pp. 11–12.

23 K. Rudolph, *Gnosis—The Nature and History of Gnosticism* (San Francisco: HarperSanFrancisco, 1987), pp. 278–279.

24 E. Kasemann, *"The Beginnings of Christian Theology,"* in R. W. Funk (ed.), *Apocalypticism* (New York: Herder and Herder, 1969), p. 37; cited in B. McGinn, *Antichrist* (New York: HarperCollins, 1994), p. 36.

25 Revelation 13:3: *Sibylline Oracles*, III; 63–74: IV; 119–124: V; 33–34.

26 Daniel 7–8; B. McGinn, *Antichrist*, p. 14; R. L. Wilken, *The Christians as the Romans Saw Them*, pp, 137–143.

27 See any biblical encyclopedia on the subject.

28 R. Graves, *The White Goddess* (London: Faber & Faber, 1961), p. 345, fn. 1.

29 We might also note that the word for "cross" (σταυρος, *stauros*) adds to 777 if the first two letters are represented by the compound letter *stau*, which was identical in appearance and value to the *episemon* or *stigma* (ς = 6), but had the phonetic value "st."

30 Irenaeus, *Against Heresies*, V; 30, in R. M. Grant (trans.), *Irenaeus of Lyons* (London: Routledge, 1985), pp. 177–178.

31 See also Isaiah 6:3.

32 M. Meyer and R. Smith (ed.), *Ancient Christian Magic*, 197.

33 M. Meyer and R. Smith(ed.), *Ancient Christian Magic*, 333.

34 M. Meyer and R. Smith (ed.), *Ancient Christian Magic*, 145.

35 M. Meyer and R. Smith (ed.), *Ancient Christian Magic*, 103–104, 118, 283.

36 M. Meyer and R. Smith (ed.), *Ancient Christian Magic*, 92.

37 J. Rohmer, *Testament—The Bible and History* (London: Michael O'Mara Books, 1988), p. 225.

chapter eleven

THE NEOPLATONISTS

T he contribution of the incomparable Plato (427– 347 B.C.E.) to Western thought is so massive that it has been said that, next to his ideas, all subsequent Western philosophy is simply a footnote. Plato recorded for posterity the teachings of his own teacher, Socrates (469-399 B.C.E.), and was himself the teacher of Aristotle (384-322 B.C.E.). He wrote extensively throughout his life, and was eventually found dead at his desk at the age of 80. The school that Plato founded at Athens was known as the Academy, and endured for centuries after his death. He placed considerable importance on geometry as a necessary preliminary to philosophy, to the extent that, over the entrance to the Academy, there was allegedly the famous inscription: "Let no one enter who doesn't know geometry"

(ΑΓΕΩΜΕΤΡΗΤΟΣ ΜΗΔΕΙΣ ΕΙΣΙΤΩ).[1] The chief doctrines of
Plato's new metaphysics can be briefly summarized as:

> . . . the immortality and the divinity of the rational soul, and
> the reality and unchangeability of the objects of its knowl-
> edge. These doctrines constitute . . . the twin pillars of
> Platonism: the architrave of those pillars is Anamnesis, the
> doctrine that learning is recollection and that the truth of all
> things is always in the soul.[2]

The recurrence of these concepts in numerous philosophies and
religions is indicative of the pervasive influence of Platonist
thought even today.

Neoplatonism is the name given to the amalgam of
Platonism and Pythagoreanism developed in the third century
C.E. It is generally attributed to Plotinus (204-270 C.E.), an
Egyptian by birth who taught philosophy in Rome from 242 C.E.
until his death. Subsequent followers of Neoplatonism included
Plotinus' disciples Amelius and Porphyry of Tyre (232-305 C.E.),
their pupils Theodorus of Asine and Iamblichus of Chalcis (242-
326 C.E.), Proclus of Athens (412-485 C.E.), and the famous
female mathematician and philosopher, Hypatia of Alexandria,
who was lynched by a relatively unphilosophical Christian mob
in 415 C.E.[3] The Neoplatonists considered themselves to be
reasserting nothing other than a true understanding of the philosophy of Plato, but actually took a syncretic approach to philosophy that drew from other sources, including Aristotle,
Pythagorean number mysticism, and theurgic magical ideas such
as those found in the *Chaldean Oracles*.[4] They also made use of a
number of philosophical writings known as Hermetica, composed around the second and third centuries C.E. and attributed
to a figure known as "thrice-greatest Hermes" (*Hermes
Trismegistos*). The most influential of these were consolidated into
the *Corpus Hermeticum*.[5]

The Neoplatonists formed part of the philosophical opposition to Christianity. Porphyry, in fact, was the author of a major polemic entitled *Against the Christians*. Despite their efforts, however, Christianity became the official religion of the Roman emperors early in the fourth century C.E. with the conversion of Constantine. In 529 C.E., the Christian Emperor Justinian suppressed all pagan philosophical schools. Neoplatonic and Hermetic philosophy both enjoyed a revival in the West during the Middle Ages.

Neoplatonists and others invoked the authority of Plato in support of arithmology, isopsephy, and related practices because of the following passage in the *Timaeus*, which describes the creation of the Kosmos from chaos:

> Before that time they were all without proportion or measure; fire, water, earth and air bore some traces of their proper measure, but were in the disorganized state to be expected of anything which God has not touched, and his first step when he set about reducing them to order was to give them a definite pattern of shape and *number*.[6]

As previously mentioned, there is another passage in the *Timaeus* that became a fruitful source of subsequent speculation. In it, Plato mentions the letter *chi* (X) in describing the creation of the Soul of the World:

> God then took the whole fabric and cut it down the middle into two strips, which he placed crosswise at their middle points to form a shape like the letter X; he then bent the ends round to form a circle and fastened them to each other opposite the point at which the strips crossed, to make two circles, one inner and one outer. And he endowed them with uniform motion in the same place, and named the movement of the outer circle after the nature of the Same,

of the inner after the nature of the Different. The circle of the Same he caused to revolve from left to right, and the circle of the Different from right to left on an axis inclined to it; and he made the master revolution that of the Same. For he left the circle of the Same whole and undivided, but split the inner circle six times to make seven unequal circles, whose intervals were double and triple, three of each; and he made these circles revolve in contrary circles relative to each other.[7]

Plato's purpose in this description is to provide a model for the explanation of the motion of the planets (the seven circles or spheres of the Different) in relation to the fixed stars (the circle of the Same). These are imagined as two circles with circumferences at right angles to each other, as if drawn on the surface of a sphere. The Neoplatonists used the example of Plato's letter *chi* (X) to speculate on the nature of the soul or the universe by analogy with the shape of letters. Proclus, in his commentary on Plato's text, says:

> The figure X . . . has a great affinity to the universe, and also to the soul. As Porphyry relates, a character of this kind, namely X, surrounded by a circle, is with the Egyptians a symbol of the mundane soul. For perhaps it signifies, through the right lines indeed, the biformed progression of the soul, but through the circle its uniform life, and regression according to an intellectual circle. . . . For the complication of the right lines indicates the union of a biformed life. For a right line itself also, is a symbol of a life which flows from on high. In order however, that we may not, omitting the things themselves, be too busily employed about the theory of the character, Plato adds "as it were," indicating that this is assumed as a veil, and for the sake of concealment, thus endeavouring to invest with figure the unfigured nature of the soul.[8]

Proclus also recounts the ideas attributed to the Neoplatonist Theodorus of Asine (fourth century C.E.), who, he said, "speculates the generation of the soul in a novel manner, from letters, and characters, and numbers." He informs us that Theodorus was drawing on the doctrines of a Neopythagorean, Numenius of Apamea, an approximate contemporary of the Gnostic Marcus, whose doctrines, as we have seen, also included Greek Qabalah in an advanced form. Theodorus uses isopsephy, *pythmenes*, Pythagorean numerology, and individual letter symbolism in an analysis of *psyche*, the word used by Plato for the soul of the world. Although neglected by Thomas Taylor in his translation, the relevant excerpt from Proclus has fortunately been translated and commented upon by Stephen Ronan in his essay, *Theodorus of Asine and the Kabbalah*:

> But Theodorus the philosopher from Asine, who was filled with the doctrines of Numenius, has treated the subject of the generation of the soul in a fairly revolutionary fashion, basing his ideas on the sounds, shapes and numerical values of the letters . . . .
>
> 1. That which comes first is justly celebrated by him as the Ineffable [*arrhetos*], Unutterable [*anaklaletos*], Source of All and Cause of the Good.
>
> 2. After this First Principle—which also transcends everything—comes the triad which, for Theodorus, determines the Intelligible Plane. He calls it the One [εν; (*h*)*en*] and it is composed:
>
> (a) of the breath [*asthmatos*] which in a particular way belongs to the word Ineffable [*arrhetos*], breath of which the rough aspirate [*h*] of *hen* [εν] is an imitation;
>
> (b) of the vault of the *epsilon* [ε] itself, taken on its own and without the following consonant;
>
> (c) and straight afterwards from the letter *nu* [ν].

3. After this triad comes another which delimits the Intellectual depth, and another which determines the Demiurgic depth . . . .

4. After this triad comes another; the Soul-Itself, the Soul-in-General, and the Soul-of-All . . . . It is this last, the Soul-of-All, which according to Theodorus, Plato proposes to describe [in the *Timaeus*] . . . .

Starting with the tetrad of the elements, he says that the Soul [ΨΥΧΗ; *psyche*] can be shown to be a tetrad [because it has four letters], and that the number in its entirety can be a geometrical number.

On the other hand, so that one does not conceive of this number as without life, one will find that in the letters at the ends of the word "Soul" [Ψ + H], there is in fact Life, if in place of the third heptad [Ψ = 700] one takes the first [Z = 7; Z + H = *ze* (*i*), "live"]. Or, instead, if one puts the fundamental numbers of the first letter [Ψ] next to this letter, one will see that the Soul is an Intellectual life. Take *zeta, omicron* and *psi* [Z, O, Ψ = 7, 70, 700]: in the middle is the circle [O] which is Intellectual, because Intellectual is the cause of the Soul. The smallest fundamental number [Z = 7] shows us that the Soul is a sort of geometrical intellect on account of the line which joins the parallel lines as a straight diagonal [Z], an Intellect which, resting on high, carries itself toward the line opposite and which manifests in a form of life which is at once non-oblique yet in an oblique manner. The largest fundamental number [Ψ = 700] is the element of the sphere. For it is certain that in any case where lines are curved [as in the letter Ψ] they will make a sphere.

After this, the fundamental numbers of the following letters *delta, mu* and *upsilon* [Δ, M, Y = 4, 40, 400], which again are three and at the same time tetradic [having a root of 4] and for this reason make up 12 [3 x 4], and produce the 12 spheres of the universe. The largest of these fundamental numbers [Y = 400] shows us that the essence of the Soul aspires to and tends to two things [due to its forked shape]—hence certain people name this letter "lover of wisdom" [*philosophos*]—but that the Soul-Itself plunges towards the depths of the two things. In any case, we too have found this title for *upsilon* amongst some of the men of great wisdom.

And the *upsilon* [Y] is common between the two spheres, the *psi* [Ψ] and the *chi* [X], the latter which because of breath [since *chi* is an aspirate], is hotter and more vitalizing, the former ones possessing these two qualities to a lesser degree. The result is that, once again, the Soul is an intermediary between two Intellects; the one anterior, the other posterior, and the fact that the letter *upsilon* is in the middle indicates the affinity and the relationship of the Soul with these two. Nevertheless, Plato more often attributed the letter *chi* to the Soul—although the letter *psi* is also a sphere—to manifest the equilibrium of the movement of the Soul, since all the straight lines are equal in the *chi*, and to render perceptible in this way the self-moved quality of the Soul. If, on the other hand, the Demiurge creates the Soul with its essence alone, then it is clear that he too is analogous to the *chi*: for the *chi* is the most primary Intellect. So, by this explanation of the letter *upsilon*, Theodorus states that the Soul proceeds and creates itself as a sort of intermediary existence between the two Intellects. This then, is how one should understand these things.

As for the last letter [in *psyche*], the *eta*, one must see it as the procession of the Soul towards the cube [because H = 8 = 2 x 2 x 2; the first cubic number in the decad] . . . . Again we have seen the appearance of the octad as derived from the dyad of the Soul.

Concerning the heptad; that which is in units [Z = 7] represents the first form of Life [*zoe*], that which is in tens [O = 70] represents the Intellectual part as cause of the circle, that which is in hundreds [Ψ = 700], and in the third and last place, represents the proper characteristic of the Soul . . . .

And since the shape of the Soul is like a letter *chi* [X], and its form is dyadic—for the division is into two—and that the dyad multiplied by the hexad, which is the fundamental number of the *chi* [600 = 6 + 0 + 0 = 6], produces the dodecad [2 x 6 = 12]. One can extract thence the twelve Primary Souls of governing rank.

These are then, more or less, the philosophical considerations of Theodorus on this subject, which he explains by basing himself upon the letters and their pronunciation—to place before your eyes what is only a small selection from a long exposition.[9]

That "long exposition," had it only survived, would probably have set out the Neoplatonic form of the Greek Qabalah, which seems from the short sample presented to have progressed even further than that of the Gnostics. Theodorus' analysis is one of the best examples of ancient Greek Qabalistic exegesis, as it incorporates an interesting range of techniques. He begins with sound, remarking that the aspirated *epsilon* that begins the Greek word *hen* (εν), "the One," is reflected in the aspirated letter *rho* (P) in *arrhetos* (αρρητος), "Ineffable." The next reference is to shape, the curved "vault" of the letter *epsilon* (ε) likened to the Platonic subcelestial arch.[10] He then uses the most obvious method of analyzing a word in numerical terms, counting the number of its composite letters. Because there are four letters in *psyche* (ΨYXH), he says that this makes its nature tetradic, and therefore similar to the four elements of Empedocles and Aristotle.

Theodorus next uses *pythmenes* to reduce the initial letter, *psi* (Ψ = 700), to its root value in the decad, represented by the letter *zeta* (Z = 7). This substitution is then used to create a *notari-chon* with the last letter, *eta* (H = 8), already a single number, since together these two letters give the Greek word *ze (i)*, "live," and also the first and last letters of the word *zoe*, "life." Several other letters are introduced by means of *pythmenes*, including *omicron* (O), *delta* (Δ), and *mu* (M). Shape is then again used by Theodorus to ascribe additional figurative meaning: *omicron* is noted as a perfect circle in shape; *zeta's* geometry portrays both non-oblique parallel lines and diagonal obliqueness; and *psi* is associated with the sphere, because its curved lines will define this shape if extended.

The second letter in Psyche's name is *upsilon* (Y), which, as Theodorus notes, is the famous "philosopher letter" of Pythagoras, so-called because its forked shape was seen to symbolize moral choice. The position of the letter *upsilon* in the word is also impor-tant for Theodorus: "common between the two spheres, the *psi* and the *chi*."

The next letter, *chi* (X), is the very symbol used by Plato in the passage of the *Timaeus* under discussion to describe the shape used in the construction of the soul, as Theodorus observes. He also notes equilibrium and duality in its cruciform shape, which, when multiplied by its root value (2 x 6), produces twelve, the number of the "twelve spheres of the universe" and the "twelve Primary Souls of the governing rank." More interestingly, *chi* is seen as "hotter and more vitalizing," because it is an aspirate. This phonetic symbolism in early Greek Qabalah appears to be based upon grammatical the-ory, like that of the Gnostics Marcus and Marsanes— further evi-dence that theories of language assisted in the continuing evolution and development of Qabalistic symbolism.

Theodorus finally comes to the letter *eta* (H), which has the value of eight and, following Iamblichus, is associated with the first cube in the decad, being the cube of two (2 x 2 x 2). From this analysis, Theodorus submits that the letters in the name of Psyche declare the very nature of the soul of the world.

The eminent Neoplatonist, Iamblichus, who had written a biography of Pythagoras and was also credited with authorship of the leading work on arithmology, *The Theology of Arithmetic*, complained that Theodorus went too far in his use of the *pythmenes* method of interpretation of words. Proclus recounts that:

> Iamblichus adds that to analyse into the primary ratios of numbers, and to dwell on these, transfers the theory from some numbers to others. For the heptad is not the same which is in units, and tens, and hundreds. This however, existing in the name of the soul, why is it requisite to introduce the disquisition of primary ratios? For thus he may transfer all things to all numbers, by dividing, or compounding, or multiplying. In short, he accuses the whole of this theory as artificial, and containing nothing sane.[11]

Iamblichus also rebutted the propositions of Numenius and Theodorus' teacher, Amelius, "whose writings contained similar opinions," by arguing, among other things, that:

> It is not safe to argue from characters. For these subsist by position, and the ancient was different from the present mode of forming them. Thus for instance the letter Z, which Numenius makes the subject of discussion, had not the opposite lines entirely parallel, nor the middle line oblique, but at right angles, as is evident from the ancient letters.[12]

This is true, for early versions of the letter *zeta* show that the upper and lower parallels of the Z were joined not by a diagonal line as they are now, but by a vertical line, more akin to the letter H turned on its side. Insofar as the observations of Theodorus were based upon the shape of the letter Z, they might equally have been made regarding the letter *nu* (N), which is simply a Z turned on its side and differing from it only by position, as Aristotle observed in his *Metaphysics*.[13]

The Neoplatonists' use of the geometry of letter shapes to illustrate philosophical concepts was in conformity with the tradition established by Pythagoras and Plato. Besides the example of Plato's *chi* in the *Timaeus*, there was also the precedent attributed to Pythagoras of the letter *upsilon* (**Y**) representing the crossroads of moral choice, and the idea naturally spread with the weight of such revered and august authority. A few brief excerpts from Proclus' commentary on the *Elements*, written by Euclid around 300 B.C.E., demonstrate the considerable overlap between mathematics and philosophy, an overlap that the Neoplatonists exploited in analyzing Greek letters according to their angles, lines, and curves.

> The straight line is a symbol of the inflexible, unvarying, incorruptible, unremitting, and all-powerful providence that is present in all things; and the circle and circular movement symbolize the activity that returns to itself, concentrates on itself, and controls everything in accordance with a single intelligible Limit. The demiurgic Nous has therefore set up these two principles in himself, the straight and the circular, and produced out of himself two monads, the one acting in a circular fashion to perfect all intelligible essences, the other moving in a straight line to bring all perceptible things to birth. Since the soul is intermediate between sensibles and intelligibles, she moves in a circular fashion insofar as she is aligned to intelligible nature, but insofar as she presides over sensibles, exercises her providence in a straight line. So much regarding the similarity of these concepts to the order of being . . . .
>
> The angle is a symbol and a likeness, we say, of the coherence that obtains in the realm of divine things—of the orderliness that leads diverse things to unity, divided things

to the indivisible and plurality to conjunction and communion. For the angle functions as a bond between the several
lines and planes, focussing magnitude upon the unextend-
edness of points and holding together every figure that is
constructed by means of it. Hence the [*Chaldean*] *Oracles*
call these angular conjunctions the "bonds" of the figures
because of their resemblence to the constraining unities and
couplings in the divine world by which things separated are
joined to one another . . . . Circular angles imitate the causes that enwrap intelligible diversity in a unity, for circular
lines ever bending back upon themselves are images of Nous
and intelligible forms . . . . Among the Pythagoreans we find
some angles dedicated to certain gods, others to others. Thus
Philolaus makes the angle of a triangle sacred to some, and
the angle of a square sacred to others, assigning different
angles to different gods, or the same angle to one god and
several angles to the same god, according to the various
potencies in him. And I think the philosopher of Asine
[Theodorus] has in mind these features of the demiurgic triangle, the primary cause of all the order among the elements,
when he sets some gods at the sides and others at the angles,
the former presiding over the forthgoing and potentiality of
things, the latter over the unification of wholes and the
reassembling into unity of things that have issued forth.
Thus do these features of the angle bring our thoughts
around to the contemplation of being. . . .

The Pythagoreans . . . refer right angles to the immacu-
late essences in the divine orders and their particular potencies, as causes of the undeviating providence that presides
over secondary things—for what is upright, uninclined to
evil, and inflexible accords with the character of those high
gods—whereas they say that obtuse and acute angles are left
in charge of the divinities that supervise the forthgoing of
things and the change and variety of their powers . . . . The

perpendicular thus is also a symbol of directness, purity, undefiled unswerving force, and all such things, a symbol of divine and intelligent measure . . . . Hence they say that virtue is like rightness, whereas vice is constituted after the fashion of the indeterminate obtuse and acute, possessing both excesses and deficiencies and showing by this more-and-less its own lack of measure . . . .

The first and simplest and most perfect of figures is the circle. It is superior to all solid figures because its being is of a simpler order, and it surpasses all other plane figures by reason of its homogeneity and self-identity . . . . Hence whether you analyze the cosmic or the supercosmic world, you will always find the circle in the class nearer the divine. If you divide the universe into the heavens and the world of generation, you will assign the circular form to the heavens and the straight line to the world of generation . . . .

The Pythagoreans assert that the triangle is the ultimate source of generation and of the production of species among things generated. Consequently the *Timaeus* says that the ideas of natural science, those used in the construction of the cosmic elements, are triangles.[14]

The symbolism referred to would have automatically attached to those Greek letters with simple geometric forms, such as *gamma* or *tau* (the right angle), *delta* (the triangle), *iota* (the perpendicular line), *lambda* (the acute angle) and *omicron* (the circle). It is easy to see how this type of reasoning was soon applied to the shapes of these and other letters by Neopythagoreans and Neoplatonists such as Numenius, Amelius, and Theodorus, the latter being the "philosopher of Asine" to whom Proclus refers in the above passage. Application of such considerations by Theodorus is evident in his exegesis on the word *psyche* quoted above, for example in his observations on the letters *zeta* (Z), *omicron* (O), and *psi* (Ψ).

On the evidence we have, the Neoplatonists must therefore be credited with stressing shape among the various qualities or attributions of letters available for Greek Qabalistic exegesis of important names or words. Geometry must also be listed with grammar as among those advances of the Hellenistic Age that led to substantial development of the symbolism of the Greek Qabalah.

Notes to Chapter Eleven

1 Olympiodorus, *Prolegomena*, 8.39–9.1; cited in G. R. Morrow (trans.), *Proclus—A Commentary on the First Book of Euclid's Elements*, foreword by I. Muller, 1992, Copyright © 1970 by Princeton University Press, 1st printing. Reprinted by permission of Princeton University Press.

2 R. E. Allen (ed.), *Greek Philosophy—Thales to Aristotle* (New York: Free Press, 1991), p. 19.

3 A. R. Burn, *The Pelican History of Greece* (London: Pelican Books, 1966), p. 393.

4 Both Porphyry and Iamblichus wrote commentaries on the *Chaldean Oracles*, a versified collection of oracles attributed to Zoroaster, but probably written in the second century C.E. by Julian the Chaldean; G. R. Morrow (trans.), *Proclus—A Commentary on the First Book of Euclid's Elements*, pp. xv–xvi.

5 W. Scott (trans.), *Hermetica* (Boulder, CO: Hermes House, 1982).

6 Plato, *Timaeus*, 53b, in D. Lee (trans.), *Plato—Timaeus and Critias* (London: Penguin, 1977), pp. 72–73.

7 Plato, *Timaeus*, 35a–36d, in D. Lee (trans.), *Plato—Timaeus and Critias*, p. 49.

8 T. Taylor (trans.), *The Commentaries of Proclus on the Timaeus of Plato*, p. 118.

9 S. Ronan, in A. McLean (ed.), *The Hermetic Journal*, No. 42, pp. 25–36. Taylor wrote, "It would be very difficult to render it intelligible to the English reader, and as in the opinion of Iamblichus, the whole of it is artificial, and contains nothing sane, I have omitted to translate it"; T. Taylor (trans.), *The Commentaries of Proclus on the Timaeus of Plato*, p. 141.

10 S. Ronan, in A. McLean (ed.), *The Hermetic Journal*, No. 42, pp. 25–36.

11 T. Taylor (trans.), *The Commentaries of Proclus on the Timaeus of Plato*, p. 141.

12 T. Taylor (trans.), *The Commentaries of Proclus on the Timaeus of Plato*, p. 141.

13 Aristotle, *Metaphysics*, 985b.

14 G. Morrow (trans.), *A Commentary on the First Book of Euclid's Elements*, ¶ 108, 129–133, 147, 166; see also Plato, *Timaeus*, 53–54.

chapter twelve

THE JEWS

reek culture and Greek thought had a huge impact on their counterparts in the Near East after the invasion of the Persian Empire by Alexander of Macedon in 334 B.C.E. Alexander and his Graeco-Macedonian army conquered Asia Minor, Syria, Judah, Egypt, Babylonia, Persia, Bactria, and parts of India, making Alexander ruler of the largest kingdom the world had ever known. Common Greek, or *koine*, quickly became the *lingua franca* spoken throughout the lands of the Alexandrian empire.

In 332 B.C.E., Alexander conquered Judah, which became known in Greek as *Judea*, the land of the Jews (see figure 21, page 172). A succession of Hellenistic dynasties ruled Judea until 152 B.C.E., when religiously motivated armed resistance led by the

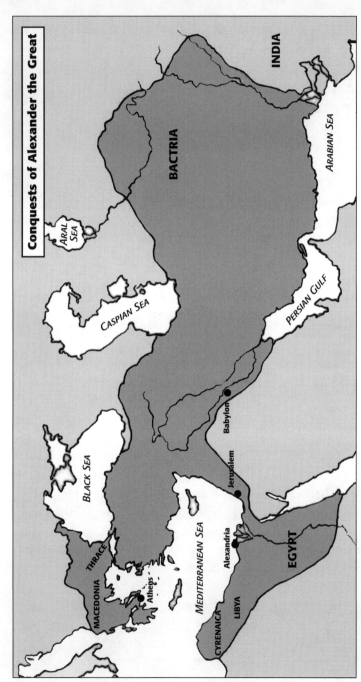

Figure 21. The conquests of Alexander the Great by 327 B.C.E.

Maccabees, or "Hammers," led to the establishment of a semi-independent state. This was conquered a century later by the Romans, who installed the hated Herod as ruler on their behalf. Under Macedonian rule, the Jews also adopted the Greek alphabetic system of numeration, which soon became well established in Judea. Jewish use of the alphabet for numbers is first found on coins of the Maccabean period (second century B.C.E.), and the system was apparently introduced even in the Temple itself, where Greek letters were also used to indicate numbers.[1] It is therefore surprising to note that many writers persist in the misconception that alphabetic numerals were first invented by the Jews, when, in fact, they were half a millennium behind the Greeks in using such a system. Because the number 15 in Hebrew would appear as IH (יה), the first two letters in IHVH or Jehovah (יהוה), the number 15 was instead written as 9 and 6 (טו). It has been suggested that the early depiction of the number 4 among the Romans as IIII rather than IV was similarly because this formed the first two letters of their supreme deity, Jupiter (IVPPITER).[2]

The influence of Greek and Hellenistic thought naturally increased as the lands conquered by Alexander were enveloped by Greek customs, ideas, and language. This is evident early on in Judaism: even the word "synagogue" is Greek. In Alexandria, the great Egyptian city on the Nile delta that Alexander founded and gave his own name, there were more Jews than in Jerusalem itself. It was in Alexandria in the third century B.C.E. that the most important books of Judaism were translated into Greek, and became known as the *Septuagint* (Latin *septuaginta*, "seventy").[3] This name is derived from the story that Ptolemy Philadelphus delegated the task to seventy-two separate translators, six from each of the twelve tribes. After seventy-two days, the story goes, each of them independently came up with identical translations.[4] This legend is useful in illustrating the belief in divine inspiration behind each letter and word of these holy books. Until the fourth century C.E. the *Septuagint* was also used by the early Christian

Church as its only version of the Old Testament. The Jewish diaspora was accelerated by the second failed Jewish revolt in 132–135
C.E., after which the irritated Emperor Hadrian expelled all Jews
from Jerusalem on pain of death, renaming the now gentile city
Aelia Capitolina.

Numerous sects and schools arose from the mixture of cultures in Alexandria during this syncretic era of Graeco-Roman
rule. Among their teachings early in the Current Era, can be dis-
cerned the origins of the Hebrew Qabalah, resulting from a merg-
er of Hebrew mysticism and Greek Neoplatonism. The latter, it
will be remembered, itself derived from a mixture of Platonism
and Pythagoreanism. Generally considered influential in this
development are the works of the Hellenistic Jewish philosopher
and theologian, Philo Judaeus (circa 30 B.C.E.–45 C.E.), who was
the leader of a large Jewish community at Alexandria in Egypt. It
was Philo who first applied Neopythagorean traditions to Hebrew
scriptures and so introduced the Greek idea of scriptural exegesis
by number to the Jews. There are numerous references in his writings that show he was acquainted with works on arithmology cir-
culating in Alexandria at the time.[5] For example, we know that
Philo was aware of isopsephy from his commentary on Genesis
17:15, in which he mentions the popular story that the name of
Abraham's half-sister and incestuous wife, Sara, was changed to
Sarra because, in Greek, the extra letter *rho,* equal to 100, alluded
to the old age to which she lived.

> Once more some of the stupid people may laugh at the
> addition of one letter worth 100 [= *rho*], and ridicule and
> make fun of it because they are unwilling to apply them-
> selves to the facts of things and follow after truth. For that
> which seems to be the addition of one letter produces all
> harmony. In place of the small (it gives) the great, and in
> place of the particular, the general, and in place of the mor-
> tal, the immortal. For through the one *rho* she is called Sara,

which in translation means "my rule," while with two *rhos* it means "ruler."[6]

Over three centuries later, the learned Jerome (342–420 C.E.) also mentions the story in his own *Hebrew Questions on Genesis*, pointing out the error inherent in it:

> Those people are mistaken who think that the name Sara was written first with one R and that another R was afterwards added to it; and because among the Greeks R represents the number 100, they surmise many absurd things about her name. At any rate, in whatever way they maintain her name was altered, it ought to have not a Greek but a Hebrew pronunciation, since the name itself is Hebrew.[7]

As mentioned earlier, the Jews eventually began to use isopsephy as a technique for interpreting the Torah, but called it by the name *gematria*, a word they derived from Greek *geometria*, or geometry.[8] Examples of *gematria* first appear in rabbinic literature in the second century C.E.[9] Against this date, it is important to note that most of the Old Testament's texts date from the Persian Period, between the exile to Babylon following the sack of Jerusalem in 587 B.C.E. to its conquest by Alexander in 332 B.C.E. Even the oldest books, including the five-volume Pentateuch attributed to Moses—Genesis, Exodus, Leviticus, Numbers, and Deuteronomy—show traces of major revision during this period.[10] Of the large number of Hebrew sacred writings, the canon of books that were eventually selected for the Hebrew Bible, or "Old Testament," as the Christians later called it, was only established after the fall of Jerusalem to the Romans in 70 C.E., by surviving rabbis at Jamnia who were anxious to preserve their religion from the catastrophe of the failed Jewish revolt.

Since even the latest texts taken into the Hebrew Bible date from the third and second centuries B.C.E., which predates the

Jewish use of Alexandrian alphabetic numerals, there are no examples of deliberate Hebrew *gematria* in the Old Testament, although subsequent Qabalists have endeavored to interpret Old Testament scriptures in this light.[11] However, the above references from Philo and Jerome are evidence of the application of Greek isopsephy as early as the first century C.E. in analysis of Old Testament writings in their *Septuagint* translation by the Greek-speaking Jews of Alexandria (for those in Judea, the everyday language was Aramaic). We have already seen how, at this time, Justin Martyr, in his *Apologia,* was also influenced by the Greek text of the *Septuagint* version to connect the sign (*semeion*) of Numbers 21:9 with the cross-shaped *chi* of Plato's *Timaeus.* Further instances recorded by Irenaeus show that, by the second century C.E., the many Hebrew names of God, by virtue of their translation into Greek, were being subjected to the principles of Greek Qabalistic exegesis wherein each letter had meaning:

> *Adonai* sometimes means "unnameable" and "admirable," and sometimes with a double Delta and an aspiration (*Haddonai*) it means "He who separates the earth from the water so that the water cannot rise up against it." Similarly *Sabaoth* with Omega in the last syllable [ΣΑΒΑΩΘ] means "voluntary," while with Omicron [ΣΑΒΑΟΘ] it means "first heaven." Just so, *Iaoth* with Omega [ΙΑΩΘ] means "fixed measure," while with Omicron [ΙΑΟΘ] it means "He who puts evils to flight."[12]

It is therefore apparent that the translation of the holy books of Judaism into Greek was a watershed in the development of the Hebrew Qabalah, since it naturally exposed these texts to the application of Hellenistic alphabetical symbolism and isopsephy for the first time. Before then, no such practice existed, or even could have existed, since alphabetic numerals were unknown to the Jews.

One such allegation of the existence of Hebrew Qabalah in the Old Testament was that the "318 men" mentioned in Genesis 14:14 was a *gematria* reference to Abraham's servant, Eliezer, whose name in Hebrew (אליעזר) was equivalent to 318. The late Gershom Scholem (1897–1982), among the leading authorities in the world on the history of the Hebrew Qabalah, acknowledged that this suggestion may have been a rabbinic response to the earlier Christian interpretation of this passage found in the Epistle of Barnabas quoted earlier, in which Greek Qabalah was used to support 318 as a reference to Jesus.[13] This early example would indicate that the adoption of isopsephy by the Jews as a technique of scriptural analysis may have been due, not only to the influence of the Neopythagoreans, Neoplatonists, and Gnostics, but also to the Christians who, by the end of the first century C.E., were distinguished from Judaism as a separate sect. In general, however, the only point about which we can be certain is, as Farbridge noted in his work, *Studies in Biblical and Semitic Symbolism*:

> It was only after the Jews came into contact with Greek philosophy that the symbolism of numbers began to play a really important part in the Jewish interpretation of the Bible. Traces of Pythagorean influence exist in the oldest Jewish-Hellenistic work, the *Septuagint*. Thus the passage in *Isaiah* XL; 26, "that bringeth out their host by number," is translated by the *Septuagint* "he that bringeth forth *his array* by number."[14]

As already mentioned, the earliest surviving Jewish Qabalist work, the *Sefer Yezirah* or *Book of Creation*, was written in a Platonic-Pythagorean spirit, probably some time between the third and sixth century C.E., certainly well after the Greek Qabalah was already established.[15] The *Sefer Yezirah* sets out each of the twenty-two letters in the Hebrew alphabet as a symbol with specific meanings and correspondences. These later formed the basis of the literal branch of the Hebrew Qabalah, that adopted the methods used by the Greeks and involved the analysis of sacred texts according to the numerical value and symbolical correspondences of each letter. The original attributions to the Hebrew letters found in the *Sefer Yezirah* are set out below. Subsequently, the order of the planets was roughly reversed similar to the older Greek system, in which Saturn, as the farthest planet, was connected with the last letter of the alphabet, *omega* (Ω); in the Hebrew alphabet, *tau* (ת) (see figure 22, page 179).

א	Air	♎︎	ל	Libra	♎
ב	Saturn	♄	מ	Water	▽
ג	Jupiter	♃	נ	Scorpio	♏
ד	Mars	♂	ס	Sagittarius	♐
ה	Aquarius	♒	ע	Capricorn	♑
ו	Taurus	♉	פ	Venus	♀
ז	Gemini	♊	צ	Aries	♈
ח	Cancer	♋	ק	Pisces	♓
ט	Leo	♌	ר	Mercury	☿
י	Virgo	♍	ש	Fire	△
כ	Sun	☉	ת	Moon	☽

Although the *Sefer Yezirah* contains the only set of combined planetary, elemental, and zodiacal attributions in ancient literature, it would be straining credibility to suggest that the system is unconnected with the previous correlation of letters to the zodiac in Hellenistic astrology, or to the widespread attribution of the seven Greek vowels to the seven planets, dating back to the

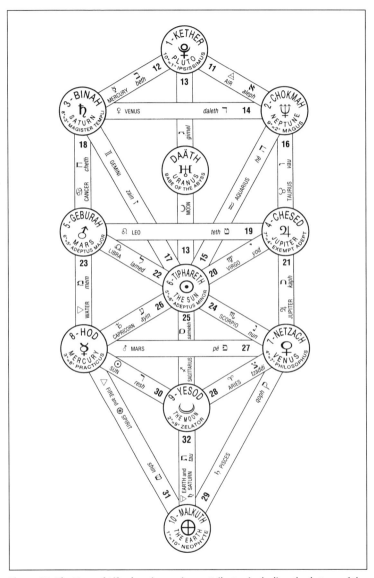

Figure 22. The Tree of Life showing various attributes including the letters of the Hebrew alphabet as used by modern magicians and Qabalists. (Reprinted from Aleister Crowley, *Magick • Book Four • Liber Aba*, second revised edition, York Beach, ME: Samuel Weiser, 1997.)

writings of Hippocrates and Aristotle. The author of the *Sefer Yezirah* apparently attempted to base these groups of symbolic correspondences upon grammatical considerations, as had been the case with the division of the Greek alphabet by the Gnostics. Since the Hebrew alphabet did not have vowels, as did the Greek, other letters had to be chosen to represent the planets. The author of the *Sefer Yezirah* therefore selected his own group of seven special letters to correspond to the number of the planets as the vowels did in Greek, namely the seven "double" letters (ב ג ד כ פ ר ת), so called because each of these Hebrew letters could allegedly be pronounced two ways. In actual fact, the suggestion that there is a double pronunciation for the letter *resh* is phonetically strained, indicative of a slightly forced fit.[16] The *Sefer Yezirah* states:

> Seven Doubles: ב ג ד כ פ ר ת. . . . Each has two sounds: *B-Bh, G-Gh, D-Dh, K-Kh, P-Ph, R-Rh, T-Th*. A structure of soft and hard, a structure of strong and weak, double because they are transposes . . . . Engrave them, carve them, combine them, as planets in the Universe, days in the Year, and gates in the Soul. From them engrave the seven firmaments, seven earths, seven weeks. Seven is therefore beloved under all heavens. How? Make *beth* king over life, bind a crown to it, and with it depict Saturn in the Universe, Sunday in the Year, and the right eye in the Soul. Make *gimel* king, bind a crown to it, and with it depict Jupiter in the Universe, Monday in the Year, and the left eye in the Soul. Make *daleth* king, bind a crown to it, and with it depict Mars in the Universe, Tuesday in the Year, and the right ear in the Soul. Make *kaph* king, bind a crown to it, and with it depict the Sun in the Universe, Wednesday in the Year, and the left ear in the Soul. Make *peh* king, bind a crown to it, and with it depict Venus in the Universe, Thursday in the Year, and the right nostril in the Soul. Make *resh* king, bind a crown to

it, and with it depict Mercury in the Universe, Friday in the Year, and the left nostril in the Soul. Make *tau* king, bind a crown to it, and with it depict the Moon in the Universe, the Sabbath in the Year, and the mouth in the Soul . . . . These are the seven planets of the Universe, the seven days of creation, and the seven gates of the Soul.[17]

After making the association between the seven planets and these seven "double" letters, fifteen letters of the Hebrew alphabet remained to be ascribed. Unfortunately for the author of the *Sefer Yezirah*, the Hebrew alphabet of twenty-two letters was less well suited to this accommodation than the Greek, since the twelve signs of the zodiac and the seven planets left only three letters for the five Aristotelian elements. Earth and ether were, therefore, simply omitted altogether. The three remaining chosen elements were attributed to the letters *aleph*, *mem,* and *shin*, which the author, according to his own strange phonetic system, designates as "matrice" letters. The last seven letters, called "single," were attributed to the signs of the zodiac in their natural sequence.

The allocation of the first letter, *aleph* (א), to the element of air may be based on Greek Qabalah, in which the equivalent letter A was the initial of the Greek word for that element (*aer*), as is evidenced in the passage concerning Adam in Zosimus' *On the Letter Omega* quoted earlier. The letter *mem* (מ) was the obvious choice for water, since "water" was the meaning of the letter-name in Phoenician and Hebrew, reflecting its origin in the Egyptian hieroglyphic for water. The third and last Aristotelian element fitted in was fire. This was ascribed to the penultimate letter before *tau* (ת), namely *shin* (שׁ) meaning "tooth." This association is also found in Greek writings, namely Revelation 21:8, where John of Patmos wrote of purification by the "tooth of fire."

In the *Sefer Yezirah*, each of the Hebrew letters is associated with the creative powers of the Kosmos. The similarity to the Gnostic teachings of Marcus and Marsanes is readily apparent, suggesting that the author of the *Sefer Yezirah* was acquainted with some form of this Gnostic doctrine. The Gnostic theory of creation by emanations is reflected in the text, in which the world is proscribed in a series of ten emanations, or *sefiroth*, in turn clearly modeled on the Pythagorean decad. Scholem however took the view that:

> While the numerical-mystical speculation of the sefiroth probably has its origins in neo-Pythagorean sources—Nicomachus of Gerasa, the celebrated author of a mystical arithmology who lived around 140 C.E., came from Palestine west of the Jordan—the idea of "letters by means of which heaven and earth were created" may well come from within Judaism itself. In the first half of the third century it is encountered in a statement of the Babylonian amora [speaker], Rab, originally of Palestine.[18] It is perfectly conceivable that two originally different theories were fused or juxtaposed in the author's doctrine concerning the thirty-two paths. This range of ideas would fit well in the second or third century in Palestine or its immediate environs.[19]

With the greatest respect to Scholem, that conclusion is manifestly against the weight of the evidence we now have. We can agree with him, as does Ronan, on the likely geographical origin of the concept, since Numenius, Iamblichus, Nicomachus, and possibly Marcus also, came from the Palestine-Syrian region; although the influence of nearby Alexandria can never be discounted as the major center of learning in the area. However, even by pushing back the *Sefer Yezirah* to Scholem's earliest possible date, the third century C.E. rather than the sixth, it is not possible to argue that this Jewish Qabalist work was even contemporaneous with the available writings from other schools that connected the alphabet with creation. In fact, all the historical evidence points to the idea originating in Gnostic doctrine, since it appears in the teachings of Marcus, who died around 175 C.E., and in those of Marsanes, that also (more likely than not) predate the *Sefer Yezirah*. Gershom Scholem makes no reference at all to Marcus in his *Origins of the Kabbalah*, or to the text of Marsanes in the Nag Hammadi codices, published only a year before his death. We have seen that the concept of the Greek alphabet taking part in the creation of the soul, or the Soul of the World, was also referred to in Neopythagorean and Neoplatonist doctrines of the same period.[20]

It is, in any event, impossible to argue a Jewish origin for the collective techniques that we now call the literal Qabalah, the system of scriptural analysis in which the mathematical and symbolic correspondences ascribed to each letter were applied to sacred texts in the search for hidden meaning, as Theodorus had done to Plato's *Timaeus*. As Stephen Ronan has pointed out, the *Sefer Yezirah* makes no reference to the numerical value or shape of letters, or to any of the other concepts of Qabalistic exegesis that had long been in use by numerous Greek writers.[21] We have seen that these aspects, such as isopsephy and other methods, evolved as part of the Pythagorean and Platonic traditions and were not adopted by the Jews until much later, when such techniques were already highly evolved. The alphabetical symbolism and associated pseudo-grammatical division of the alphabet that appear in the *Sefer Yezirah* are also Greek concepts that were already well developed as early as the Hellenistic Age. Considering all the evidence, there is nothing to support Scholem's attempt to split off the particular concept of the alphabet's creative role in the *Sefer Yezirah* from the acknowledged Greek influences in the rest of the work. Indeed, in the *Encyclopaedia Judaica*, for which he wrote a detailed discussion of the Jewish literary evidence on the point, Scholem simply concluded that the *Sefer Yezirah* was written by a devout Jew endeavoring to "Judaize" *non-Jewish* Gnostic or Pythagorean speculations that suited his spirit.[22]

A further technique of Hebrew Qabalah was *temurah*. This involved substituting some letters for others, according to various set systems of pairs, until (hopefully) a recognizable new word was created. For example, one of these systems, called *athbash* (אתבש), is so called because it involved taking each word and changing the first letter of the alphabet (א) to the last (ת), the second (ב) to the penultimate (ש), and so on. Thus, under this system, the word *Sheshak* (ששך) in Hebrew scripture becomes *Babel* (בבל), and, therefore, allegedly a hidden reference to Babylon.[23] This system was almost certainly developed by the Jews, since it was unlikely to produce any meaningful word in Greek due to the use of vowels in that language. The pairing of letters in *temurah* does, however, reflect the earlier allocation of pairs of Greek letters to parts of the body by the Gnostic, Marcus, and to the signs of the zodiac by Hellenistic astrologers, as recorded by Vettius Valens.[24] An early example of *temurah* cited by Scholem is found in a Hebrew-Greek magical amulet dating from the second to fourth century C.E., that includes a verse from the Hebrew text of Deuteronomy (28:58), but interestingly, even this is in Greek transcription.[25]

In summary, the historical evidence shows that the earliest manifestation of the literal Hebrew Qabalah, the set of correspondences seen in the *Sefer Yezirah*, was not a new idea, but, at best, an adaptation to the Hebrew alphabet of existing Greek Qabalistic practice already many centuries old. The Greeks, who loved to play with words, in addition to being the first to ascribe their letters to the constellations, zodiac, planets, and elements, and to create extensive alphabetic symbolism and correspondences, were also responsible for the development of other aspects of the literal Qabalah later used by the Jews, such as Qabalistic exegesis, alphabetic numerals, isopsephy, *notarichon*, and *pythmenes* or *aiq beker*. This last fact has been too often ignored by Hebrew Qabalists, both ancient and modern, who, unfortunately, have been generally unaware of their historical debt to the Greeks. Greek Qabalists such as Marcus, Marsanes, and Theodorus knew and used an entire coherent system of Greek alphabetical symbolism and exegesis, and made no mention whatsoever of any similar system of Hebrew Qabalah. Indeed, there is no evidence that one even existed at that time.

The Qabalist school of Judaism really has its beginnings over a millennium later, emerging suddenly in the 13th century C.E. in southern France and Spain. The doctrines of the Jewish Qabalah can be found in the major thirteenth century collection of related writings known as the *Zohar*. It claims, however, to derive its inheritance from earlier texts, including the *Sefer Yezirah*, and from other literature of Jewish Gnosticism. These included speculations of Merkabah mysticism (*merkabah* being the name for the divine chariot or throne appearing in 1 Ezekiel), in which the ecstatic visionary rose through the regions of the seven palaces or heavens (*hekhaloth*) to arrive at the throne of God, clearly similar to the ascent journeys described in Gnostic texts and the Greek magical papyri.[26] Despite the considerable lapse of time, therefore, the Hebrew Qabalah of the Middle Ages was linked to earlier tradition by its reference to these texts and subsequent related commentaries.

As was indicated in the introduction to this book, the literal Qabalah we have been discussing is a combination of scriptural interpretative techniques that formed only a small part of the philosophy and doctrines of the Qabalah as a sect of Judaism. An analysis of the Greek, Gnostic, or other foreign influences on the entire spectrum of the Hebrew Qabalah, as opposed to what extent that school was evolved from internal speculation within Judaism, is a study outside the scope of this book and a topic on which Scholem and others have already written authoritatively. For our limited present purposes, it is sufficient to note that Hebrew Qabalist doctrines reached their pinnacle of importance in Judaism in Europe during the Middle Ages. Consequently they also had a huge influence on Western magical tradition, which drew heavily on Jewish esoteric lore, and as a source for the inner gnosis of orthodox Christian thought.

Notes to Chapter Twelve

1 *Shek.* 3.2; cited in G. Scholem, *Kabbalah* (Jerusalem: Keter Publishing House, 1974), p. 337.

2 W. Halsey (ed.), *"Numerals and Systems of Numeration,"* in *Collier's Encyclopaedia.*

3 Augustine, *City of God*, XVIII; 42 (London: Penguin, 1984), p. 820; the full title is *Vetus Testamentum Graece Iuxta Septuaginta Interpretes.*

4 J. Rohmer, *Testament—The Bible and History* (London: Michael O'Mara Books, 1988), p. 125.

5 D. Runia, *Philo of Alexandria and the Timaeus of Plato* (Leiden: Brill, 1986), vol. 1, pp. 169–170; M. Stone (ed.), *Jewish Writings of the Second Temple Period* (Assen: Van Gorcum, 1984), p. 256.

6 Philo, *Questions and Answers on Genesis*, III; 54, in R. Marcus (trans.) (London: William Heinemann, Ltd., 1953), p. 254.

7 C. T. R. Hayward (trans.), *Saint Jerome's Hebrew Questions on Genesis* (Oxford: Clarendon Press, 1995), p. 49.

8 M. Farbridge, *Studies in Biblical and Semitic Symbolism* (Hoboken, NJ: Ktav Publishing House, 1970), p. 93.

9 G. Scholem, *Kabbalah*, p. 337.

10 J. Rohmer, *Testament*, p. 111.

11 The first recorded use of Hebrew letters as numbers is under the Maccabees in the second century B.C.E., and only the very latest book included in the Jewish Bible, the anti-Hellenic Apocalyptic book of Daniel, can be dated this late.

12 Irenaeus, *Against Heresies*, II; 35, in R. M. Grant (trans.), *Irenaeus of Lyons* (London: Routledge, 1985), p. 122. Apparently further evidence of the association discussed earlier, between the letter *delta* and the element of water, arising from the fact that only five consonants were used in the words for the five Aristotelian elements.

13 G. Scholem, *Kabbalah*, p. 338.

14 R. Ottley, *Isaiah According to the Septuagint*, vol. 1, p. 221; cited in M. Farbridge, *Studies in Biblical and Semitic Symbolism*, p. 97.

15 G. Scholem, *"Sefer Yezirah,"* in *Encyclopaedia Judaica.*

16 For a discussion on the difficulties in the phonetic system used by the author, see G. Scholem, *Origins of the Kabbalah* (Princeton: Princeton University Press, 1990), pp. 30–31, and sources there cited.

17 *Sefer Yezirah*, IV; 1–12.

18 Citing *Berakhoth*, 55a.

19 G. Scholem, *Origins of the Kabbalah*, pp. 28–29.

20 Signs of the idea can even be traced as far back as the early Pythagoreans, who had pointed out "the interval from *alpha* to *omega* in the alphabet . . . is equal to that of the

whole system of the universe"; Aristotle, *Metaphysics*, 1093b, H. Treddenick (trans.) (Cambridge: Harvard University Press, 1962), p. 301.

21 S. Ronan, *Theodorus of Asine and the Kabbalah*, in A. McLean (ed.), *The Hermetic Journal,* No. 42 (London: Privately published, 1988), p. 33.

22 G. Scholem, *"Sefer Yezirah,"* in *Encyclopaedia Judaica*; see also *Kabbalah*, pp. 27–28, in which Scholem notes the Greek origin of several terms in the book, including the permutations of YHW (יהו) as a transliteration of IAO. In his *Origins of the Kabbalah*, pp. 32–33, fn. 55, Scholem notes that the historian Reitzenstein, on the basis of a comparative study of the letter-mysticism of the period, was of the view that the book was of Hellenistic origin, and to be dated as early as the second century C.E.; R. Reitzenstein, *Poimandres* (Leipzig: Teubner, 1904), p. 291.

23 Jeremiah XXV; 226, LI; 41; cited in G. Scholem, *Kabbalah*, p. 338.

24 In particular the Hebrew *temurah* known as AL-BaM; F. Dornseiff, *Das Alphabet in Mystik und Magie*, p. 84.

25 G. Scholem, *Origins of the Kabbalah*, p. 29, fn. 48.

26 Ronan, *Theodorus of Asine,* pp. 21–23. See also Naomi Janowitz, *The Poetics of Ascent— Theories of Language in a Rabbinic Ascent Text* (Albany: State University of New York, 1989).

chapter thirteen

GREEK QABALISTIC
EXEGESIS

e have seen that the
Greeks had, over a thou-
sand years, evolved a variety of different techniques
that they used in order to
find extra layers of meaning in important names, words, and
phrases, seeking out messages from the gods. Beginning with the
pictorial symbolism of some individual letters, the letters of the
alphabet attracted additional symbolism and various sets of correspondences. The creation of alphabetic numerals and the development of isopsephy added to this symbolism the possibilities of
mathematical permutation and Pythagorean number mysticism.
Magical numbers passed on their qualities to words of equivalent
value, and magical names and words added to the qualities of
numbers associated with them. There were also other means of

wordplay independent of mathematics, such as palindromes, puns, anagrams, and acronyms. Qabalistic exegesis, or the literal Qabalah, constitutes the application of these combined techniques and symbolism to each individual letter of a specific word or name in the search for extra levels of meaning. Fortunately, as we have seen, some examples have survived from the ancient world that show how the collective principles of the Greek Qabalah were used this way in practice.

Although we know isopsephy and individual letter symbolism were both of great antiquity and in widespread use by the Hellenistic Age, the combination of these and other techniques in detailed letter-by-letter analysis of words—usually the names of deities—is not evidenced until much later. It appears that the Gnostics were central to the synthesis and development of this aspect of Greek Qabalah, because they provide the earliest instances of Qabalistic exegesis. The passages from Irenaeus and Hippolytus preserving the teachings of Marcus show that the name of Jesus may have been among the first to be analyzed in this way, not later than the second century C.E. In the *Pistis Sophia*, compiled around 300 C.E., we find Jesus himself giving his disciples an exegesis of the name IAO, the Greek name for Yahweh or Jehovah:

> This is its interpretation: Iota, the Universe came out; Alpha, they will turn them; Omega, will become the completion of all completions.[1]

Theodorus' elaborate and extensive analysis of the word *psyche,* set out earlier, shows that by the fourth century C.E., in the hands of the Neoplatonists, Qabalistic exegesis had flowered fully as a technique. It is impossible for us now to ascertain if the literal Qabalah was evolved principally by one school, such as the Gnostics, Neopythagoreans, or Neoplatonists, or the extent to which these schools were indebted to a common source, such as popular Hellenistic divination and magic.

The Carthaginian satirist, Martianus Capella, who flourished around 400 C.E., provides us with another excellent example of how the Greek Qabalah was used in practical application. It is found in his major work, titled *On the Marriage of Mercury and Philology*, that was for centuries a popular textbook on the so-called "seven liberal arts": arithmetic, geometry, music, astronomy, grammar, dialectic, and rhetoric. Each of these arts was personified by Martianus in his essays as a deity. In one such essay, for instance, the goddess Arithmetic, who is accompanied by Pythagoras as her guide, calculates the number 717 on her fingers; the goddess Philosophy then explains that this is Arithmetic's way of greeting Jupiter by his own name, since the Greeks called Jupiter "the Beginning" (H APXH = 717).[2]

Martianus provides a detailed exegesis of two other divine names, utilizing several of the techniques of Greek Qabalah, including individual letter symbolism, isopsephy, the rule of nine, and Pythagorean numerology. The relevant passage occurs when the goddess Philology ("love of learning") resorts to divination by numerology in order to determine whether Mercury will be a suitable husband:

> And so, she sought from the numbers to discover whether a marriage would be beneficial and whether the winged swiftness of the celestial whirlwind would unite with her by a suitable bond of marriage. She counted up on her fingers the letters of her own name and that of the Cyllenian [Mercury]—not the name which the conflicting stories of different nations had given him, not the name which the different rituals of peoples, varying according to the interests and cults of each place, had created, but that name which Jove himself had settled upon him by a celestial proclamation at his birth and which the faulty research of man had claimed was made known only through the ingenuities of the Egyptians. She took from each end of his name the

bounding element which is both the first and the perfect terminus of number. Next came the number which is worshipped as Lord in all temples for its cubic solidity. In the
next position she took a letter which the Samian sage regarded as representing the dual ambiguity of mortal fate.
Accordingly, the number 1218 flashed forth.

Diminishing this number by the rule of nine, by substituting units for tens, she cleverly reduced it to the number
three. Her own name, which was set out in numeral form as
724, she reduced to the number four; these two numbers
(three and four) are marked by a harmonious relationship
with each other. For the number three is certainly perfect,
because it may be rationally arranged as a beginning, a middle, and an end; it alone both makes a line and defines the
solids (for solids are defined by length and depth); further-
more, the triplication of the number three is the first to yield
a cube from the odd numbers. Who does not know the
threefold harmonies in music? And an odd number is attributed to masculinity. All time changes in a threefold sequence
[past, present, and future]; the number three is also the
seedbed of perfect numbers, namely of six and of nine, by
different forms of connection [3 x 2 and 3 x 3]. It is therefore properly associated with the god of rationality.

But Philology, because she is herself a most learned
woman, although she is reckoned among the female (even)
numbers, yet is made perfect by complete computation. For
the number four with its parts makes up the whole power of
the decad itself [1 + 2 + 3 + 4 = 10] and is therefore perfect
and called quadrate, as is the Cyllenian himself, with whom
are associated the four seasons of the year, the regions of
heaven, the elements of the earth. That celebrated oath of
old Pythagoras, who did not refrain from swearing "by the
tetrad"—what does that signify except the number of perfect
ratio? Within itself it contains the one, the duad, the triad,

and is itself the square of two, within which proportions the musical harmonies are produced . . . . Thus, in her examination of agreement among numbers, the clever maiden was delighted.

Then she joined them with each other, and three joined to four makes the heptad. But this number is the perfection of the celestial rationality, as the fullness of the sevens testifies. For what else is shown by the passage of the fated climacteric, by the circuits and movements of the planets, and by the viability of the fetus in the seventh month in the darkness of the womb? . . . Thus the numbers represented by their names were in concord. Therefore the concord established between them bound their nuptial union with a true proportion, so that the maiden delighted in a marriage so advantageous to herself.[3]

During the Middle Ages, scholars searched without success to discover Mercury's "divine name" and explain this passage, which, like that in Revelation, had become an enigma to subsequent generations. It was finally unraveled in 1599 by the brilliant young Dutchman—he was then just 17 years old—Hugo Grotius (1582-1645), later to become famous as both a religious scholar and as the founder of international law. The "first and the perfect terminus of number" is 9, which completes the first Pythagorean decad. It is called "perfect" because it is the square of three and is represented by the letter *theta* (Θ). Next comes the number worshipped "as Lord in all temples for its cubic solidity." We saw earlier that Iamblichus and Theodorus refer to eight as "the first cube" (2 x 2 x 2), as does Plutarch, when noting its attribution by the Pythagoreans to the god Poseidon.[4] The number suggested is 800, being 8 (the first cube) multiplied by 100 (the square of 10), and the value of the letter *omega* (Ω = 800). The "Samian sage" is none other than Pythagoras himself, who came from the island of Samos. According to Pythagoras, the letter that represented the "dual ambiguity of mortal fate" was the crossroads letter, *upsilon* (Υ).

This then gives us the letters for the name Thouth, or Thoth (ΘΩΥΘ), the Egyptian name for Hermes Trismegistus, or Mercury. The name adds to 1218. Similarly, the Greek letter values for Philology (ΦΙΛΟΛΟΓΙΑ) add to 724. By application of the rule of nine, 1218 and 724 reduce to three (1 + 2 + 1 + 8 = 12 = 1 +2 = 3) and four (7 + 2 + 4 = 13 = 1 +3 = 4) respectively. These, when added together, form seven. These numbers are then explained by Martianus in terms of their qualities, according to the extensive traditional correspondences found in Greek arithmology for each of the numerals of the Pythagorean decad. It will be recalled that Martianus' use of this technique is similar to the older account of traditional Pythagorean numerology given by Hippolytus and quoted earlier.

The examples of Theodorus and Martianus show exactly how the techniques of the Greek Qabalah were applied in practice in the ancient world. Although it would, therefore, have been a simple matter to use Greek Qabalah according to the methods of the ancients, regrettably these original sources do not appear to have been known or referred to by the authors of most modern New Age books on Pythagorean numerology, ennead mysticism, Qabalah, and the like. For those who are interested in these areas, the numerical values of Greek letters have been summarized in the tables at the end of this book, together with all those instances of the use of letter symbolism actually authenticated in ancient history and referred to earlier in the text. The best early source for the arithmological correspondences for the decad is undoubtedly *The Theology of Arithmetic,* attributed to Iamblichus.[5] So-called "Pythagorean" numerology, or the rule of nine technique used by the Gnostics and others, that is the foundation of the simplified numerology still in use today, has also been described in the passage by Hippolytus quoted above with sufficient clarity to need no further explanation.

To sum up, we know that the Greek Qabalah incorporated at least the following techniques:

Number of letters: The simplest way of reducing a word to numeral analysis, involving counting the number of letters in a word. This approach appears often in the Greek magical papyri, where magical names or words are expressly noted as having seven letters, the same number as the planets, or some other important number, such as one hundred, being the square of the decad. The position occupied by any given letter in a word, and its relationship to those around it, was a further possible cause for comment.

Individual letter symbolism: The interpretation of a word according to the symbolism or correspondences ascribed to individual letters by tradition; often based on the shape or numerical value of the letter.

Isopsephy or **gematria**: The addition of the letters in a word or phrase to achieve a numerical value. This number was either of importance in itself, or used to connect it with another word or phrase of equal value.

Arithmology: The interpretation of numbers in the primary decad, to which words or letters were reduced by various methods, according to traditional philosophical associations and attributions given to each of those numbers or letters by Pythagoras, and extended by his followers in later centuries.

Pythmenes or **aiq beker**: The reduction of the numerical value of each letter to its primary root in the numbers 1 to 9. Each of these numerals or letters might then be subjected to some other technique, such as interpretation in terms of their traditional Pythagorean attributions. Theodorus shows that this method also served to connect letters of the same root value, for example those with the value of 700, 70 and 7, thus tripling the possibilities for symbolism and exegesis.

Pythagorean numerology or ***the rule of nine*:** An extension of *pythmenes*, by means of which the root values of letters in a word were further mathematically reduced by addition in order to obtain a single value from 1 to 9 for the whole name or word. Alternatively, the whole value of a word could be divided by nine, and the remainder used for interpretive purposes. In the earliest account of the technique by Hippolytus, any repetition of a letter or long vowel sound was discounted.

***Grammatical groupings*:** The preliminary division of the letters in a name or word into established groupings, before applying the rule of nine or other techniques of Qabalistic analysis. These groups were usually grammatically based, such as aspirates, vowels, semi-vowels, and mutes, although the three "double letters" were also identified as a separate group. The number of vowels in a word was particularly noteworthy, since these were perceived as the most powerful letters due to their connection with the seven planets. Aspirated pronunciation was also a notable quality, reflecting breath, life, and spirit.

***Left-hand numbers*:** A belief that words with a value in isopsephy of less than 100 carried a negative connotation.

***Odd and even numbers*:** A similar practice invoked after applying the rule of nine, based on the view that odd numbers were masculine, ascending, and positive, and even numbers were feminine, descending, and negative. This was apparently in use among the Egyptians in particular, and derived from the Pythagoreans' columns of cognates and the qualities ascribed to the monad and duad.

Notarichon: A Greek word denoting abbreviation or acrostic, in which a letter's symbolism was derived from the fact that it was the initial of a particular word. By extension, a whole phrase was reduced to a word formed by its initials, or a word used in abbreviation for a phrase. Sometimes an abbreviation was formed from both the first and last letters in a word.

Notes to Chapter Thirteen

[1] G. Horner (trans.), *Pistis Sophia* (London: Macmillan Co., 1924), p. 180.

[2] W. H. Stahl and others (trans.), *The Quadrivium of Martianus Capella,* 729, in *Martianus Capella and the Seven Liberal Arts*, Vol. I (New York: Columbia University Press, 1977), p. 150.

[3] W. H. Stahl and others (trans.), *The Marriage of Philology and Mercury*, Book II; 101, in *Martianus Capella and the Seven Liberal Arts*, Vol. II, pp. 35–37.

[4] Plutarch, *On Isis and Osiris*, X; 354f.

[5] Recently republished in translation: R. Waterfield (trans.), *The Theology of Arithmetic* (Grand Rapids, MI: Phanes Press, 1988).

c h a p t e r   f o u r t e e n

CONCLUSION

he symbolism of letters is inherent in the history of the alphabet itself and in its origins in the pictographic scripts used by the Egyptians, Mesopotamians, Mycenaeans, and Minoans. The use of alphabetic letters as symbols for philosophical and cosmological concepts was first pioneered by Pythagoras and Plato, and later extended by the Greeks throughout their history, particularly in the Classical and Hellenistic Ages. This practice eventually came to include a whole range of ideas and objects, such as musical notes, parts of the human body, angels, elements, planets, stars, and signs of the zodiac.

Collateral to this was the development of alphabetic numerals. These were conceived by the Greeks, although they may have been influenced by a similar numerology of language apparently in use earlier among the Assyrians. One of these numerical systems, the Alexandrian or Milesian, was spread throughout the lands of the ancient world, along with all other aspects of Greek culture, by the conquests of Alexander the Great in the third century B.C.E. The system of alphabetic numerals, together with its natural partner, the contemporaneous popular numerology of the Pythagoreans, eventually developed into a comprehensive philosophy and system of linguistic analysis. The ancient and ever-evolving symbolism of Greek letters combined with the sciences of isopsephy and arithmology to form a system that we may loosely call—for want of a better term—the Greek Qabalah, evidenced, as we have now seen, in numerous examples from the ancient world.

The use of alphabetic numerals and Greek Qabalah was introduced to other peoples of the Mediterranean during the Hellenistic Age, an age culturally syncretic by nature. During this period, there was also further speculation on the symbolism of Greek letters arising from advances in diverse fields such as alchemy, grammar, and geometry. Combinations of the letters of the Greek alphabet were seen as capable of controlling the gods themselves. These appear in innumerable magical papyri, chants, charms, and amulets. By the first and second centuries of the Current Era, the alphabet had become clearly identified with the powers of heaven, and its letters were seen by various religious groups as elders, angels, and aeons. The Gnostics developed Greek Qabalah extensively, as can be seen in the surviving teachings of figures such as Marcus, Monoimus, and Marsanes. Gnostic influence in particular led to the use of Greek Qabalah in the early Christian Church, where it is found in the writings of the earliest Church Fathers, including Justin, Tertullian, Hippolytus, Irenaeus, Lactantius, Jerome, and Augustine. Examples of Greek Qabalistic symbolism still survive in the Christian Church. In the third and fourth centuries C.E., Neoplatonists such as Amelius and

Theodorus also adopted and developed Greek Qabalistic principles to underpin and explain their theories.

In the same period, Near Eastern Christian and Gnostic doctrines, in conjunction with the wholesale impact of Hellenistic culture and philosophy on Jewish mysticism, influenced Jewish texts that were fundamental to the later evolution of the Hebrew Qabalah. A pivotal point in this development was the translation of the sacred books of Judaism into Greek in the *Septuagint*. This, in turn, led to the application of Greek Qabalistic techniques to Hebrew literature. At the same time, the adoption of the Alexandrian numerical system by the Jews, and its concurrent adaptation to the Hebrew alphabet, created the possibility for indigenous isopsephy to be applied to texts in Hebrew. The hiatus of Qabalah in Judaism during the Middle Ages, together with a contemporaneous resurgence of interest in Neoplatonism, in turn had a major and lasting effect on Christian gnosis and the Western magical tradition.

Thus it is to the ancient Greeks that we are indebted for the doctrine we today know only by its Hebrew name, the *Qabalah*. As the original basis for the technique of literary analysis by alphabetic symbolism and numerology, Greek Qabalah represents a body of knowledge and a field of study that can well and truly stand on its own, just as it did for the ancients who used it. It is therefore to be hoped that the current work will help future authors avoid the unnecessary and regrettable error of confusing the ancient Greek and later Hebrew Qabalah. It is equally hoped that the preliminary research presented here, together with the accompanying citation of original sources and historical dates where possible, will provide those interested with a corpus of helpful reference material and a more reliable academic base for further work in the area than has previously been available.

— KIEREN BARRY

a p p e n d i x   I

TABLES OF
CORRESPONDENCES

Table 1. Origins of Greek Alphabet
in Phoenician Alphabet and Egyptian Hieroglyphics

Greek Letter		Greek Letter Name	Original Phoenician Letter	Original Egyptian Hieroglyphic
A	α	alpha	aleph	ox
B	β	beta	beth	house
Γ	γ	gamma	gimel	
Δ	δ	delta	daleth	door
E	ε	epsilon	heh	
F	ϛ	digamma; episemon	waw	prop
Z	ζ	zeta	zayin	
H	η	eta	cheth	courtyard, fence
Θ	θ	theta	teth	
I	ι	iota	yod	
K	κ	kappa	kaph	
Λ	λ	lambda	lamedh	
M	μ	mu	mem	water

*Table 1. Origins of Greek Alphabet
in Phoenician Alphabet and Egyptian Hieroglyphics (cont.)*

Greek Letter		Greek Letter Name	Original Phoenician Letter	Original Egyptian Hieroglyphic
N	ν	nu	nun	snake
Ξ	ξ	xi	samekh	
O	o	omicron	ayin	eye
Π	π	pi	peh	
Q	Q	qoppa	qoph	
P	ρ	rho	resh	head
Σ	σ ς	sigma	shin	
T	τ	tau	tau	cross
Y	υ	upsilon	waw	prop
Φ	φ	phi		
X	χ	chi		
Ψ	ψ	psi		
Ω	ω	omega	ayin	eye

Table 2. Numerical Values Ascribed to Greek Alphabet

Greek Letter		English Equivalent	Alexandrian or Milesian Value	Herodianic or Acrophonic Value	Ordinal Value
A	α	A	1		1
B	β	B	2		2
Γ	γ	G	3		3
Δ	δ	D	4	10	4
E	ε	EE	5		5
F	ς	W	6		-
Z	ζ	Z	7		6
H	η	H	8	100	7
Θ	θ	TH	9		8
I	ι	I	10	1	9
K	κ	K	20		10
Λ	λ	L	30		11
M	μ	M	40	10,000	12
N	ν	N	50		13

Table 2. Numerical Values Ascribed to Greek Alphabet (cont.)

Greek Letter		English Equivalent	Alexandrian or Milesian Value	Herodianic or Acrophonic Value	Ordinal Value
Ξ	ξ	X	60		14
O	ο	O	70		15
Π	π	P	80	5	16
Q	Q	Q	90		-
P	ρ	R	100		17
Σ	σ ς	S	200		18
T	τ	T	300		19
Y	υ	U	400		20
Φ	φ	F	500		21
X	χ	KH	600	1,000	22
Ψ	ψ	PS	700		23
Ω	ω	OO	800		24

Table 3. Angels and Magical Names Ascribed to Greek Alphabet

Greek Letter		24 Elders or Angels	Magical Name of Letter	
A	α	Achael	ΑΚΡΑΜΜΑΧΑΜΑΡΙ	Akrammachamari
B	β	Banuel	ΒΟΥΛΟΜΕΝΤΟΡΕΒ	Boulomentoreb
Γ	γ	Ganuel	ΓΕΝΙΟΜΟΥΘΙΓ	Geniomouthig
Δ	δ	Dedael	ΔΗΜΟΓΕΝΗΔ	Demogened
E	ε	Eptiel	ΕΝΚΥΚΛΙΕ	Enkyklie
Z	ζ	Zartiel	ΖΗΝΟΒΙΩΘΙΖ	Zenobiothiz
H	η	Ethael	ΗΣΚΩΘΩΡΗ	Eskothore
Θ	θ	Thathiel	ΘΩΘΟΥΘΩΩ	Thothouthoth
I	ι	Iochael	ΙΑΕΟΥΩΙ	Iaeouoi
K	κ	Kardiel	ΚΟΡΚΟΟΥΝΟΩΚ	Korkoounook
Λ	λ	Labtiel	ΛΟΥΛΟΕΝΗΛ	Louloenel
M	μ	Merael	ΜΟΡΟΘΟΗΠΝΑΜ	Morothoepnam

Table 3. Angels and Magical Names Ascribed to Greek Alphabet (cont.)

Greek Letter		24 Elders or Angels	Magical Name of Letter	
N	ν	Nerael	ΝΕΡΞΙΑΡΞΙΝ	Nerxiarxin
Ξ	ξ	Xiphiel	ΞΟΝΟΦΟΗΝΖΞ	Xonophoenax
O	ο	Oupiel	ΟΡΝΕΟΦΑΟ	Orneophao
Π	π	Pirael	ΠΥΡΟΒΑΡΥΠ	Pyrobaryp
P	ρ	Rael	ΡΕΡΟΥΤΟΗΡ	Reroutoer
Σ	σς	Seroael	ΣΕΣΕΝΜΕΝΟΥΡΕΣ	Sesenmenoures
T	τ	Tauriel	ΤΑΥΡΟΠΛΙΤ	Tauropolit
Y	υ	Umnael	ΥΠΕΦΕΝΟΥΡΥ	Ypephenoury
Φ	φ	Philopael	ΦΙΜΕΜΑΜΕΦ	Phimemameph
X	χ	Christuel	ΧΕΝΝΕΟΦΕΟΧ	Chenneopheoch
Ψ	ψ	Psilaphael	ΨΥΧΟΜΠΟΙΑΨ	Psychompoiaps
Ω	ω	Olithiel	ΩΡΙΩΝ	Orion

Table 4. Symbolism and Notarichon Ascribed to Greek Alphabet

Greek Letter		Meaning by Notarichon	Other Symbolism
A	α	man, air, source, east, north, cherubim	beginning, source, God, Apollo, Zeus, Jesus
B	β	king, help	duality, second, Artemis, Isis, Rhea
Γ	γ	Gaia, earth, born	Moon, Hecate, the Fates
Δ	δ	decad, west, God	tetraktys, pudenda, Hermes, the four elements
E	ε	build	Apollo, Sun, justice, ether, quintessence
Z	ζ	Zoe, life	Athena, the seven planets
H	η	Hera	Poseidon, the first cube
Θ	θ	God, death, Thoth, rushing one (Mars)	the nine Egyptian gods, the universe
I	ι	Jesus, jot	line, decad, perfection, primal man, Rod of Moses, Ten Commandments
K	κ	Lord, Caesar	
Λ	λ	lion	ratio, progression

Table 4. Symbolism and Notarichon Ascribed to Greek Alphabet (cont.)

Greek Letter		Meaning by Notarichon	Other Symbolism
M	μ	Mary, south, myriad	middle
N	ν		
Ξ	ξ	Zeus (on Thera)	
O	ο		circle, heaven
Π	π	Father, fire, flaming one (Mars)	
P	ρ		old age
Σ	σ ς	Savior	
T	τ		cross
Y	υ	Son	moral choice
Φ	φ	voice, sound	
X	χ	Chronos, Christ	world soul
Ψ	ψ	Psyche, soul	Holy Spirit
Ω	ω	Oceanus, Orion	end, Saturn

Table 5. Parts of the Human Body, Zodiacal Signs, and Grammatical Groups Ascribed to Greek Alphabet

Greek Letter		Part of the Body	Grammatical Group	Sign of Zodiac
A	α	head	Intermediate Vowel	♈
B	β	neck	Intermediate Mute	♉
Γ	γ	shoulders and hands	Intermediate Mute	♊
Δ	δ	breast	Intermediate Mute	♋
E	ε	diaphragm	Short Vowel	♌
Z	ζ	back	Double Semi-Vowel	♍
H	η	belly	Long Vowel	♎
Θ	θ	thighs	Aspirate Mute	♏
I	ι	knees	Intermediate Vowel	♐
K	κ	legs	Inaspirate Mute	♑
Λ	λ	ankles	Single Semi-Vowel	♒
M	μ	feet	Single Semi-Vowel	♓
N	ν	feet	Single Semi-Vowel	♈
Ξ	ξ	ankles	Double Semi-Vowel	♉

Table 5. Parts of the Human Body, Zodiacal Signs,
and Grammatical Groups Ascribed to Greek Alphabet (cont.)

Greek Letter		Part of the Body	Grammatical Group	Sign of Zodiac
O	o	legs	Short Vowel	♉
Π	π	knees	Inaspirate Mute	♋
P	ρ	thighs	Single Semi-Vowel	♌
Σ	σ ς	belly	Single Semi-Vowel	♍
T	τ	back	Inaspirate Mute	♎
Y	υ	diaphragm	Intermediate Vowel	♏
Φ	φ	breast	Aspirate Mute	♐
X	χ	shoulders and hands	Aspirate Mute	♑
Ψ	ψ	neck	Double Semi-Vowel	♒
Ω	ω	head	Long Vowel	♓

*Table 6. Alphabetic and
Other Correspondences Ascribed to Seven Planets*

Greek Letter	Gnostic Heaven	Word of Power	Planet	Archangel	Attribute	Direction
A	First	EIA	Moon	Michael	Peace	East
E	Second	EIIAK	Mercury	Gabriel	Grace	North
H	Third	MIIAK	Venus	Raphael	Power	West
I	Fourth	SEMIIAK	Sun	Suriel	Will	South
O	Fifth	ARTORE	Mars	Raguel	Truth	Down
Y	Sixth	ARTORAN	Jupiter	Anael	Glory	Up
Ω	Seventh	NARTORAK	Saturn	Saraphuel	Healing	Center

*Table 7. Alphabetic and
Other Correspondences Ascribed to Five Elements*

Greek Letter	Element	Qualities	Greek God	Platonic Solid
Γ	Earth	Cold and Dry	Hades	Cube
Δ	Water	Cold and Wet	Chronos	Icosahedron
Θ	Ether	All	[Zeus]	Dodecahedron
Π	Fire	Hot and Dry	Ares	Tetrahedron
P	Air	Hot and Wet	Dionysus	Octahedron

DICTIONARY OF ISOPSEPHY

Note on the Format of Entries

THE ATTACHED DICTIONARY IS A LIST OF examples of isopsephy, arranged in numerical rather than alphabetical order. Some numbers have no words of equal value yet located, in which case the entry is left blank. As described in chapter 2, isopsephy is the practice whereby the Alexandrian numerical values of each Greek letter are added up so as to turn a phrase, name, or word into a single number. Other phrases, names, or words totaling the same value were then seen as connected in some way. For example, Irenaeus equated the Dove (Greek *peristera*) with the Alpha and Omega, since both add up to 801. In cases such as this, a purely coincidental equality of values is used for the purposes of allegory or exegesis. This is the principle use of simple isopsephy. However, in a few rare instances, a name or word is deliberately chosen to equal a particular numerical value (or vice versa). For example, this is probably the case with the solar Gnostic deity Abraxas, whose name totals 365, the number of days in the year.

The greatest risk in using isopsephy is confusing examples of the former with the latter.

For those unfamiliar with Greek, the following points should be noted when working with isopsephy:

1. In Greek, the sound N (*nu*) was written as G (*gamma*) when it appeared before either a G (*gamma*) or an X (*xi*). While this did not alter the pronunciation of the relevant sounds as NG or NX, it does alter the isopsephy. An example is the Greek word *sphinx*, which is written as *sphigx* (σφιγξ), with a value of 773.

2. The letter *beta* is sometimes used for the sound V, as in the Greek transliteration of Jehovah (ιεχωβα).

3. The Greeks did not use a separate letter for the aspirated H sound in English. Hence Hermes is written as *Ermes* (Ηρμες), and Hector as *Ektor* (Εκτωρ), and the word for holy (*hagios*), as *agios* (Αγιος).

4. As in Latin, the number, gender, or case (nominative, accusative, genitive, and so on) of a noun or adjective results in a change in the word-ending. For example, the Greek word for "bright" is spelled *phoebus* (φοιβος) if describing a single male person or male-gendered noun (hence Phoebus Apollo, a Homeric epithet of the Sun god), but becomes *phoebe* (φοιβη) for the feminine singular, *phoebon* (φοιβον) for the neuter singular, *phoeboi* (φοιβοι) for the male plural, and so on. These endings also vary according to which of several different declensions, or types, a noun or adjective might belong, and according to its case.

5. Accents, which were introduced by Aristophanes of Byzantium in the third century B.C.E. to assist in pronunciation, are here omitted, since they were not used by the ancient Greeks in isopsephy, and are an unneccesary burden in the present context.

6. The Greek letter *digamma*, so called because its shape resembled two letters *gamma* (Γ) placed on top of one another (F), fell into disuse and was retained as a numerical sign only, used for the number six. It became gradually simplified in form until it was no more than a large comma, the *episemon* or as it was later known, *stigma* (ς). This is almost identical in appearance, not only to the miniscule form of the letter *sigma* (σ, ς) used when it appears at the end of a word, but also to a semi-compound letter known as *stau*, that was used in later Byantine Greek to represent the sound of S and T together. Depending on the symbol with which the "ST" sound was written, it was possible to count it as either *sigma* plus *tau* (500), or as *stau* (= *stigma* = 6), giving a different isopsephy. A particularly important example is found in the Greek word for "cross," *stauros* (σταυρος), which totals 777 if the first two letters are taken as *stau/stigma*, but 1271 if these letters are counted in full. Where the former process has been used here, the word has been marked with an asterisk; hence σταυρος* = 777 and σταυρος = 1271.

1		16	Up, on (εια)
2		17	And (ηδε)
3		18	Youth, manhood; Hebe (ηβη)
4		18	Arrows (ιη)
5	Him/her/itself; mostly (ε)	19	Behold! Lo! (ιδε)
5	Had, Hadit (Egyptian deity) (Αδ)	19	Food; prey (ηια)
		19	One must (δει)
6	Father (Galatians 4:6) (αββα)	20	Form; idea; way; nature (ιδεα)
6	If (εα)	20	Now; therefore (ηδη)
7		20	Force, strength (βιη)
8	Truly; where, how; if; I was; the (defnite article) (η)	21	Liberty; fearlessness (αδεια)
		21	The force (η βια)
8	At least; indeed (γε)	22	Long (δηθα)
9	Today (James 4:3) (αγε)	22	Woody mountain; wood (ιδη)
9	But; thus (δε)		
9	Earth; Gaea, Earth goddess (Γεα)	22	Hearth; house; altar; Hestia; Vesta (εστια*)
10		23	The earth (η γαια)
11	Earth; Gaea, Earth goddess (Γη)	24	Hadit (Αδιθ)
		25	Asunder, through (διαι)
11	One, the same; voice; arrows; violets (ια)	25	Out of; because of (εκ)
		25	Divine (θεια)
11	If (αι)	25	Privately (ιδια)
11	Youth; manhood (ηβα)	26	Forever; immortal (αιει)
12	Earth, land (αια)	27	
12	Now; manifestly (δη)	28	How, why; anyhow (κη)
12	Astonishment; envy (αγη)	29	Softly, gently (ηκα)
12	Treasury (γαζα)	30	Ten (δεκα)
13	Strength, force (βια)	31	And; especially (και)
13	His, hers (εη)	32	Salt (αλα)
13	If (ηε)	33	
14		34	Baal (Βααλ)
15	Goddess; a view (θεα)	34	Live! The numerals 7-10 (ζηθι)
15	Earth; Gaea, Earth goddess (Γαια)		
		35	Milk (γαλα)
15	Asunder; through (δια)	36	
15	Thou art; if (ει)	37	Heat; escape (αλεα)
16	Forever, immortal (αει)	37	Olive tree; olive (ελαα)
16	Dirt (αζη)	38	

39	Rush; impact (αικη)	52	Wickedness, vice (κακια)
39	Madness (αλη)	52	Healing (ιαμα)
40	It seemed good (εικε)	52	Mother (μαια)
41	Up; on high (αμ)	52	Pillar, stone; stele (στηλη*)
41	Handle; weak side (λαβη)	52	Wicked women (κακαι)
41	Forgetfulness (λαθα)	52	Beautiful (pl.) (καλα)
41	To the sea (αλαδε)	53	Message (αγγελια)
42	Law (Acts 25:15) (δικη)	54	
42	Ill-treatment (αικια)	55	One; with, within (εν)
42	Assembly (αλια)	55	Magic (μαγια)
42	Together, at once (αμα)	55	A forgetting (ληθη)
42	Troubles, evils (κακα)	55	Much (αγαν)
43	Leda (Ληδα)	55	Books (βιβλια)
43	Loss, damage (βλαβη)	56	Dana, the Celtic mother-goddess (Δανα)
43	In vain (εικη)		
44	Piercing (λιγα)	56	Bite, sting (δηγμα)
45	Tomb; chest; sheath (θηκη)	56	If (εαν)
46	Splendor; pride (αγλαια)	56	Sight, spectacle (θεαμα)
46	Adam (Αδαμ)	56	Booty, plunder (ληιη)
46	Injustice (αδικια)	56	Garment, robe (ειμα)
46	Surge; storm (ζαλη)	56	To wonder, praise (αγαμαι)
46	Delights (θαλεα)	57	Evening (δειλη)
46	Booty, plunder (λεια)	58	He, she, it was; if (ην)
47	Olive tree; olive (ελαια)	58	Plentifully (ηλιθα)
47	Herd, flock (αγελη)	58	Promiscuously (μιγδα)
48	Not (μη)	58	Yes; truly (νη)
48	Troop, band (ιλη)	58	I say (ημι)
49	A throw (ημα)	59	To breathe (αημι)
49	Somehow (αμη)	59	Force; defensive power (αλκη)
49	Great (μεγα)		
50	A wind (αημα)	59	To be at leisure; to lie in wait (ημαι)
51	Happiness; a feast (θαλια)		
51	If (αν)	60	Fear, terror (δειμα)
51	One, the same (μια)	60	Magic (μαγεια)
51	Step; throne (βημα)	60	Step (ιθμα)
52	Blood; life (αιμα)	60	Mark, brand; point; letter name of *stigma* (στιγμα*)
52	Arise! Upwards; above; on high (ανα)		
		61	There; that (ινα)
52	Brightness, luster; daylight; torch (αιγλη)	61	Yes; truly (ναι)
		62	Pain, grief (ανια)

62	Long (δην)
62	Drunkenness (μεθη)
62	But (αλλα)
62	Ignorance (αμαθια)
62	Athene (Doric) (Αθανα)
63	Female (θηλεια)
63	Abundantly (αδην)
63	War-cry (αλαλα)
63	Proof (δειγμα)
64	Truth (αληθεια)
64	Birth; generation (γενεα)
65	I am; to be, come to pass, exist (ειμι)
65	Six; out of, from (εξ)
65	Slowly (βαδην)
65	Scream; sound (κλαγγη)
65	With, within; through (ειν, ενι)
65	There; where; when (ενθα)
65	Name of Zeus (Ζην)
66	Damage, loss (ζημια)
66	Chatterer (βαβαξ)
67	Abundantly (αδδην)
67	Storm (αελλα)
67	Certainly (θην)
68	To send off; to utter; to desire (ιημι)
68	Medea (Μηδεια)
69	Athena (Αθηνα)
69	Praise, reknown (αινη)
69	Point; highest point; perfection (ακμη)
69	Otherwise (αλλη)
70	Letter name of *xi* (ξι)
70	Any one, a certain one (δεινα)
70	The (the definite article) (ο)
70	Purity (αγνεια)
70	Athene (Homeric) (Αθηναα)

71	Goat (αιξ)
72	The truth (η αληθεια)
72	Leap, bound (αλμα)
72	A talking (λαλια)
72	Much; wholly (μαλα)
73	Change (αλλαγη)
74	To learn; to know (δαηναι)
75	In nature; in idea (εν ιδεα)
76	Athene (Αθηνη)
76	Goddess (θεαινα)
76	Ornament, statue (αγαλμα)
77	
78	Letter name of *lambda* (λαμβδα)
78	Spear, javelin (αιγανεη)
79	Prime of life; manhood; age; time (ηλικια)
79	Will; courage (λημα)
79	Athens (Αθηναι)
79	Silently (ακην)
79	Seawater (αλμη)
80	War-cry; voice; prayer; battle; ox-hide; shield (βοη)
80	Athena; Athens (Αθηναια)
80	Io, priestess of Hera; the rapture-cry of the Greeks (Ιο)
81	Shot, wound (βλημα)
81	As (οια)
81	IAO, Gnostic name of God (IAO)
82	Thorn; spine (ακανθα)
82	Knot (αμμα)
82	Shamelessness (αναιδεια)
83	Necessity; fate (αναγκη)
83	Sorrow (αλγημα)
84	Wrong, injury (αδικημα)
85	Letter name of *gamma* (γαμμα)
85	Eleven (ενδεκα)
85	Life (ζοη)

85	To know (οιδα)	99	Letter name of *digamma*
86	Sixteen (εκ–και–δεκα)		(διγαμμα)
86	Kindness (ενηειη)	99	Listening; report; sermon
86	And one (και εν)		(ακοη)
87		99	Amen; truly, in truth
88	Victory, conquest; the god-		(Hebrew) (AMHN)
	dess Nike (Νικη)	99	Knowledge; teaching of the
88	How? Where? Why?		Mysteries (μαθημα)
	Somehow; anywhere; anyway	99	Thread (νημα)
	(πη)	100	Feast of the dedication of the
89	Bridal chamber; palace		temple (εγκαινια)
	(θαλαμη)	100	Stalk of corn (καλαμη)
90	Letter name of *pi* (πι)	100	Him, her, it (μιν)
91	Destruction, ruin (δηλημα)	100	Lust (λαγνεια)
91	With the heel (λαξ)	101	Ra, the Egyptian Sun god
91	Very much (λιαν)		(Ρα)
92	Snare, trap (παγη)	101	The love (η αγαπη)
92	Carelessness (αμελεια)	102	Prayer; curse; destruction
92	Doubt (δοιη)		(αρα)
92	Wreath (στεμμα*)	102	Madness, frenzy (μανια)
93	Love (αγαπη)	103	Softness, weakness
93	Will (θελημα)		(μαλακια)
93	Words; oracles (επη)	104	For (γαρ)
93	End, top; foot (πεζα)	105	Circle, coil; twisted (ελιξ)
93	Lazy, stupid (βλαξ)	105	Chase, hunting (αγρα)
93	Legend, myth (αοιδη)	106	Spring, prime (εαρ)
93	By necessity (αναγκηι)	106	Child's play (παιδια)
94	Mixture (μιγμα)	106	To seem; to believe (εοικα)
94	Nowhere; never (μηδαμα)	106	Moon (μηνη)
94	Necessity; fate (αναγκαιη)	106	The goddess Rea (Ρεα)
95	On; at; by reason of; during;	107	Nothing; no one (μηδεν)
	near; over; at hand (επι)	107	To satiate (αμεναι)
95	Indeed; certainly (μεν)	107	Execration (αναθεμα)
96	Morning; east (ηοιη)	108	Nothing; no one (μηδεμια)
96	The victory (η νικη)	108	Whole; perfect (ολη)
97	Fetter (πεδη)	109	Air; mist, cloud (αηρ)
97	Lioness (λεαινα)	109	Hera, Juno (Ηρα)
98	Month, new moon (μην)	110	Him, her, it (νιν)
98	To be propitious (ιλημι)	110	Of stone (λιθαξ)
98	Said (ελεγεν)	110	Consecrated gift (αναθημα)

110 Promiscuously (αναμιγδα)

111 Nine (εννεα)

111 Knowledge, discipline (παιδεια)

111 House, temple (οικια)

112 King, prince, lord, master (αναξ)

112 Contest, desire (αμιλλα)

113

114

115 Riddle (αινιγμα)

115 Master, rabbi (ραββι)

115 Star (αστηρ*)

115 Disregard (αλογια)

115 To flow (ρει)

116

117 Beast (θηρ)

117 Mouth; tongue; point (στομα*)

118 Origin; root (ριζα)

118 Dogma (δογμα)

119 Struggle (Ephesians 4:12) (παλη)

119 Even now (ακμην)

119 To another place (αλλην)

120 Being (ον)

120 Libation (λοιβη)

120 Master, rabbi (ραββει)

120 To be within (ενειμι)

121 Attack, rage (οιμα)

121 Head; goddess of death or fate (Καρ)

121 Disobedience (απειθεια)

121 Bad men (κακοι)

121 Unnatural lust (κιναιδεια)

122 Head, summit (καρα)

122 End, point, height (ακρα)

123

124

125 Waves (οιδμα)

125 His, hers (εον)

126 Heart (κεαρ)

126 To wonder; to praise (αγαο–μαι)

126 Black (μελαν)

127 Egeria (Ηγερια)

127 Salve (αλειμμα)

128 Heart; goddess of death or fate (Κηρ)

128 Ether, spirit (αιθηρ)

129 A suffering (πημα)

129 Axe (Matthew 3:10) (αξινη)

129 Motion (κινημα)

129 Hesitation (στραγγεια*)

130 Knowledge; skill (ιδρεια)

130 A violet (ιον)

131 Pan; all (Παν)

131 Priestess (ιερεια)

131 Change, exchange (αμοιβη)

131 Birth, origin; seed (γονη)

131 Dove (πελεια)

132 Folly (Luke 6:11) (ανοια)

132 All, whole (απαν)

133

134 Holy, sacred (αγιον)

135 Splendor, glory; principle; honor (δοξα)

135 Ignorance (Acts 3:17) (αγνοια)

135 Unanimously (αμοθει)

136 Choice (εκλογη)

136 To wonder; to praise (αγαιομαι)

136 Heart (καρδια)

137 Arcadia (Αρκαδια)

137 To be leader (ηγεομαι)

137 Black (μελαινα)

137 The hesitation (η στραγγεια*)

138 Lake; sea (λιμνη)

138 Promise (επαγγελια)
138 To be offered (ανακειμαι)
139 The dove (η πελεια)
140 Lust; delight, joy (ηδονη)
141 Belly, womb (κοιλια)
142 Vessel, receptacle (Matthew 13:48) (αγγειον)
142 Manna (μαννα)
142 Savior; paean (παιαν)
142 Once (απαξ)
142 Day; time; fate (αμαρ)
143 The glory (η δοξα)
143 Youthful spirit (νεοιη)
143 Heart (καρδιη)
144 The choice (Romans 11:7) (η εκλογη)
144 Abram, Father of Israel (Αβραμ)
144 The heart (η καρδια)
146 Wife, spouse (δαμαρ)
146 Drama, play (δραμα)
146 Thought, intellect (διανοια)
146 Ill-repute (αδοξια)
146 To go away (αμειμι)
146 Foundation; cause; prop, defense (ερμα)
147 To heal (ακεομαι)
147 Day; time; fate (αμερα)
148
149 House; temple (οικημα)
149 Word, saying (ρημα)
149 Accuracy; perfection (ακριβεια)
149 Day; time; fate (ημαρ)
150 Elsewhere; else (αλλοθι)
150 Trench, ditch (αμαρη)
150 Said (ειπεν)
151 Dust, ashes (κονια)
151 Eye; image (ομμα)
151 From (απο)

152 Mary (Μαρια)
152 Downfall (ρηγμα)
152 Protection (αλκαρ)
153 To wander, doubt (αλαομαι)
154 Day; time; fate (ημερα)
154 Gabriel (Γαβριηλ)
155 Spring, fountain (πιδαξ)
155 Seeker (μαστηρ*)
156 lambda + lambda (λαμβδα + λαμβδα)
157 To avoid (αλεομαι)
157 Knowledge; science; art (επιστημη*)
158 Circe (Κιρκη)
159 Man, warrior (ανηρ)
159 Lamb (Luke 10:3) (αρην)
160 Hand; power, force (παλαμη)
160 Prize (αθλον)
160 Combat; desire (αμιλλημα)
161 Intercourse (ομιλια)
161 To get healed (αλθομαι)
161 Furrow (αλοξ)
161 Climax; staircase (κλιμαξ)
162 Happy, blessed (μακαρ)
162 Promiscuously (αναμιξ)
162 Mound; cloak (αναβολη)
163 Chamber; vault (καμαρα)
163 Love-charm (στεργημα*)
164 Solitude, desert (ερημια)
164 Calm (νηνεμια)
165 Wrong, injury (αδικιον)
165 From the sea (αλοθεν)
166
167
168 Promise (2 Peter 3:13) (επαγγελμα)
168 The force; the hand (η παλαμη)

207 Prison (ανακειον)
207 Height, swelling (εξαρμα)
208
209 Beauty, excellence (καλλονη)
209 Earth (πεδον)
209 Woe (αση)
209 Work; poem, book (ποιημα)
210 Strength, force (ις)
210 Fertile (πιον)
211 Hail Pan! (ιο Παν)
211 Equilibrium (ισα)
212 Fate, destiny (αισα)
213 Hades, Pluto (Αδης)
213 Unbroken (ααγης)
213 Unfruitfulness (ακαρπια)
214 Silently, secretly (σιγα)
214 Ignorant (αδαης)
214 Twice, double (δις)
215 One; one alone; toward (εις)
215 Name of Zeus (Διας)
215 Earth (γαιας)
216 Intercourse (επιμιξια)
217 Suffering (κακοπαθεια)
218 Vengeance (ποινη)
218 Pederasty (παιδεραστια*)
218 Impulse; onset (ορμη)
218 Fearless (αδεης)
218 Much, many (πολλη)
218 Equilibrium (ιση)
218 Jesus (abbrev.) (ΙΗΣ)
219 Sand, desert (θις)
219 Foundation (θεμελιον)
220 Whole, perfect (ολον)
220 House, temple (οικον)
221 Fate; destiny; death (Μοιρα)
221 Dream, vision (οναρ)
221 Silence, stillness (σιγη)
221 Offering bowl (αμνιον)
222 Ibis (ιβις)

222 Of earth (γαιης)
223 Hades, Pluto (Αιδης)
224 Shield of Jupiter or Minerva; storm (αιγις)
224 Bright, white, swift; not working (αργον)
225 Deed, action (πραγμα)
225 Hammer (ραιστηρ*)
225 Child (παιδιον)
226 The equilibrium (η ιση)
227 Trust (παραθηκη)
227 Star (αστρον*)
228 Work, labor; great work (εργον)
229 The silence (η σιγη)
230 Peak (ριον)
230 Theban (θηβαις)
230 House, temple (οικιον)
231 Salt (αλς)
231 Shadow, darkness; phantom, specter, shade (σκια)
231 Name (ονομα)
232 Threshold; step; foundation (βαθρον)
232 Perseverence (λιπαρια)
232 Stone (λαας)
232 Isaac (Ισαακ)
232 Salt (αλας)
233 To strive (αμιλλαομαι)
233 To deny (αναινομαι)
233 Oracle (λογιον)
234
235 Sacrifice; temple; ritual; mystery (ιερον)
235 The trust (η παραθηκη)
236
237 To choose (Hebrews 11:25) (αιρεομαι)
238 Tomb (ηριον)
238 The Theban (η θηβαις)

239 Endurance; victory (καμ–
μονιη)

240 Of the dead (ενεροι)

240 Lion; smooth; linen (λις)

241

242 Ill-will, enmity (κακονοια)

242 Receptacle; urn, coffin
(λαρναξ)

243 Offering (Mark 7:11) (κορ–
βαν)

244

245

246

247 The Beast (Revelation 13:11)
(θηριον)

247 Image (εικασια)

247 Steel (αδαμας)

248

249 Sandal (πεδιλον)

249 Sign, omen; tomb (σημα)

249 Great, mighty (μεγας)

249 Name of Aphrodite
(βασιλεα)

249 Us (ημας)

249 Breath (αμπνοη)

250 Sacrificial victim (ιερειον)

250 Before; in front; outside (προ)

250 Intoxication; debauch
(κραιπαλη)

250 He, she, it falls (ρεπειν)

251 Purity (ειλικρινεια)

251 Experience, knowledge, skill
(εμπειρια)

251 Thong, strap; girdle of Venus
(ιμας)

251 Raven (κοραξ)

252 Altogether (παμπαν)

253 Inaction (απραξια)

254 Letter name of *sigma*
(σιγμα)

254 Change (James 1:17) (παρ–
αλλαγη)

255 Month (μεις)

255 Licentiousness (ασελγεια)

256 Virginity (παρθενια)

256 House (στεγασμα*)

256 True (αληθης)

257 Pillar (σταμις*)

258 Shepherd (ποιμην)

258 Key (κλης)

259 Man (αρρην)

259 Queen, princess; kingdom
(βασιλεια)

259 Destiny (ειμαρμενη)

259 Passionate desire (ορμημα)

259 Ignorant (αμαθης)

259 They were (ησαν)

260

261 Child of the Sun (Ηλιαδης)

261 Loss (Acts 27:22)
(αποβολη)

262 Doubt (απορια)

263 We (ημεις)

264 Of truth (αληθειας)

264 The virginity (η παρθενια)

264 Justice, law; the goddess
Themis (Θεμις)

265 Key (κλεις)

265 A sending; apostle's office
(αποστολη*)

266 Way, journey (πορεια)

267 Bound by an oath (εναγης)

267 Nothing (μηδεις)

267 The kingdom (η βασιλεια)

268 Glorious (αγακλεης)

268 Key (κληις)

269 Lightning-flash (στεροπη*)

270

271

272 Union; the goddess

273	Harmony (Αρμονια)	286	We (αμμες)
273	Oracle; speech (βαξις)	287	Title of Zeus (βαγαιος)
273	In order (εξης)	288	Semele, mother of Dionysus (Σεμελη)
274	Leader; reverence; abomination (αγος)	288	Path (στιβος*)
275	Andromeda (Ανδρομεδα)	289	Shape, form; beauty; nature (ειδος)
275	Satiety (αδος)	290	Eaten, consumed (εδεστος*)
275	One perfect (εν ολον)	290	Magi, magicians (αοιδες)
275	His, her own (εος)	291	Child, son, daughter (παις)
276	Black (μελας)	291	Healing; remedy (ακος)
276	Temple of Hermes (Ερμαιον)	292	Most holy (ζαθεος)
277	To deny (αρνεομαι)	292	Pollution (2 Peter 2:20) (μιασμα)
278		293	Heart, understanding (στηθος*)
279	Temple, altar; foundation (εδος)	293	Violent, mighty (βιαιος)
279	Fear (δεος)	294	Of the gods; holy, sacred (θειος)
280	Arrow; poison; one (ιος)	294	Young, fresh (νεαλης)
280	Unto thee (σοι)	294	Rose (ροδον)
281	Shit, filth (κοπρια)	294	Church, assembly (εκκλησια)
281	Divine law (οσια)	295	Pitcher, urn (καδος)
281	All, entire (πας)	296	End; snare (πειραρ)
281	Wizard (γοης)	296	Obedience (πεισα)
281	Heart (στερνον*)	296	Six times (εξακις)
281	Lamb (αρνιον)	297	
281	Sickness (ασθενεια)	298	Sword (σπαθη)
282	All, whole, entire (απας, πασα)	299	Holy art thou (*Corpus Hermeticum* I 31) (αγιος ει)
282	Folly; despair (απονοια)	299	The child (η παις)
282	Life; a bow (βιος)	300	Armor, weapon (οπλον)
283	All, whole, entire (απασα)	301	Salt (αλος)
284	Holy, sacred (αγιος)	301	Selene, Moon (Σεληνη)
284	God, deity (θεος)	302	Youth (ηιθεος)
284	Shining, brilliant; noble, divine (διος)	302	Maenad; raving (μαινας)
284	Of earth (γαιος)	302	Blind (αλαος)
285	Godless, infidel (αθεος)	303	
285	A spell (βασκανια)	304	Selene, Moon (Σηληνη)
286	House, temple (σκηνη)		
286	Black (μειλας)		

304 Sorrow, pain (αλγος)

304 Chosen (λογας)

305 Guardian spirit; devil; genius (with Socrates) (δαιμονιον)

305 Speech (λεξις)

306 Trust, faith (πιστις*)

306 Boy, young man (μειρακιον)

307 Dove (περιστερα*)

307 Mockery (εμπαιγμονη)

307 Missile (βελος)

308 Nail (ηλος)

308 Wrath (μηνις)

308 Harlot (πορνη)

308 Selene, moon (Σεληναια)

308 Laughter (γελος)

309 Letter name of eta (ητα)

309 Kingdom (βασιλειαν)

309 Delusion, stupor; evil, woe; guilt (ατη)

309 Ares, Mars (Αρης)

309 The Moon (η Σεληνη)

310 Threshold (βηλος)

310 Mercy, pity (ελεος)

310 Ship, vessel (πλοιον)

310 Why? how? Any one; every one (τι)

310 Nose (ρις)

311 Letter name of beta (βητα)

311 God-like (θεοειδης)

311 Body; life (σομα)

311 Sun; east; Helios; of the sea (Αλιος)

311 Propitious; gentle (ιλαος)

311 Ill, evil, wicked (κακος)

311 Left, left-hand (λαιος)

311 Unity (ομονοια)

311 Mine; ours (αμος)

311 Covetousness (πλεονεξια)

312 Angel, messenger (αγγελος)

312 Manifest, clear (δηλος)

312 Wizards (θελγινες)

313 Dew, dewdrop (ερση)

313 Madness (παρανοια)

313 Secret, unknown (αδηλος)

313 To listen (ακροαομαι)

314 Magus, wizard (μαγος)

314 Book; letter (βιβλος)

315 Twenty (εικοσι)

315 The Egyptian god Hadit (Αδιτ)

315 Right; lawful; just (δικαιος)

315 The goddess Eris; strife, discord (Ερις)

315 The dove (η περιστερα*)

316 Letter name of zeta (ζητα)

316 Fornication (πορνεια)

316 Rope (σειρα)

316 Sun; east; Helios (Αελιος)

317 Profane; unholy (βεβηλος)

318 Letter name of theta (θητα)

318 Helios (Ηλιος)

318 Why? (τιη)

318 Dearest (κηδιστος*)

318 Number of servants of Abraham

319 Stone (λιθος)

319 Wickedness (πονηρια)

320 Rainbow; the goddess Iris (Ιρις)

321 Beautiful, favorable; omen (καλος)

321 Temple (ναος)

321 The raven (ο κοραξ)

322 Downward; against (κατα)

322 Armor (Ephesians 6:11) (πανοπλια)

322 People (δημος)

322 Cause (αιτια)

323 Foresight (προμηθεια)

323 The goddess Eris; the strife, discord (η Ερις)
324 Pure, sacred, holy (αγνος)
325 Hope, expectation (ελπις)
325 Glory, honor (κλεος)
325 Just (δικαιοις)
325 New; youthful (νεος)
325 Of one (ενος)
326 Life; intercourse (διαιτα)
326 Divine things; oracles; worship (τα θεια)
326 Horn, antlers; mountain peak (κερας)
326 Flesh, meat (κρεας)
327
328 Birth; generation (γενος)
329 Newborn (νεηγενης)
329 Goddess of death or fate (Καρης)
330 Flower (ανθος)
330 Equilibrium (ισον)
331 Projection; defense; armor; spear (προβλημα)
331 The Roman god Janus (Ιανος)
331 Another (αλλος)
332 Might, power (μεγεθος)
333 Girl, maiden (παιδισκη)
333 The hope (η ελπις)
333 Excess (1 Corinthians 7:5) (ακρασια)
333 Wantonness, dispersion (ακολασια)
334 Passage (παρακομιδη)
334 Hecate (Εκατη)
334 Tribe, race (εθνος)
335
336 To worship (Romans 1:25) (σεβαζομαι)
337

338
339
340 Delta (δελτα)
340 Horned (κεραστης*)
341 Worthy (Revelation 3:4) (αξιος)
341 Of earth (γηινος)
341 Pestle (κοπανον)
342 Pallas (Athene); brandisher; virgin, maiden-priestess (Παλλας)
342 Demigod (ημιθεος)
343 Poor (πενης)
343 A spell (γοος)
344 Way, path; threshold (οδος)
344 River (ρειθρον)
344 Magical (μαγικος)
345 Empty, void (κενος)
345 Order, rank (1 Corinthians 15:23) (ταγμα)
346
347 Headdress (κρηδεμνον)
348 Prayer, entreaty (λιτη)
348 Eight (ογδοας)
349 Israel (Ισραηλ)
350 Sprung from Zeus (διογενης)
350 The Pallas; name of Athene (η Παλλας)
350 Victory, conquest (νικος)
350 Empty, void (κενεος)
351 New, strange (καινος)
351 Beauty, excellence (καλλος)
351 Sand (αμμος)
351 The wizard (ο γοης)
351 Throat (λαιμος)
351 Maiden (ταλιθα)
351 Thou (ταν)
351 Redeemer (ακακητα)
352 Lamp; light, sun (λαμπας)

352 Folly (ματια)
352 Image (Romans 9:20) (πλασμα)
352 The way (η οδος)
352 The life (ο βιος)
352 Opposite, against (αντα)
353 Hermes, Mercury (Ερμης)
354 Indivisible (αμερης)
354 Lustful (λαγνος)
355 Word; oracle (επος)
355 Guide (οδηγος)
355 Magician; bard (αοιδος)
355 Most holy; abominable (εξαγιστος)
355 Fox (κιναδος)
356 Arrow (οιστος*)
356 Male; strong (αρσεν)
357
358 Estimate; esteem; honor, dignity (τιμη)
359 Helper (Hebrews XIII 6) (βοηθος)
359 Male; strong (αρσην)
359 Perfect and perfect (ολον και ολη)
360 Letter name of *omicron* (ομικρον)
360 Mithras (Μιθρας)
360 Vengeance (οπις)
360 The victory of truth (η νικη αληθειας)
360 Sickle (Revelation 14:14) (δρεπανον)
360 Suffering (παθος)
360 Number of degrees in a circle (360)
361 Flesh, body (Revelation 19:18) (σαρξ)
361 A monad (μονας)

361 Distant (απιος)
361 Lamb (αμνος)
361 The child (ο παις)
362 Tender, gentle (μαλακος)
363 Curve; atom (ογκος)
364 Hermaphrodite (εναρης)
365 Abraxas, Abrasax (Αβραξας, Αβρασαξ)
365 Mithras (Μειθρας)
365 The god Belenos (Βεληνος)
365 Desire; spirit, courage (μενος)
365 Pile of dust, ashes (σποδια)
365 The river Nile (Νειλος)
365 Voluptuary, sodomite (κιναιδος)
365 Middle, center (μεσον)
365 Number of days in the solar year (365)
366 Nymph, nereid (νηρης)
366 Sixfold (εξαπλοον)
367 Visible; bright, manifest (εναργης)
367 Hercules (Ηρακλης)
368 Gentle, kind (ηπιος)
369 Camel (καμηλος)
369 Foundation (θεμελιος)
369 Goods, treasure (κτημα)
369 Earthen vessel (πιθος)
369 Wandering (πλανης)
369 Instructed ones (μαθηται)
369 The monad (η μονας)
370 House; temple (οικος)
370 Whole; temple (ολος)
370 The many (οι πολλοι)
370 The (definite article) (το)
371 Rope (καμιλος)
371 Name of Apollo (Λοξιας)
371 Birth (γενετη)

372 Bliss; power (ολβος)
373 Logos; word (λογος)
373 Siren (Σειρην)
373 Confusion (αταξια)
374 Deceit, treachery (δολος)
374 Bright, white; swift; lazy (αργος)
374 The pain (ο αλγος)
375 Sincere (1 Peter 2:2) (αδολος)
375 Sometimes (οτε)
376
377 Curse; accursed (καταθεμα)
377 Wand (ραβδος)
377 Cassandra (Κασανδρα)
378 North wind; north (Βορεας)
378 Watch-tower (σκοπη)
378 Expectation (Philippians 1:20) (αποκαραδοκια)
378 Another beast (Revelation 13:11) (αλλο θηριον)
379 Shit (μινθος)
380 Dagger; sword; liar (κοπις)
380 In truth (τοι)
380 Because (οτι)
380 Nineveh (Νινος)
380 The daemons, spirits (δαιμονες)
381 To invoke (επικαλεισθαι)
381 Watch-tower (σκοπια)
382 Depth, abyss (λαιτμα)
382 Erebus, the dark nether-world (Ερεβος)
383 Of the earth (επιγειος)
383 Frost, cold (ριγος)
383 Sign, wonder (Revelation 15:1) (σημειον)
384 Countenance, face (ρεθος)

384 The magician (ο μαγος)
384 All-truth (παναληθες)
384 Chosen (λογαιος)
384 Summer (θερος)
385 Stranger (ξενος)
385 Fresh; holy, sacred (ιερος)
385 Fascination (κηληθμος)
386 Seven (επτα)
386 Dark, black (κελαινος)
386 End, goal (περας)
386 Solid (στερεος)
387 The Devil (Διαβολος)
387 Of the Beast (θερος)
388 The Sun (ο ηλιος)
389 Long-lived; fresh; quick (διερος)
390 Deceitfulness (*Corpus Hermeticum,* XIII 7) (απατη)
390 Mind, reason; understanding (νοος)
390 Way, road (οιμος)
390 City, citadel (πολις)
391 Evening; west (εσπερα)
391 Barren (στειρος*)
391 Epithet of Athena (Πολιας)
392 Ancient (παλαιος)
392 The people (ο δημος)
393 Equivalent (αμοιβος)
393 Eleventh (ενδεκατη)
394 Unborn; barren (αγονος)
395 Two hundred (διακοσιοι)
395 Cities (πολιες)
396 Horned (κεραος)
397 All black (παμμελας)
397 Serpent sacred to Aesculapius (παρειας)
397 The people (πληθος)
397 Magic; witchcraft (γοητεια)

398	New birth (*Corpus Herme-ticum* III 26) (παλιγγενεσια)	412	Libation (σπονδη)
399	Shit (ονθος)	412	Pleasant, sweet (ηδυ)
399	To endure (τληναι)	413	Voice, speech (αυδη)
399	Inheritance (κληρονομια)	413	Step, pace; basis, foundation (βασις)
400	Ram (κριος)	413	The spell (η γοος)
400	Wine (οινος	414	Darkness; twilight (αμολγος)
400	Grain (κοκκος)		
400	Vinegar (οξος)	414	Perfection; virtue (αρετη)
401	Pure, perfect (καθαρος)	414	Mad; lustful (μαργος)
401	Icarus (Ικαρος)	414	Grief, sorrow (πενθος)
401	The god Pan; all (Πανος)	414	Names of Dionysus, Bacchus (Θεοινος)
401	Time, season (Revelation 1:3) (καιρος)		
		414	Honest, straightforward (ευθυ)
402			
403		414	The way (η οδος)
404	On the right hand; favorable (ενδεξιος)	415	Way, path (αγυια)
		415	Lover of boys (παιδεραστης*)
405	Archer (εκηβολος)		
405	Most good (παγκαλος)	415	All-holy (παναγιος)
405	Well (ευ)	415	Part (μερος)
406	Eve (Ευα)	416	Ungodly (ασεβης)
406	Perfection (εντελεια)	417	Mysteries; sacrifices; sacred rites; temples (τα ιερα)
407	Letter name of *stau* (σταυ*)		
407	The inheritance (Isaiah 58:14) (η κληρονομια)	417	Keeping off evil (αλεξικακος)
407	Commandment (επιταγη)	418	Such are the words (ειδε τα επη)
408	Worship; glory (σεβας)		
408	Coitus; offspring (κοιτη)	418	The not, the nothing (το μη)
408	Festival of Sarapis (Σαραπιεια)		
		418	Foundation, base; shoe (κρηπις)
409	Exodus; way out, gate; mouth; end (εξοδος)	418	Pallas Athene (Παλλας Αθηνη)
409	Defeat (ησσα)		
410	Dirt, filth (πινος)	418	Cut, stroke (τομη)
411	Three (τρια)	418	To be Hermes; I am Hermes (Ηρμες ειμι)
411	Thorned (John 19:5) (ακανθινος)		
		419	The great (το μεγα)
412	Splendor, brilliance; ray, beam (αυγη)	419	The Egyptian god Tuat, Thoth (Θυαθ)

419 Health (υγεια)

419 Steep, straight; erect (ιθυ)

420 The Egyptian goddess Isis (Ισις)

420 Mistress, lady (δεσποινα)

420 Bacchante (θυια)

420 Hawk (κιρκος)

420 Ring, circle (κρικος)

420 Practice, skill (τριβη)

420 Evil, ruin (ατηρια)

420 May you live (Christian catacombs) (ΖΗΣΕΣ)

421 Smoke, vapor (καπνος)

421 Incredible (απιθανος)

421 A howling (ιυγη)

422

423 Solitary; desert (ερημος)

423 Curse (καταρα)

423 Shaft, spear (πελτη)

423 To deceive by false reasoning (παραλογιζομαι)

424 Ambrosia, food of the gods (αμβροσια)

425 Attendant; deacon (διακονος)

425 Child, scion (ερνος)

425 Love; a longing (ιμερος)

425 Prophecy, oracle (θεο–προπια)

426 Seed; descent, origin; off-spring (σπερμα)

426 Offence (σκανδαλον)

427 Prayer, entreating (δεησις)

428 Curse (Revelation 22:3) (κατανaθεμα)

428 Wall; veil (περιβολαιον)

428 Progress, growth (προκοπη)

429 To set up, erect; consecrate, charge (ανατιθημι)

429 Love, desire (ποθος)

429 Hygeia, goddess of health (Υγεια)

430 United, joined; friend (αρθμιος)

430 Law (νομος)

430 Universal; Catholic (καθολικος)

430 Bird; prophecy (ορνις)

430 Number (αριθμος)

430 Kind; simple (ευηθη)

431 Lawless; pagan (ανομος)

431 Brother, sister (κασις)

432 Priesthood, body of priests (ιερατεια)

432 Foundation (καταβολη)

432 Everywhere, wholly (παντα)

433

434 Wantonness (στρηνος*)

435 The sodomite (ο κιναιδος)

436 Unholy, wicked (ανιερος)

436 Light; fire, flame (σελας)

436 Ram (αρνειος)

437

438 Goodness, simplicity (ευηθεια)

438 Dry (ξηρος)

438 Matter (*Corpus Hermeticum*, III 18) (υλη)

438 Everywhere, wholly (παντη)

439

440 Letter name of *mu* (μυ)

440 Five (πεντε)

440 A showing forth (αποδειξις)

440 Horse; chariot (ιππος)

440 Current, stream (ροος)

440 The foundation (η καταβολη)

440 Limit; mountain (ορος)

440 Cybele (variant of) (Κυβηβη)

440 The house; the temple (ο οικος)

440 Everywhere (απαντη)

441 Triumphant, beautiful (καλλινικος)

441 Courage (τολμα)

441 Consort, wife (οαρος)

442 Sea (θαλασσα)

442 Blessed (Revelation 1:3) (μακαριος)

442 Ecstasy (εκστασις*)

443 The Logos; the Word (ο λογος)

443 Sun-bright; pure; manifest (ειλικρινης)

444 Offering (Matthew 27:6) (κορβανας)

444 Flesh and blood (σαρξ και αιμα)

444 Oedipus (Οιδιπος)

445 Temperence (εγκρατεια)

445 Dead; corpse (νεκρος)

445 Divine being, guardian spirit; devil; death; genius (with Socrates) (δαιμονος)

446 One hundred (εκατον)

446 End, goal (τερμα)

447 Seventeen (επτα–και–δεκα)

447 Female (θηλυ)

448 Remnant, residue (Romans 9:27) (καταλειμμα)

448 The true (ο αληθινος)

449 Prayer, vow (ευγμα)

449 Semen (θορος)

449 Womb (μητρα)

449 Hole, aperture (τρημα)

449 Warrior (πολεμιστης*)

449 Mocking (εμπαιγμος)

449 Upright, erect (ορθος)

450 Toward, to, at (προς)

450 Letter name of *nu*; now; the Egyptian goddess Nu, Nuit (νυ)

450 Offering, sacrifice (θυμα)

450 Axis; firmament (πολος)

450 Feast of the tabernacles (σκηνοπηγια)

450 The ecstasy (η εκστασις*)

450 The sea (η θαλασσα)

450 Song at a banquet (σκολιον)

451 Marvel; admiration (Revelation 17:6) (θαυμα)

451 Square (πλαισιον)

451 Deed, action (πραξις)

451 Silver Star (αστρον* αργον)

451 Gentle, kind (πραος)

451 Beetle (κανθαρος)

451 Seed (σπορα)

452 Wickedness (αλιτρια)

452 Lance-bearer (δεξιολαβος)

453 Failure, error (αμαρτια)

453 Mistress, lady (ανασσα)

454 Wine (μεθυ)

454 Demeter (Δαματηρ)

455 Divine, god-like; possessed (δαιμονιος)

456 Mother (μητηρ)

456 Righteous judgment (Romans 2:5) (δικαιοκρισια)

456 Hurled by Zeus (διοβολος)

456 Bond (ζευγμα)

457 Reaper (αμητηρ)

457 Spark (σπινθηρ)

457 Ten horns (Revelation 12:3) (δεκα κερατα)

457 Exchange (Matthew 16:26) (ανταλλαγμα)

458
459 Glorious, honored (ενδοξος)
459 The seed (*Corpus Hermeticum,* XIII 2) (η σπορα)
460 Sunrise, east (ανατολη)
460 Youth, warrior (ορκος)
460 Gematria, isopsephy (γεμα–τρια)
460 Horned (κερεινος)
460 Remaining (λοιπος)
461 The failure, the error (η αμαρτια)
461 Woman, mistress (γυνη)
461 Demeter, Ceres (Δημητρα)
461 Temple of Hecate (Εκατειον)
462 Will (θελησις)
463 Symbol; letter name of *episemon* (επισημον)
463 The will (το θελημα)
463 Bed (ευνη)
463 Priest of Artemis (εσσην)
464 The mother (η μητηρ)
465 Ascent; stairway (αναβασις)
465 Robe, cloak (πεπλος)
465 Cybele (Κυβελη)
466 Diaspora, dispersion (διασ–πορα)
466 End; sign (τεκμαρ)
466 The river Styx (Στυξ*)
466 Infinite (απειρος)
467 Mistake, failure (διαμαρτια)
468 Demeter, Ceres (Δημητηρ)
468 Teaching of the Mysteries; knowledge (μαθησις)
469 The Egyptian goddess Nuit (Νυιθ)
469 Resurrection (αναστασις*)

470 Dark, gloomy (ερεμνος)
470 Bosom; womb; depth; vagina (κολπος)
470 Suffering (πονος)
470 Not (ου)
470 The will (η θελησις)
471 Cancer, crab (καρκινος)
471 Mind, heart (πραπις)
471 Be satisfied (εξαρκομενον)
471 Circles (κυκλα)
472 Trident (τριαινα)
473 Genesis; origin; birth (γενεσις)
473 Spell, charm (ιυγξ)
474 Two (δυο)
474 To sacrifice (θυειν)
475
476 Dedication (αναθεσις)
476 Nectar, the drink of the gods (νεκταρ)
477 Repentance (μετανοια)
477 The curse (το αναθεμα)
478 Heart, mind, soul; life, spirit (ητορ)
479 Exorcist (εξορκιστης*)
479 But not (ουδε)
480 Fate, destiny; death (μορος)
480 Many, mighty (πολλος)
480 Lawful (νομιμος)
480 Evoe! The Bacchic cry (ευοε)
480 Equal (ισος)
480 Wealth, prosperity (ευθενια)
481 The beginning (η γενεσις)
481 IAOU, Gnostic name of God (variant of) (ΙΑΟΥ)
481 Father, Son and Holy Spirit by notarichon (Πατηρ, Υιος, Αγιον Πνευμα) (Π. Υ. Α.)

481 Raiment (Revelation 4:4) (ιματιον)

482 Immortal (αθανατον)

482 Giver (δοτηρ)

482 Of life (βιου)

482 Magic wheel; whirling motion; rhombus (ρομβος)

482 Consummation; Pythagorean name for the number ten (παντελεια)

483 Avenger (παλαμναιος)

484 Ruin, defeat (ολεθρος)

484 Of God (θεου)

485 Abomination (Revelation 17:5) (βδελυγμα)

485 IEOU, Gnostic name of God (IEOY)

485 The all-holy (ο παναγιος)

485 The repentance (η μετανοια)

485 Health; wealth (ευθενεια)

486 Honey (μελισσα)

486 Stone (πετρα)

486 Gladness (Hebrews 1:9) (αγαλλιασις)

487 The Beast (το θηρ)

487 The mouth; the point (το στομα*)

488 To provide for (προβλεπο– μαι)

488 Health; wealth (ευθηνεια)

489 Father (πατηρ)

490 Slavery (ειρερος)

490 Not (ουκ)

490 Being (το ον)

490 Prosperous course (ευοδια)

491 Shield (σακος)

492 Mason (λιθολογος)

492 Descent, lineage (πατρια)

492 Name of Dionysus, Bacchus (Βρομιος)

492 Left; of the left hand (αριστερος*)

493

494 Measure (μετρημα)

495 War (πολεμος)

495 Child (τεκνον)

495 Does ritual; brings to perfection, accomplishes (επιτελειν)

496 The heart (το κεαρ)

497

498 Shrine (σηκος)

498 Hymen (Υμην)

498 Motion (κινησις)

498 The heart (το κηρ)

499 Throne (θρονος)

500 Robe (ενδυμα)

500 Now; therefore (νυν)

500 The number (ο αριθμος)

501 Fifteen (πεντε–και–δεκα)

501 Jasper (ιασπις)

501 The whole, the universe; Pan (το παν)

501 Mistress (ποτνα)

501 Surge (σαλος)

501 Left, on the left (σκαιος)

502 Air, breath (αυρα)

502 Winged (ποτανα)

503 A rising of a star (επιτολη)

504 The Good (Corpus Hermeticum, I 26) (το αγαθον)

504 Disk (δισκος)

504 Divine; inspired by God (θεσπις)

504 Twelve (δυοδεκα)

504 Waters; moist (υγρα)

505 Dream, vision (ονειρος)
505 Hail to thee! (ουλε)
505 Little child (τεκνιον)
505 Hydra, water-serpent (υδρα)
505 Warlike (πολεμιος)
505 Five + six (πεντε + εξ)
506
507 Impotence (αδυναμια)
508
509 Speech; law (ρητρα)
509 Touch (αφη)
510 Letter name of *phi* (φι)
510 Door, threshold (θυρα)
510 Will (βουλη)
510 The goddess Night, daughter of Chaos; night (Νυξ)
510 Mine, of me (μου)
510 Nemesis, goddess of vengeance; anger (Νεμεσις)
510 Knight (ιππηλατα)
510 Anyone, everyone (τις)
510 Kronos, Saturn (Κρονος)
511 Sensual pleasure; luxury (ευπαθεια)
511 Mistress (ποτνια)
511 Cup; shell (καλυξ)
511 Anywhere (αμου)
511 The rising of a star (η επι–τολη)
512 Rest, end (παυλα)
512 The equalities (τα ισα)
512 Delicate (παναπλος)
512 The waters (η υγρα)
513 Throat (λαυκανια)
513 Destroyer (ολετηρ)
514 Good, kind; favorable (εσθλος)
514 Destined, fated (μοιριδιος)
514 Thoughtlessness (αβουλια)

514 Sixty (εξηκοντα)
515 Maiden, virgin; Virgo (παρθενος)
515 He, she, it is (εστι)
516 The goddess Hestia, Vesta; hearth, house; altar (Εστια)
516 Sixfold (εξαπλοος)
517 Priest; one praying (αρητηρ)
517 Door, threshold (θυρη)
518 Mistake, error (εξαμαρτια)
518 Not (ου μη)
518 Sorrow, grief (λυπη)
518 Gate, door (Matthew 7:13) (πυλη)
518 The door (John 10:9) (η θυρα)
518 The elect (οι κλητοι)
518 The bad woman (η κακη γυνη)
519 The word (το ρημα)
519 The seed, the semen (ο θορος)
519 The day; the fate (το ημαρ)
519 Bond, fetter (δεσμος)
520 Slavery, bondage (δουλεια)
520 Hatred; hateful thing (μισος)
520 Passage (πορος)
520 Cup (κυλιξ)
520 Everywhere (παντοθι)
521 Shining, brilliant; magnificent; manifest (λαμπρος)
521 Silence, stillness (σιγηλος)
521 Of the temple (ναου)
521 Wide (ευρεια)
522 Angel-like (ισαγγελος)
522 A fasting (ασιτια)
523 Daughter (επικληρος)

523 The goddess Hestia, Vesta (Εστιη)

524 Torment; test (βασανος)

525 Holiness (αγιασμος)

525 Passage; entrance (παροδος)

525 Wickedness (2 Peter 2:7) (αθεσμος)

525 Of tears (δακρυ)

526 I will be (εσομαι)

527 Shadowy (σκιοειδης)

527 Temple of Sarapis (Σαραπιειον)

528 Kingly, royal (βασιλειος)

528 Fresh (ερσηεις)

528 Island (νησος)

528 The goddess Hestia, Vesta (variant of) (Ιστιη)

529 Corinth (Κορινθος)

529 None, nothing (ουδεν)

529 Fettered, captive (δεσμιος)

530 Thunder (βροντη)

530 Harm (σινος)

530 Yoke, union (ζυγον)

530 None, nothing (ουδεμια)

531 Goddess; mistress (κυρια)

531 Altogether (πανυ)

531 Evil, suffering (το κανον)

531 Light, splendor (ακτις)

532 Letter name of *alpha* (αλφα)

532 Veil (καλυμμα)

532 Pain, grief (οδυνη)

532 Enduring, patient (ταλας)

532 Atlas (Ατλας)

533 Thunderings (Revelation 4:5) (βρονται)

534 Force, power (σθενος)

534 None, nothing (ουθεν)

535 Comb; pudenda (κτεις)

535 Treachery (προδοσια)

535 Lord; God (vocative) (κυπιε)

536

537

538 Non-being (το μη ον)

538 Thought (νοησις)

539 Period, cycle; circumference (περιοδος)

540 Division (διαιρεσις)

540 Messenger; guide (πομπος)

540 Feather (πτιλον)

540 Justice, judgment; separation (κρισις)

540 Teacher (διδασκαλος)

540 None, nothing (ουδενια)

541 Priapus, god of generation (Πριαπος)

541 Sprout, bud; growth; origin (βλαστη)

541 Knight; mounted (ιπποτα)

541 Maiden (ταλις)

541 The beautiful; the beauty; the virtue (το καλον)

542

543 Delightful (τερπνη)

544 Without object (ατελης)

544 Prophecy, oracle (θεοπροπιον)

545

546 Stele, pillar, stone (στηλη)

546 Current, river (ρευμα)

547 Opportunity (ευκαιρια)

548 Force (ρυμη)

548 Friend, mistress (φιλη)

548 Sister (αδελφη)

549 Urn, cup, vessel (φιαλη)

549 The archangel Auriel (Αυριηλ)

549 Word, speech (φημα)

550 Arrow (τοξον)

550 By (υπο)

550 Cythereia, surname of Aphrodite (Κυθερεια)

551 Will (βουλημα)

551 Love (φιλια)

551 On all sides, about, around (αμφι)

551 Vapor (Acts 2:19) (ατμις)

552 The angel Satan (Σαταν)

552 The magic wheel; the whirling motion; the rhombus (ο ρομβος)

553

554 Letter name of *stigma*; mark, brand; point (στιγμα)

555 Separation; division (διακρισις)

555 Desire; lust (επιθυμια)

555 Foundation; image (ιδρυμα)

555 Necronomicon, or book of the dead (νεκρονομικον)

556 All-desired (πανιμερος)

556 Speech; omen, oracle (φημη)

557 Leader; teacher (καθηγητης)

557 The urn (η φιαλη)

558 None, nothing (μη–τις)

558 Counsel, wisdom (μητις)

558 Perfect, complete (τελειος)

558 Solstice; change (τροπη)

559 Ninety (ενενηκοντα)

559 The father (ο πατηρ)

560 Champion; prince (προμος)

560 One who wills; a wizard (θελητης)

561 Carelessness (ραθυμια)

561 Efflux (ρυαξ)

562 Verily (Hebrews 2:16) (δηπου)

563 Poimandres, tutelary figure in the *Hermetica* (Ποιμανδρης)

563 Daphne (Δαφνη)

564 Deity, divine being (το θειον)

564 Godlike (ισοθεος)

564 Head; end, point; source (κεφαλη)

564 Hardness of heart (σκληροκαρδια)

565 Freedom (ελευθερια)

565 Sacred, holy (σεμνος)

565 The void, the space (το κενον)

565 From every side (παντοθεν)

566 Disciple (μαθητης)

567

568

569 Passage (πορθμος)

569 Denial (αρνησις)

569 The throne (ο θρονος)

570 Of the temple (οικου)

570 Seventy (εβδομηκοντα)

570 Fornicator (πορνος)

570 Mandrake (μανδραγορας)

571 Order, arrangement (ταξις)

571 Father, ancestor (γενετης)

572

573

574 Wood; spear; war; warrior (δορυ)

574 Good fortune (ευκληρια)

575 Year (ετος)

575 Who am I? (τις ειμι?)

576 Breath; spirit; inspiration (Revelation 1:10) (πνευμα)

577 Cassandra (Κασσανδρα)

578 Wicked (πονηρος)

578 A making, creating; poetry (ποιησις)

578 Chamber (τεγος)

579 Obedience (υπακοη)

579 Flame, fire (φλεγμα)

579 The order (*Corpus Hermeticum,* XI 2) (η ταξις)

580 True, real (ετεος)

580 Courage, daring (θαρσος)

580 Fire; lightning (πυρ)

580 Rotten (σαθρος)

580 Pit (σιρος)

580 Hair (φοβη)

580 To destroy (ολλυμι)

580 Much; mighty (πολυ)

580 Udder (ουθαρ)

581 Wheel (αμπυς)

581 Deadly; of death (θανασιμος)

581 Reality (υπαρ)

582 Giver (2 Corinthians 9:27) (δοτης)

583

584 Woman (γυναιον)

585 Across; beyond (υπερ)

585 The god of oracles (η φαμαιθεια)

586 Wreath (στεμμα)

586 Lance, spear (ξυστον*)

587 Foundation (πυθμην)

588 Will (ιοτης)

589 Kiss (φιλημα)

589 A howler (γοητης)

590 Circle (κυκλον)

590 The whole; the perfect (το ολον)

590 Bright (Moon) (φοιβη)

591 The dream, the vision (το οναρ)

591 Eight (οκτας)

592 Holiness, sanctity (αγιοτης)

592 Traveller (οδιτης)

592 Sword; iron (σιδηρος)

592 Divinity, godhead (θεοτης)

592 Divinity (αγαθοτης)

592 The Graeco-Egyptian god Sarapis, Osiris-Apis (Σαραπις)

593 Voice (φλογγη)

593 Immortal (αβροτον)

594 Dawn (περιορθρον)

595 Child (τεκος)

595 Perfect, complete (εντελες)

595 Center; sting (κεντρον)

595 The thing; the deed (το πραγμα)

595 Sirius, the dog-star (Σειριος)

596 Eighty (ογδοηκοντα)

596 Forgiveness (παρεσις)

596 End; passage from life (περασις)

596 The Graeco-Egyptian god Sarapis, Osiris-Apis (Σεραπις)

597

598 Abyss (κητος)

598 Entire, perfect (ολοκληρος)

598 Cloud (Revelation 1:7) (νεφελη)

598 Perfect, complete (εντελης)

598 The eight (η οκτας)

599

600 Sister (κασιγνητη)

600 Thou (συ)

600 World, universe (κοσμος)

600 One hundredth, hundredth (δεκατος)

600 Success, well-doing (ευπρα–για)

600 Swine, pig (υς)

600 The godhead (η θεοτης)

600 Tortuous (σκολιος)

601 Prophet (μαντις)

601 Unholy (1 Timothy 1:9) (ανοσιος)

601 The name (το ονομα)

601 Epithet of Dionysus (Υας)
602 Father (αττα)
602 Divinity (θειοτης)
602 Unbelief (απιστια)
602 Stars (αστρα)
603 Emission of seed; orgasm (εκποιησις)
603 Infallible proof (Acts 1:3) (τεκμηριον)
603 The oracle (το λογιον)
604 The end (η περασις)
605 End, result; death; full power (τελος)
605 Flight; omen (πτερον)
605 Shady, shaded (σκιερος)
605 Sacrifice; temple, oracle; mystery, sacred rite (το ιερον)
605 Brave, noble (ευς)
606 Temptation (πειρασις)
606 Omen (τερας)
606 Young man (νεανισκος)
606 The perfect (η εντελης)
607 Cleopatra (Κλεοπατρα)
608 Monster (φηρ)
608 Epithet of Dionysus (Υης)
609 Star (Revelation 1:16) (αστηρ)
610 Letter name of *chi* (χι)
610 Wood; spear; cross (ξυλον)
610 The teacher (ο διδασκαλος)
610 Winged (πτεροεν)
611 Whip, scourge (μαστιξ)
611 Assassin (σικαριος)
611 Mouth; speech; point (στομα)
611 Triad (τριας)
611 Wanderer (μεταναστης*)
611 The summit (το ακρον)
612 Zeus (Ζευς)
612 Womb; belly (γαστηρ)

612 Enough (επιτηδες)
612 Sweet, joyous (ηδυς)
613 Servant, slave (οικετης)
614
615 Three (τρεις)
616
617 Pure, guiltless; shining; purifying (ευαγης)
617 The Beast (το θηριον)
617 All-begetter (vocative); epithet of Pan (παγγενετορ)
618 Oracle (ομφη)
619 Undertaking; straight, true (ιθυς)
619 Fear, defeat (κακοτης)
619 Delphi (Δελφοι)
619 To raise up, to excite (ανιστημι)
619 Sun + Moon; Helios + Selene (Ηλιος + Σεληνη)
619 The sign, the seal (το σημα)
620 Bacchante (θυιας)
620 A sacrifice (θυσια)
620 Web; thread; semen (Orphic) (μιτος)
620 Perfect, complete (τελειος)
621 Of flesh; sensual (σαρκικος)
621 Terror (φοβημα)
621 To save, guard (ρυομαι)
621 The Iynges, a group of divinities appearing in the *Chaldean Oracles* (Ιυγγες)
622 Winged (ποτανον)
623 To will (βουλομαι)
623 Justice (δικαιοτης)
623 Thought, reasoning (λογισμος)
623 Hesitation (στραγγεια)
624 To swear, take an oath; affirm solemnly (διομνυμι)

624 Heap of dust, ashes (σποδος)
625 Within (Luke 17:21) (εντος)
626 The Egyptian god of the Sun at midnight, Keph-Ra (κεφρα)
627
628 Harsh, cruel (σκληρος)
628 To be learned (μαθητος)
628 Reverent (ευσεβεια)
629
630 The hesitation (ηστραγγεια)
630 All-devourer (vocative); epithet of Pan (παμφαγε)
630 Adjuration (επιθειασμος)
630 Ram (κτιλος)
630 Precious, honored (τιμιος)
630 Kind; simple; silly (ευηθης)
631 Death (θανατος)
631 Olympia (Ολυμπια)
632 Immortal (αθανατος)
632 Purity (αγνοτης)
632 Failure, defeat (πταισμα)
632 Thirty (τριακας)
633 Spear (προβολαιος)
633 Dress; vessel; ornament (σκευη)
633 Harmony (εναρμοστια*)
634 Baptism (βαπτισμα)
634 The Holy Trinity (η αγια τριας)
634 Epithet of Dionysus (Ιυγγης)
635 Strong, mighty (σθεναρος)
635 Master, Rabbi (ραββουνι)
636
637 Unborn (αγενητος)
637 Mortal (θνητος)
637 Self-disciplined; strong (Titus 1:8) (εγκρατης)
638 Accomplished (επιτελης)

639
640 Mouse (μυς)
640 Watcher, guardian (σκοπος)
640 Urn, coffin (σορος)
640 The archangel Raphael (Ραφαηλ)
641 Slave (λατρις)
642
643 Thief (κλεπτης)
644 Dew, dewdrop (δροσος)
644 Emmanuel (Εμμανουηλ)
645 Godlike (αντι–θεος)
646
647 Female, effeminate (θηλυς)
647 To understand (επισταμαι)
648 Initiation, celebration; mysteries (τελετη)
648 The House of Truth (δομος αληθειας)
648 The Truth + Spirit (η αληθεια + πνευμα)
648 The Kingdom of Peace (η βασιλεια ειρηνης)
649 Seeker (μαστηρ)
649 Fight, battle (μαχη)
650 Strength, vigor (κικυς)
650 With, to (συν)
651 Ship (ναυς)
651 Worthless (σαπρος)
651 Of flesh; sensual (σαρκινος)
651 Intelligence, insight; science, art (επιστημη)
652
653
654 One initiated (μυστης*)
655 Eleventh (ενδεκατος)
655 Pleasant, delightful (τερπ–νον)
656 Artemis (Αρτεμις)

656 Messiah (Μεσσιας)
656 The initiation; the Mysteries; the celebration (η τελετη)
657 Messenger (μεταγγελος)
657 Love-charm (στεργημα)
658 Soul, mind, heart; under-standing (φρην)
658 Half (ημισυ)
659 Invincible (ανικητος)
659 Dew; foam (αχνη)
659 Blood (λυθρον)
659 Sufficiency (2 Corinthians 3:5) (ικανοτης)
660 Child; birth (τοκος)
660 Fire; flame (φλοξ)
661
662 Belly, womb (νηδυς)
662 Sanctuary (ανακτορον)
663 Enduring (τολμηεις)
663 Beloved (αγαπητος)
664 A mocker (εμπαικτης)
664 Sixfold (εξαπλησιος)
665 Ancient of Days (Παλαιος Ημερον)
665 Sirius, the dog-star (ο Σειριος)
666 The Great Beast (το μεγα θηριον)
666 Transmission (παραδοσις)
666 The Graeco-Egyptian god Sarapis, Osiris-Apis (ο Σεραπις)
666 Titan (τειταν)
666 Latin (adjective) (λατεινος)
666 The heart, the soul, the mind (η φρην)
666 Five times (πεντακις)
666 I am a god on earth (θεος ειμι επι γαιης)

666 Sum of the first six Roman numerals, D + C + L + X + V + I (666)
667 The Scarlet Woman (η κοκκινη γυνη)
668 Test; means of judging (κριτηριον)
668 Mushroom (μυκης)
668 Spider (φαλαγγιον)
669
670 Coitus; marriage-bed; off-spring (κοιτος)
670 Precincts of the temple (τεμενος)
670 Groin (ιξυς)
670 The manifestation (η επι–φανεια)
670 The universe, the world (ο κοσμος)
671 Paradise (παραδεισος)
671 Thirteen (τρισ–και–δεκα)
671 Bread (αρτος)
671 Unripe (ομφαξ)
671 Perfect, complete (παντελες)
672 Ox (βους)
672 Trust (πεποιθησις)
673 Fear (ταρβος)
674 He-goat (τραγος)
674 Setting forth; purpose (προθεσις)
674 All, perfect (παντελης)
674 In six parts (εξαχη)
675 Earth (ουδας)
675 Divine being; genius (with Socrates) (το δαιμονιον)
676 Thirteen (τρεισ–και–δεκα)
676 Creator; poet (ποιητης)
677

678 Witchcraft, medicine (φαρ–μακεια)

679 Incense, medicine (θυος)

679 Mother (παιδουργια)

679 The river Styx (Στυγος*)

679 The star (ο αστηρ)

679 Wanton, lustful (μαχλη)

680 Son (υιος)

680 Destruction; death (φθορα)

680 Another (Acts 7:18) (ετερος)

681 Perfect (2 Timothy 3:17) (αρτιος)

681 Abyss, depth (βυθος)

681 Essence (ουσια)

681 Buddha (βουδδας)

682 Path (τριβος)

682 Of the whirling motion; of the magic wheel (ρυμβου)

683 Intercourse (συνηθεια)

683 Sender of lightning (σττεροπηγερετα*)

684 Secret rite, mystery (μυστηριον*)

685 Shouting; Bacchic; rejoicing (ευιος)

685 Star (τειρος)

685 Union; couple (ζευγος)

686 Immense (απλετος)

687 War-like (στρατιος*)

688 Cup (ποτηριον)

689 The archangel Michael (Μιχαηλ)

689 None, nothing (ουδεις)

690 Lightning (αστραπη)

690 Cord; chord (τονος)

690 South; south wind (νοτος)

690 The perfect (ο τελειος)

691 Power, force; victory, dominion (κρατος)

691 Knowledge; science; history (ιστορια)

691 North; a bear (αρκτος)

692 Pure; perfect (ακρατος)

692 Cube (κυβος)

693

694 None, nothing (ουθεις)

695 Destruction; ruin; corruption (διαφθορα)

695 Double, twofold (διπαλτος)

695 Excess; passage (υπερβολη)

696 The True Sun (Αληθινος Ηλιος)

697

698

699 Without understanding (ανοητος)

700 The equilibrium (το ισον)

700 Chosen, picked out (κριτος)

700 Age, antiquity (παλαιοτης)

700 Priest (προπολος)

700 Purple-red, crimson; phoenix (φοινιξ)

700 Chronos or Christ (abbreviated); the chi-rho (XP)

701 Letter name of tau (ταυ)

701 Crystal, glass (υαλος)

701 Beloved (στερκτος*)

701 Command, shout (1 Thessalonians 4:16) (κελευσμα)

702 Strong, mighty (κραταιος)

702 Delight, joy (χαρα)

703 Oppressive; deep; loud; cruel; mighty (βαρυς)

704 Mad; wandering (πλαγκτος)

704 Tragic (τραγικος)

704 In the nether world (υπεν–ερθεν)

704 Abyss, depth (κευθος)

705 Power (δυναμις)
706 Never-failing (εκατηβολος)
706 Pillar (στυλος*)
707 War-engine (μηχανη)
707 Strongest, best, mightiest (κρατιστος*)
707 Pan + Spirit (Παν + Πνευμα)
708 Winged, fleet (πτηνος)
708 Battle (υσμινη)
709 Purity (καθαροτης)
709 Fun (υθλος)
709 Origin, cause (αρχη)
709 War-cry; battle (αυτη)
710 Letter-name of *psi* (ψι)
710 Holy Spirit (Πνευμα Αγιον)
710 Willingness, desire (προ–θυμια)
711 Spear, lance (λογχη)
711 Wholly, utterly (αχρι)
711 Muse (Μουσα)
712 Love of boys (παιδεραστια)
712 Surge; surf (ραχια)
712 Sacrifice, slaughter (σφαγη)
712 Wantonness (υβρις)
712 Manifold universe (παντοιας)
712 Angels (αγγελους)
713 Perfect; wholly (1 Thessa-lonians 5:23) (ολοτελης)
713 All-powerful; epithet of Pan (παγκρατης)
713 The power (η δυναμις)
714 Congregation (αγυρις)
714 Dagger (ξιφιδιον)
714 Forerunner (Hebrews 6:20) (προδρομος)
715 Hand, side; close fight; brav-ery; power (χειρ)

715 Dream, vision (ενυπνιον)
715 To have intercourse (with) (συνειμι)
715 Woman (2 Timothy 3:6) (γυναικαριον)
715 Ineffable (ανεκλαλητος)
716 Hail! (χαιρε)
716 Child; child-birth (λοχεια)
716 Humble (ταπεινος)
717 To shun (παρατεισθαι)
717 The beginning; name and number of Zeus (Martianus Capella) (η αρχη)
718 Form (Philippians 2:6) (μορφη)
718 Endurance, patience (Revelation 1:9) (υπομονη)
719 Soul; will; mind, spirit; heart (θυμος)
719 Chariot; vessel (οχημα)
719 Hammer (ραιστηρ)
719 Purity (καθαριοτης)
719 Cause, occasion (αφορμη)
719 Myth (μυθος)
719 Amphora (αμφορα)
720 Hiereus; priest (ιερευς)
720 The Holy Spirit (ο Αγιος Ανεμος)
720 Seed, birth (σπορος)
720 Spirit of God (Θειον Πνευμα)
720 Sacred IEOU (ιερον IEOY)
720 Medusa (Μεδουσα)
720 Wolf (λυκος)
720 Atonement; vengeance (τισις)
720 Space; position (τοπος)
720 Mind, understanding (νους)
721 Star (αστρον)
721 Shaft, stem (καυλος)

722 Sword (ρομφαια)

722 Hero, prince (αριστευς*)

722 Everywhere (εκασταχοθι)

722 The creatures (τα οντα)

723 Change; intercourse (συναλλαγη)

724

725 By hand (χειρι)

725 Bright, brilliant; white (λευκος)

725 Last, extreme (τερμιος)

725 Earthquake (Revelation 6:12) (σεισμος)

725 The word; the oracle (το επος)

726 Unutterable (αναυδος)

726 The Messiah (ο Μεσσιας)

727 Splendid, glorious (επικυδης)

727 Wonderful (Isaiah 9:6) (θαυμαστος*)

727 Brightness (Hebrews 1:3) (απαυγασμα)

728 Double, twofold (διδυμος)

729 The rock + the trust (η πετρα + η παραθηκη)

729 Ship; vessel (σκαφη)

729 Kephas, the name given by Jesus to Peter (Κηφας)

729 The Perfected Work (ευεργεσια)

729 Abominated (στυγνος*)

730 Fiery, active (Revelation 1:16) (οξυς)

730 To receive (δεχομαι)

730 Critic (Hebrews 4:12) (κριτικος)

731

732 Cup (κυμβος)

733 Anubis, the Egyptian god of the dead (Ανουβις)

733 A seeking, quest (ζητησις)

734 Ordeal (πειρατηριον)

734 Feminine (γυναιος)

734 Forerunner (προδρομος)

735 Hidden, precious (αποθετος)

735 Ill-will; dislike (δυσνοια)

735 The center (το μεσον)

735 Guardian; bishop (επισκοπος)

736 Battle of the gods (θεομα–χια)

737 Indolence (ραδιουγημα)

738 An acquiring; possession, goods (κτησις)

739 Way, path (κελευθος)

740 Foundation, creation (κτισις)

740 Circle, wheel; cycle; eye, disk (κυκλος)

740 Sanctuary of God (Αγιασμα Θεου)

740 The God over All (Plato) (ο επι πασι Θεος)

740 Of Demeter, Ceres (Δημητριος)

741 Visible (ορατος)

741 The five (Platonic solids) (τα πεντε)

741 Celestial (ουρανον)

741 Spells, enchantments (καταδεσις)

742 Invisible (αορατος)

742 Man, mortal (βροτος)

742 The ox (ο βους)

743 Watcher, guardian (εποπτης)

743 Immortal, divine (αβροτος)

744 Word of Power (ενεργης λογος)

744 Threshold, entrance (ουδος)

745 Brain (μυελος)

745 Feast of Dionysus (Διονυσια)

745 Slaughter of the Magi (μαγοφονια)

746 Free will; means; power; fortune (εξουσια)

746 Mark; character (χαραγμα)

746 Secret; mystic (μυστικος*)

747 The curse (το καταθεμα)

748 War-engine (μηχανημα)

748 Of the Muses; music, dance (Μουσικη)

748 Truth (ασφαλεια)

748 Simple; smooth, naked (ψιλη)

749 Quiet, idle (λεγαμυος)

749 Dolphin (δελφις)

749 Easy path; prosperous course (ευοδος)

750 Scorpion (σκορπιος)

750 House (στεγασμα)

750 Foot (πους)

750 Of the law (της δικης)

751 Of the father (πατρος)

751 Pillar (σταμις)

751 All-honored (παντιμος)

751 The abyss (ο βυθος)

752 The mother (of Dionysus) Semele (η μητηρ Σεμελη)

753 Sword (μαχαιρα)

753 Revolution (περιτροπη)

753 Violence (υβρισμα)

753 The angel Satan (Σατανας)

753 The sign, the mark (το σημειον)

754 Fiery, active (ζαφλεγης)

755 Stone (πετρος)

756 Unchangeable (Hebrews 7:24) (απαραβατος)

757 Accursed (επαρατος)

758 Eye; eyelid (βλεφαρον)

759 A sending; apostleship (Romans 1:5) (αποστολη)

760 Secret, unseen, occult (αφανης)

760 Destiny, fate; death (ποτμος)

760 The Egyptian goddess Nuit (Νυιτ)

760 Song, hymn (υμνος)

760 In sacrifice (θυματι)

760 The south; the south wind (ο νοτος)

761

762 Full knowledge (περιφανεια)

762 Speed (σπουδη)

763 Lightning-flash (στεροπη)

763 Naked (γυμνος)

763 Mediator (μεσιτης)

763 Pearl (μαργαριτης)

763 Anarchy (αναρχια)

764 Lightning (αστεροπη)

765 Erinys, the god of vengeance; destruction, revenge; fury (Ερινυς)

766 Warlike (ενναλιος)

767 The sacrifice, the victims (τα εντομα)

767 Weak; inferior (υποδεης)

768

769 Will; mind, thought (φρονημα)

769 Feminine (γυναικειος)

769 Pythian; Delphian; epithet of Apollo (Πυθιος)

770 Vow, prayer (κατευγμα)

770 Sea (ποντος)

APPENDIX II

770 Whole, perfect (ουλος)
770 Voice, speech (οψ)
770 Winged (πτεροεις)
771 Light; life; sunlight (θαος)
771 Eight hundred
(οκτακοσιοι)
771 Winged (ποτανος)
772 Accuser (κατηγορος)
772 Failure, defeat (σφαλμα)
773 Filth (σκυβαλον)
773 Wet, moist (υγρος)
773 Round, curved (γυρος)
773 Justice (δικαιοσυνη)
773 Sphinx (σφιγξ)
774 Goat-footed (αιγιπους)
774 Slave (δουλος)
775 Messenger of the gods; guide
(διακτορος)
775 Knight (ιππευς)
775 Heart (στερνον)
775 South-east; south-east wind
(ευρος)
776 Darkness; twilight (κνεφας)
776 Hymen, the god of marriage
(Υμεναιος)
777 The cross (σταυρος*)
778 A sound (ηχος)
778 Winged (ποτηνος)
779 Unsaid; unknown; secret,
holy; abominable (2
Corinthians 12:4)
(αρρητος)
779 Kamephis, Egyptian sage
appearing in the *Hermetica*
(Καμηφις)
780 Serpent (οφις)
780 Many; mighty (πολυς)
780 Lord of the sea; of the sea
(ποντιος)
780 Gateway (πυλος)

780 Corn, wheat; food (σιτος)
780 Hole (τορμος)
780 Fear (τρομος)
780 The Gnostic goddess Sophia;
wisdom (Σοφια)
781 Meditation (συννοια)
781 Light, splendor (φεγγος)
781 The sphinx (η Σφιγξ)
782 Path (στιβος)
783
784 Eaten, consumed (εδεστος)
785
786 Proper (Hebrews 11:23)
(αστειος)
787 Heart; understanding
(στηθος)
787 Magic (μαγευτικη)
788 Beggar (προικτης)
789 Countless (αναριθμητος)
789 The myth (ο μυθος)
789 The soul (ο θυμος)
790 Husband (παρακοιτης)
790 Tamed, tame (τιθασος)
791 Keeping silence
(ευστομος*)
791 Wanton, lustful (μαχλον)
791 Three hundred
(τριακοσιοι)
791 New, fresh (ποταινιος)
792 Wife (παρακοιτις)
792 To utter (Acts 2:4)
(αποφθεγγομαι)
793
794 Path; advance (προσοδος)
795 Hephaestus, Vulcan
(Ηφαιστος*)
795 War, battle (πτολεμος)
795 Epithet of Zeus (πολιευς)
796
797

248

798

799 Transgression; wantonness
(υπερβασια)

799 To sound forth (εξηχεομαι)

799 Scourge (φραγελλιον)

800 *Omega*; the End, the Last
(Ω)

800 Lord; god (κυριος)

800 Faith (πιστις)

800 Swine (συς)

800 Sleep (υπνος)

800 The Great Power; title of the
Gnostic, Simon Magus (η
Δυναμις Μεγαλη)

800 Of the world, of the universe
(κοσμου)

801 Dove (περιστερα)

801 Rope (σπαρτον)

801 *Alpha* + *Omega*; Beginning
and End; First and Last (A +
Ω)

802

803

804 Visible, manifest (εμφανης)

804 Danger (κινδυνος)

805 To sing (Revelation 5:9)
(αδω)

805 Delightful (τερπνος)

806 Gog (Revelation 20:8) (Γωγ)

806 Divine Wisdom; divine
Sophia (θεια σοφια)

807 Infinite, endless
(απεραντος)

807 Four (τεσσαρα)

808 Knavish (φηλος)

808 Ego, I (εγω)

809 Surname of Bacchus (Αττης)

809 Blood, gore (λυθρος)

809 Veil (παραπετασμα)

809 The dove (η περιστερα)

810 Wand (ριψ)

810 Disorder (τυρβη)

810 Beloved (φιλος)

810 Name of Aphrodite
(Κυπρις)

810 To gather together in one
(Ephesians 1:10) (ανακε–
φαλαιοομαι)

810 To say (βαζω)

810 Io! The rapture-cry of the
Greeks (ΙΩ)

811 IAO, Gnostic name of God
(*Pistis Sophia*) (ΙΑΩ)

811 Needle (ραφις)

811 Breast (μαστος)

811 To fart (βδεω)

811 To perceive, to know (αιω)

812 Dark; blind (αμαυρος)

812 Dearest (κηδιστος)

812 Sphere (σφαιρα)

812 Song, poem (ωδη)

812 To live (βιω)

812 Magic wheel; whirling
motion; rhombus (ρυμβος)

813

814 West; sunset (δυσις)

814 The Word of Power
(Hebrews 4:12) (ο ενεργης
λογος)

814 The Divine Wisdom; the
divine Sophia (η θεια
σοφια)

815 Life; Eve (*Septuagint*) (ζωη)

815 Force, power (παρασκευη)

816 Five hundred
(πεντακοσιοι)

816 Loving (στεργης)

816 Mercy (ελεημοσυνη)

817 Penalty (θωη)

817 Without love (αστεργης)

817 Reverent (ευσεβες)
818 Thoth, the Egyptian god of wisdom and magic (Θωθ)
818 Enduring, magic (τολμηρος)
818 Wanton; luxurious (υβριστικος*)
819 To see (ειδω)
819 Rhythm, order (ρυθμος)
820 Strong, mighty (πυκνος)
820 Way; direction (τροπος)
820 Reverent (ευσεβης)
820 The sacrifice (το θυμα)
820 To overcome, force (βιαζω)
820 The sphere (η σφαιρα)
821 To doubt (διζω)
821 Daughter (θυγατηρ)
821 First matter; element; letter (στοιχειον*)
822 To consecrate (αγιαζω)
822 Spheres (σφαιραι)
823 The life (η ζωη)
824 Free (ελευθερος)
825 The stone, the rock (ο πετρος)
825 Sanctuary (αδυτον)
825 New (Mark 2:21) (αγναφος)
825 Cloud, heaven (νεφος)
826 To come; to return (ερχο–μαι)
827 Headless (ακεφαλος)
827 Spell, charm (γοητευμα)
828 Shining (ην–οψ)
828 Scepter, staff (σκηπτρον)
828 Exceeding great (2 Peter 1:4) (μεγιστος)
829 Splendor, glory (λαμπροτης)
830 Folly (ματαιοτης)

831 Phallus (φαλλος)
831 Rage, fury; Bacchic frenzy (λυσσα)
831 Pyramid (πυραμις)
831 Of death (θανατου)
832 Traitor (προδοτης)
832 *Alpha* and *Omega*; Beginning and End; First and Last (A και Ω)
832 Beloved by God (θεοφιλης)
833
834 Twelve (δωδεκα)
834 Horned (κεραστης)
834 Loved by Zeus (διιφιλος)
834 Victim, sacrifice (σφαγιον)
834 To receive (δεχεσθαι)
834 Delivering, freeing (ελευθεριος)
835 To yield, retire (εικω)
835 Shining; glorious (φαιδιμος)
836 Pyramids (πυραμεις)
837 The delights (τα τερπνα)
838
839 To laugh (γελαω)
840 Sword (ξιφος)
840 Watcher, guard (ουρος)
840 Microcosm (μικροκοσμος)
840 A setting free (λυσις)
841 *Alpha* + *Mu* +*Omega*; Beginning, Middle and End (A + M + Ω)
841 To seek, wish (μαω)
841 One in Three (μονας εν τριαδι)
841 Three in One (τριας εν μοναδι)
842 Wound, defeat (τραυμα)
842 Fear (φοβος)
843

844 Sad, sorry (δυσκηδης)
844 Oedipus (Οιδιπους)
844 The two (το δυο)
844 The slave (ο δουλος)
845 Palace, temple (δωμα)
845 My God! (ελωι)
845 To strive (2 Timothy 2:5) (αθλεω)
846 Lightning, thunderbolt (κεραυνος)
846 Phantom (σκιαγραφια)
846 Mytilene (Μυτιληνη)
847 West; darkness; reign of darkness (ζοφος)
847 To charm, enchant; to blind, seduce (θελγω)
848 King, prince (βασιλευς)
848 Prudence (πινυτη)
849 To will; to have power (εθελω)
849 Most holy; abominable (εξαγιστος)
849 Form, figure; nature (σχημα)
849 The ineffable (ο αρρητος)
849 Letter name of *omega*; the End; the Last (ωμεγα)
849 The Great Universe (μεγας κοσμος)
849 The Perfect Man (ο τελειος ανηρ)
849 The Three in One (η τριας εν μοναδι)
849 The One in Three (η μονας εν τριαδι)
850 My God! (ελωει)
850 Arrow (οιστος)
850 The serpent (ο οφις)
850 Dirt, filth (ρυπος)

850 Eleusis (Ελευσις)
850 Of fire (πυρος)
850 To vomit (Revelation 3:16) (εμεω)
851 Prophet, priest (προμαντις)
851 Three-headed (τρικρανος)
851 Narcissus (Ναρκισσος)
851 Transitory (προσκαιρος)
852 Letter name of *omega*; the End; the Last (ωμηγα)
852 Thirty (τριακοντα)
852 Female slave (δμωη)
852 Name of Apollo; bright, pure (φοιβος)
852 The immortal (το αθανα– τον)
853 Tower (πυργος)
854 Assembly; combat, contest; labor (αγων)
854 Subject to trial (Romans 3:19) (υποδικος)
855
856 Silent, mute (ανεω)
856 To call (καλεω)
857
858 Initiation (μυησις)
858 Half (ημισυς)
859 An offering (παροχη)
859 Thrice-great (τρισμεγας)
860 Faithful (πιστος)
860 Night; nether world (σκοτος)
860 Simple; smooth; naked (ψιλον)
861 Deep sleep, trance (κωμα)
861 The being first-born (πρεσ– βυγενεια)
861 Exceedingly mighty (υπερμηκης)
861 Night-hawk (χαλκις)

861 Seraphim (σεραφειμ)

861 Aeon; eternity (Αιων)

861 Phallic (φαλλικος)

861 The Egyptian god Apophis (Αποφις)

861 Assurance, confirmation (βεβαιωμα)

862 Presence (παρουσια)

862 Symbol (συμβολον)

862 Priesthood (ιερατευμα)

863 To charm, fascinate; to seduce (κηλεω)

864 Altar (θυσιαστηριον*)

864 Joiner's square; corner-stone (γωνια)

864 Holy of holies; of the saints (αγιων)

864 Jerusalem (Ιερουσαλημ)

864 Temple of the gods (Θεων)

864 Throne of Abraxas (Θρονος Αβραξας)

865 Letter name of *epsilon* (εψιλον)

865 Girdle; loins (ζωνη)

865 To adorn, glorify (αγαλλω)

865 Beyond measure (περισσος)

865 An angel of Satan (2 Corinthians 7:7) (αγγελος Σατανα)

866 Adonai, Hebrew name of God (Αδωναι)

866 Feast of Adonis (Αδωνια)

867 Dagger (εγχειριδιον)

867 Passionate, wanton (υπερβιος)

867 Lord, master (δεσποτης)

868 Fear; passion (πτοησις)

868 Loving knowledge (φιλομαθης)

869 Inborn; natural (συγγενης)

869 Cloak (φαινολης)

869 To lead away (εξαγω)

870 Shining; fiery (αιθων)

870 Journey; army (στολος)

870 Reed (φλοος)

871 Chaos (Χαος)

871 Pain, sorrow (αχος)

871 Secret, dark (σκοταιος)

871 Web; cloak (φαρος)

871 To purify (αγνιζω)

871 Against one's will (ακων)

872

873 Majesty (σεμνοτης)

874

875 Sword, knife (φασγανον)

875 Mirror (εσοπτρον)

876 Arrow (τοξευμα)

876 Eve of the Sabbath (προσ–αββατον)

877 Whirling (στροφας*)

877 Child (βρεφος)

878 Flaming, blazing (φλογεος)

878 Spear, lance; sword (εγχος)

878 The Graeco-Egyptian god Hermanubis, Hermes-Anubis (Ερμανουβις)

878 Thunderbolt (σκηπτος)

879 Epithet of Apollo (Δελφινιος)

880 Sorrow; burden (αχθος)

880 Companion; lover (ο φιλος)

880 Column, pillar (κιων)

880 Solid (στερεος)

880 Of union (ζυγου)

881 Formed, molded (πλαστος)

881 Flashing (στεροψ*)

882 To live; to preserve life (βιοω)

883 Pillar (παραστας)

883 Inexcusable (Romans 1:20) (αναπολογητος)

884 Chariot (διφρος)
884 Red (ερυθρος)
884 Fifty (πεντηκοντα)
885 Leo, lion (λεων)
885 Barren (στειρος)
885 Image (εικων)
885 To move, change, continue, begin (κινεω)
886 The Principle of the Father (Δοξα Πατρος)
886 Judgment (δικαιωμα)
887
888 Jesus (Ιησους)
888 I am the Life (η ζωη ειμι)
888 Hated by the gods (δυσθεος)
888 Excessively mighty (υπερμενης)
889 Boaster (Romans 1:20) (αλαζων)
890 Massacre; dagger (φονος)
890 Olympus (Ολυμπος)
890 Odyssey (Οδυσσεια)
890 Dust (κονιορτος)
891 To smite (παιω)
891 Heaven; Uranus (Ουρανος)
891 Most excellent (φεριστος*)
892 Dissolution, end; start (αναλυσις)
893 Bacchus (βακχος)
894 Mark, sign; knowledge (γνωμα)
895 All-devouring; epithet of Pan (παμφαγος)
895 To divide (νεμω)
895 Inspiration of God (2 Timothy 3:16) (Θεοπνευστος*)
896 Feast of Aphrodite (Αφροδισια)
897 Incantation; spell (επωδη)

898 To make new (καινιζω)
898 The seven stars (οι ζ αστερες)
899 Amazon (Αμαζων)
899 Ill-will; jealousy (φθονος)
899 Capacious (υποδεξιος)
899 The nothing; the zero (το ουδεν)
900 Letter name of rho (ρω)
900 Bloody (φοινος)
900 The union (το ζυγον)
901 Letter name of stau (σταυ)
901 Iacchus, Bacchus (Ιακχος)
901 Care; season; prime of life (ωρα)
901 Atys (Ατυς)
901 Mind, understanding (γνωμη)
901 The death (τον θανατον)
902 Mad (παρανους)
903 Bacchus (βακχιος)
903 Experienced, knowing (δαημων)
904 Ferryman (πορθμευς)
904 Continual, constant (ενδελεχες)
905 Guardian spirit; demon; fate; genius (with Socrates) (δαιμων)
905 Marriage-bed (λεχος)
905 To flow (ρεω)
905 Freedman (απελευθερος)
905 Demiurge (Δημιουργος)
905 Wide, broad (ευρυ)
905 With the just (τοις δικαιοις)
906 Four (τετρας)
906 Ashes (τεφρα)
907 Continual, constant (ενδελεχης)

908 To call up, summon (ανακαλεω)

908 Vault, crypt (κρυπτη)

908 Archer; saver (ρυτηρ)

908 Leisure (σχολη)

908 Terror (φυζα)

908 Heliopolis, City of the Sun (Ηλιου πολις)

908 Suffering, patient (τλητος)

909 To sacrifice, offer; to do, act (ερδω)

909 Lover of boys (παιδεραστης)

909 True, real (σαφης)

910 Fiery (πυρινος)

910 Bloody (φοινιος)

911 Axle, wheel (αξων)

911 Backbone (ραξις)

911 Joy, grace (χαρις)

911 The Hours (Ωραι)

911 To raise (αιρω)

911 Wholly, utterly (αχρις)

911 Center (ομφαλος)

911 Position (στασις)

911 Drop (ψιας)

911 Bloom of youth (ωρια)

912 To do, effect; to sacrifice (ρεζω)

913 Rest (ερωη)

913 Madness (παραφρονια)

913 Mean; weak; bad (χερης)

914

915 To unite, join (ζευγνυμι)

915 Beyond destiny (υπερμορον)

915 To account righteous (δικαιοω)

916

917

918 Poppy; poppy-juice (μηκων)

918 Moses (Μουσες)

918 The king (ο βασιλευς)

919 Swift (λαιφηρος)

919 The grace (η χαρις)

919 The word (το φημα)

920 To give forth, burst forth; to yield (αναδιδωμι)

920 Will (βουλησις)

920 Egg (ωον)

921 Cover, lid; potion (πωμα)

921 The whole (συμπας)

921 Copper disc (χαλκος)

921 Rod, staff; law, canon (κανων)

922

923 To awaken; to excite; to raise (εγειρω)

923 To yield, empty oneself, surrender oneself (ενδιδωμι)

924

925 Secret, dark (σκοτεινος)

925 Before, in front; earlier; superior (προτερος)

926 The voice, the oracle (το φημη)

927 Creature, beast; image (ζωον)

928 Wantonness (στρηνος)

929 Near; at hand (σχεδον)

929 Ineffable; secret (απορρητος)

930 Practical wisdom (φρονις)

930 Phoenix (φοινικος)

930 To come (ερχεσθαι)

930 In void (*Corpus Hermeticum*, II 10) (εν κενω)

930 Egg (ωιον)

931 Immutable (Hebrews 4:18) (αμεταθετος)

931 To threaten (Acts 4:17) (απειλεω)

931 The Aeon (*Corpus Hermeticum*, XI 2) (ο Αιων)

931 Ambrosia and nectar; food and drink of the gods (αμβροσια και νεκταρ)

932 Veil; covering (καλυπτρα)

933

934

935 Purple (φοινικεος)

936 Ecstasy (εκστασις)

937 Goat-footed (τραγοσκελης)

938 Compassionate (συμπαθης)

938 Tribe (φυλη)

938 Avenger; Alastor (αλαστωρ*)

939

940 Certain; true (Acts 21:24) (ασφαλης)

940 Destroyer (δηλημων)

940 Receptacle; chariot (οχος)

941 Io Pan! Hail Pan! (Ιω Παν)

941 Wanton, lustful (μαχλος)

942

943 Warrior (πολεμιστης)

943 Rest (Revelation 4:8) (αναπαυσις)

943 To mock; to deceive (εμπαιζω)

944 Thrice-greatest; epithet of Thoth (τρισμεγιστος*)

945 To fear (οκνεω)

945 To receive (εισδεχομαι)

946 The Spirit (1 Corinthians 15:1) (το Πνευμα)

947

948 To purify (καθαριζω)

948 Hermaphrodite (ανδρογυνος)

948 Mercy, pity (ελεητυς)

948 Deceiver (ηπεροπευς)

948 Force, might (ρωμη)

949 Destruction, death (φθορος)

949 Veil (καταπετασμα)

950 Red (πυρρος)

950 Of Thoth, Hermes (Ερμεω)

950 Of All (*Corpus Hermeticum*, I 27) (ολων)

950 The fire (το πυρ)

950 The udder (το ουθαρ)

951 Circle; edge (αντυς)

951 To summon, invoke (επικαλεω)

951 Folly (μωρια)

951 The reality (το υπαρ)

952 Bloodless (αναιμων)

953 Destroyer (διαλυτης)

954

955 Son (κελωρ)

956 Anointing (αλειψις)

957 My ecstasy (εκστασις* εμου)

958 Old man (γερων)

959 Oppression (θλιψις)

959 Staff; message (σκυταλη)

960 The circle (το κυκλον)

960 Marriage; a mixing together (συμμιξις)

960 The river Styx (Στυξ)

961 To desire (μενεαινω)

961 Adulterous (μοιχαλις)

961 The heaven; the circle (ο ουρανος)

961 Winged (πτεροεσσα)

962 Cup; bowl (κισσυβιον)

962 Cup; bowl (τρυβλιον)

962 To lead astray (πλαναω)

962 Perfect Trinity (Τριας Τελεια)

963 Resurrection (αναστασις)

963 Art; work of art (τεχνη)

964 Silence in ritual; good repute (ευφημια)

965 To do, make, cause, create (ποιεω)

965 The ecstasy of me (η εκστασις* εμου)

966

967 To lift up; to prophesy; to accept; to destroy (αναιρεω)

967 Foundation; matter (υποστασις*)

968 Mad (φρηνοβλαβης)

969 Chief shepherd (2 Peter 5:4) (αρχιποιμην)

969 Image; vision; idol (ειδωλον)

969 High Priest (Μεγας Ιερευς)

970 Of earth (χοικος)

971 Self; alone (αυτος)

971 To understand (οραω)

971 Ambition (φιλοτιμια)

972 A vanishing (αφανισις)

973 Exorcist (εξορκιστης)

973 Hermaphrodite; bisexual (αρρενοθηλυς)

974 Foundation (υποθεσις)

974 To deceive (2 Corinthians 4:2) (δολοω)

975 Serpent, dragon (Revelation 12:9) (δρακων)

975 To be wanton (στρηνιαω*)

975 The Demiurge (ο Δημιουργος)

975 The perfected; the end (το τελος)

976

977

978 Nourishment (τροφη)

979 Thyrsus, the wreathed staff of the Bacchantes (θυρσος)

980 Innocent (αθψος)

980 Eye; vision (οψις)

980 Six and fifty (εξ και πεντηκοντα)

981 Of wisdom (σοφιας)

981 The axis (ο αξων)

982 Ancient, primeval (αρχαιος)

983

984

985

986 Left; of the left hand (αριστερος)

986 Heavenly (επουρανιος)

986 Dangerous, difficult (χαλεπος)

986 Unprofitable (Matthew 25:30) (αχρειος)

987 Old; old man (πρεσβυς)

988

989 Hardship, misery (μοχθος)

990 Hammer (τυκος)

991 To enter, go into (εισ–πορευομαι)

991 Hollow vessel; ship (σκαφος)

991 Watcher, guard (φυλαξ)

992 Enjoyment (Hebrews 11:25) (απολαυσις)

993 Sustenance (διατροφη)

993 Accursed (καταρατος)

993 Aphrodite, Venus (Αφροδιτη)

993 Perfect Word (λογος τελειος)

994 Master (σοφιστης*)

995 Begetter (τοκευς)

996 Joyous (ευγαθητος)

997

998 Bride; maiden; nymph, nereid (νυμφη)

998 The Virgin of the World, a

figure in Gnostic theogony (Κορη Κοσμου)

999 My wrath (Hebrews 3:11) (τη οργη μου)

999 Ineffable place (το αρρητον)

999 The ineffable; the secret (ο απορρητος)

999 Ineffable God (Θεος ανεκλαλητος)

999 Restriction (κατοχη)

1000 Nail (τυλος)

1000 Of the Lord, of God (Κυριου)

1000 Thus (ως)

1001

1002

1003 To renew (Colossians 3:10) (ανακαινοω)

1004 Work of art (τεχνημα)

1004 Dionysus (Διονυσος)

1004 Mind of Zeus (anagram of Dionysus) (Νους Διος)

1004 The baptism (το βαπτισμα)

1005 Dawn; east (εως)

1005 To gain by toil; to suffer (πονεω)

1005 Swift-footed (χαλαργος)

1005 The deliverer (ο ρυομενος)

1005 Nero (Νερων)

1005 Killed his own mother (of Nero; Suetonius, *Twelve Caesars*, XXXIX 2) (ιδιαν μητερα απεκτεινε)

1005 Epithet of Dionysus (Υευς)

1006 The bride (η νυμφη)

1006 The Virgin of the World, a figure in Gnostic theogony (η Κορη Κοσμου)

1006 Votive, involved in prayer (ευκταιος)

1007 To worship (σεβω)

1008 Teacher (παιδευτης)

1008 Prayer (προστροπη)

1008 Belly (προτμησις)

1008 Archer (τοξοτης)

1008 Dawn; east (ηως)

1008 The avenger (ο αλαστωρ*)

1009 Dawn, twilight (αμφιλυκη)

1009 End (ποδεων)

1009 Earthly (χθονιος)

1010 Wonder-tree (σιλλικυπριον)

1010 Confusion (ταραχη)

1010 Naked; simple; smooth (ψιλος)

1010 The number of me (ο αριθμος μου)

1011 Four (τεσσαρες)

1011 To change, alter (αλλοιοω)

1011 Oppression; pride (βαρυτης)

1011 Communion; intercourse (κοινωνια)

1011 In three parts (τριχα)

1011 Apollo (Απολλω)

1011 Wide (Matthew 7:13) (πλατυς)

1011 Lukewarm (Revelation 3:16) (χλιαρος)

1012 Tomb (τυμβος)

1013 Prayer; vow; wish; curse (ευχη)

1013 Hosts, armies (σαβαωθ)

1013 To be godless (Jude 15) (ασεβεω)

1013 Archangel (αρχαγγελος)

1014 Seal; sign (1 Corinthians 9:2) (σφραγις)

1014 Straight, true (ευθυς)

1015 Real, true (ετυμος)

1015 To dare (θαρρεω)

1015 Monster (πελωρ)

1015 Ripe; gentle; a friend (πεπων)

1016 To yield (παρεικω)

1016 To shut to (Luke 13:25) (αποκλειω)

1017 Absolute power (δεσπο–συνη)

1018 Persephone (Περσεφονη)

1018 Interpretation (ερμηνευσις)

1019

1020

1021 Union, pair (συζυγια)

1021 Apostle (αποστολος)

1021 Mighty (κρατυς)

1021 The prayer; the vow; the wish (η ευχη)

1022 Without a leader (αναρχος)

1023 To go (βασκω)

1023 Communion (μετοχη)

1024 Baseness (ταπεινοτης)

1025 Wanton (υπερκοπος)

1026

1027 Fivefold (πεντα–πλασιος)

1028 Winged (ποτητος)

1029

1030 Encounter, visit; prayer (εντευξις)

1031 Bacchic frenzy; rage (λυττα)

1032

1033

1034 Sodomite (1 Corinthians 6:9) (αρσενοκοιτης)

1035 A sending (πεμψις)

1035 Swift; excellent (σπουδαιος)

1036 Pandora (Πανδωρα)

1037 Downcast, despised (κατηφης)

1037 Abundance; satiety (πληθωρη)

1037 Conciousness (συνειδησις)

1038 To veil (σκιαζω)

1038 Moonless (σκοτο–μηνιος)

1038 Laughter (γελως)

1039 Sacrificer (θυοσκοος)

1040 Wise (σοφος)

1040 Microcosm (Μικρος Κοσμος)

1040 Macrocosm (Κοσμος ο ολος)

1040 The goddess Night, daughter of Chaos (Νυκτος)

1040 Everywhere (πανταχη)

1041 Body, existence, life (σωμα)

1041 Psalm (ψαλμος)

1041 Witness (μαρτυς)

1042 Nonsense (φλυαρια)

1043 Blame (ψογος)

1044 A slave (δμως)

1045 Wall (τειχιον)

1045 Daily (Matthew 6:11) (επιουσιος)

1046

1047

1048 End, death (τελευτη)

1049 The thyrsus, the wreathed staff of the Bacchantes (ο θυρσος)

1050 Stroke; image; type (τυπος)

1050 Race; tribe; sex (φυλον)

1051 Rope (καλως)

1051 Highest; last (υπατος)

1052

1053 First-born (πρεσβυγενης)

1053 Saith the Lord (Hebrews X 30) (λεγει Κυριου)

1054 Unknown (αγνως)
1055
1056
1057
1058 The treasure (ο θησαυρος)
1059 Fatherhood (πατροτης)
1059 Pleroma; fullness (Πληρωμα)
1059 Great Paraclete, Great Comforter (μεγας παρακλητος)
1059 The Great Circle; the Mighty Eye (ο μεγας κυκλος)
1059 Mysteries (μυστηρια)
1060 I bring to you (σε αναγω)
1060 Zion (Σιων)
1060 Desirous; lover, adherent (επιθυμητης)
1060 Rope, cord (σχοινιον)
1060 Spell (φιλτρον)
1060 Priests of Zeus (τομουροι)
1061 All-productive (παμφορος)
1061 Apollo (Απολλων)
1062 The Ages (Αιωνας)
1062 The True Word (ο λογος ιθυς)
1063 Splendor (φαντασια)
1064 Egypt (Αιγυπτος)
1064 To have power (σθενω)
1064 *Alpha + Alpha* (αλφα + αλφα)
1065 Understanding, knowledge (συνεσις)
1065 Adonis (Αδωνις)
1065 Ignorance (1 Peter 2:15) (αγνωσια)
1066
1067
1068

1069 The viewpoint (η αποψις)
1070 Manifold (Ephesians 3:10) (πολυποικιλος)
1070 Not (ουχ)
1071 Bull, ox (ταυρος)
1071 Tomb; astonishment (ταφος)
1071 Division (φαρσος)
1071 Nakedness (γυμνοτης)
1072 Fourteen (τεσσαρες–και–δεκα)
1072 Unutterable; horrible; huge (αφατος)
1072 Abyss (βυσσος)
1073 Abyss; bottomless pit (Revelation 9:11) (αβυσσος)
1073 Buttock (γλουτος)
1073 Bisexual, hermaphrodite; name of God (*Corpus Hermeticum,* III 21) (Αρσηνοθηλυς)
1073 Auspicious, favorable (ευφη–μον)
1074 Prophecy (Revelation 1:3) (προφητεια)
1075 Of Dawn (Εωος)
1076 Free; sacred (αφετος)
1077 Alive, vital (ζωος)
1078 To sift (Luke 22:31) (σινι–αζω)
1079
1080 Lance, spear (ξυστον)
1080 Threefold (τρισσος)
1080 The Holy Spirit (το Πνευμα Αγιον)
1081 Undesired; involuntary (αβουλητος)
1081 Lord, master (ορχαμος)

1081 Way (τροχια)

1082 The prophesy (η προφετια)

1083

1084 Lovely (ευηρατος)

1084 Heart (σπλαγχνον)

1084 To bewitch (Galatians 3:1) (βασκαινω)

1085 IAO SABAO; God of Hosts (*Papyri Graeci Magicae*) (ΙΑΩ ΣΑΒΑΟ)

1085 Fear (ορρωδια)

1086 Four hundred (τετρακοσιοι)

1086 Blessed (ευλογητος)

1087

1088

1089 All-seeing (παντοπτης)

1089 Dead (φθιτος)

1090 Answer; hypocrisy (υποκρισις)

1090 The god Chronos, Saturn; time (Χρονος)

1090 Thorn (2 Corinthians 12:7) (σκολοψ)

1090 Secret, mystic (μυστικον)

1091 United (συναορος)

1092

1093

1094

1095 Temple of Athena (Παρθενων)

1095 To make war (πολεμοω)

1096

1097

1098 Top, summit; crown of the head (κορυφη)

1099

1100

1101 Joke (σκωμμα)

1102

1103 Vulture (γυψ)

1104 Earthy (επιχθονιος)

1104 Master (επιστατης)

1105 Eros, Cupid; love, desire (Ερως)

1105 Wanderer (μεταναστης)

1105 Warlike (φιλοπολεμος)

1105 Wide (ευρυς)

1106 Precarious (σφαλερος)

1107

1108 Hero; demigod (ηρως)

1109

1110 Sacrificial (θυστας)

1110 Wise (πινυτος)

1110 Raw, savage (ωμος)

1110 The Microcosm (ο Μικρος Κοσμος)

1110 The Macrocosm (ο Κοσμος ο ολος)

1111 Letter name of *iota*; a jot (ιωτα)

1111 Absolute power; tyranny (τυραννις)

1112 Altar; step (βωμος)

1112 In every direction (παντα–χοι)

1113

1114 Sweat (Luke 22:2) (ιδρως)

1115 To dare (θαρσεω)

1115 Poor (Luke 21:2) (πενιχρος)

1116

1117

1118 Love (φιλοτης)

1119 Of Mytilene (Μυτιληναιος)

1119 The teaching of God (η διδαχη Θεου)

1120 To seek (ζητεω)

1121

1122 Of double form; epithet of Bacchus (διφυες)

1123
1124 The most high (υπιστη*)
1125 To bring down; to lead to a place (καταγω)
1126
1127 Harmony (ευαρμοστια)
1128
1129 To abide by one's oath (εμπεδορκεω)
1130 Unknown (αγνωστος*)
1131
1132
1133 Night (ευφρωνη)
1134 Chance (συγκυρια)
1135 All-seeing; manifest (εποψιος)
1135 An observation (σκεψις)
1136 The river Alpheus (Αλφευς)
1136 Mid-heaven (μεσουρανος)
1136 One in four (μονας εν τετραδι)
1137
1138 Reason, pretence (σκηψις)
1138 Will; thought (φρονησις)
1139 Womb (δελφυς)
1139 Of laughter (γελωτα)
1140 Cup-bearer (οινοχοος)
1140 To initiate into the Mysteries; to end (τελεω)
1141 Eternal (αιωνιος)
1141 Destruction (συντριμμα)
1142 The Delphic Oracle (λογος Πυθιος)
1142 Do what thou wilt (αγε το θελημα σου)
1142 Restoration; perfection (καταρτισις)
1142 Web (υφασμα)
1142 The abyss (ο βυσσος)
1143 The abyss (ο αβυσσος)

1144 Violent; mighty (σφοδρος)
1145 Excellent (περιουσιος)
1146 Centaur (κενταυρος)
1146 The will (η φρονησις)
1147 Putrefaction (σηπεδων)
1147 Infinite essence (ουσια απειρος)
1147 Heavenly virgin (παρθενος ουρανια)
1148 One initiated (μυστης)
1148 To banish (αγηλατεω)
1149
1150 Treasure; power (πλουτος)
1150 Beloved (ευφιλες)
1151 Pure, without spot (Hebrews 9:4) (αμωμος)
1152
1153 Beloved (ευφιλης)
1154
1155
1156
1157 Warrior; warlike (μαχητης)
1158
1159 Magician; a refrain (επωδος)
1160 Staff (σκιπων)
1161 Pretext; cause; prediction (προφασις)
1161 Staff (σκυλατις)
1161 Without law (Romans 2:12) (ανομως)
1162
1163 Words of ill omen; lamentation (δυσφημια)
1164 Son of God (Υιος Θεου)
1164 The Egyptian goddess Nephthys (Νεφθυς)
1165 To accomplish, bring to an end (εκτελεω)
1166
1167

1168

1169 Union (συνδεσμος)

1170 Secret, hidden, occult
(κρυπτος)

1170 The Egyptian god Horus
(Ωρος)

1171 Swiftness (ταχος)

1171 Royal, kingly; lord, master
(τυραννος)

1171 Watch, guard (φρουρα)

1172 Teacher (παιδαγωγος)

1173 The river Styx (Στυγος)

1174 Slain (ανδροφθορος)

1175

1176

1177 Sender of lightning
(στεροπηγερετα)

1177 Evening wind (ζυφος)

1178 Secret rite, mystery
(μυστηριον)

1179

1180 Descendent; sprout (μοσχος)

1180 To accept (προσδεχομαι)

1181 To study, practice (μελεταω)

1181 Warlike (στρατιος)

1181 Incorruptible, immortal
(αφθαρτος)

1182 To first trust (Ephesians
1:12) (προελπιζω)

1183 To delude (απαταω)

1184

1185 Fortress (τειχος)

1185 Vivid, animated (ζωηρος)

1186

1187

1188 Useless (τηυσιος)

1189 The beginning (υπαρχη)

1189 Hexagonal; sextile
(εξαγωνος)

1190 Threefold (τριπλους)

1190 Eight (οκτω)

1191

1192

1193 Ancient, legendary
(παλαιφατος)

1193 To unite (συμμιγνυμι)

1194

1195 Beloved (στερκτος)

1195 The cloud, the heaven (το
νεφος)

1196 Sorcery (γοητευσις)

1197 Sorceress (γοητευτρια)

1198 Thyrsus-bearer
(ναρθηκοφορος)

1198 Beloved (προσφιλης)

1199

1200 Pillar (στυλος)

1200 Reed; rope, cord (σχοινος)

1200 Entire; sure (σως)

1200 To water (υω)

1200 Light, lamp (λυχνον)

1201 Evil, mean; sorry (φαυλος)

1201 Mightiest; best (κρατιστος)

1201 Hammer (σφυρα)

1202

1203

1204 To sink; to enter (δυω)

1205 To singe, dry up (ευω)

1206

1207

1208 To make peace (Colossians
1:20) (ειρηνοποιεω)

1209 To sacrifice, burn, slay (θυω)

1209 Torch-bearer (δαδουχος)

1210 Triumphant (υπερκυδας)

1210 Foolish (μωρος)

1211

1212 To perceive; to illuminate
(αυγαζω)

1212 Giver (δωτηρ)

1213
1214
1215
1216 Prince, hero (αριστευς)
1216 Everywhere (εκασταχοθι)
1217
1218
1219 Fish; the Sibylline Acrostic
(Augustine, *City of God*)
(ιχθυς)
1219 Tragedy (τραγωδια)
1219 Watch, guard (φρουρημα)
1219 The *Omega*; the End; the
Last (το ωμεγα)
1219 The Word of the Father (ο
Λογος εκ Πατρος)
1219 Joy and gladness (χαρα και
αγαλλιασις)
1219 Poseidon, Neptune
(Ποσειδων)
1219 Hexagonal; sextile
(εξαγωνικος)
1220 To perfect (τελειοω)
1220 Sweet savor, perfume
(Ephesians 5:2) (ευωδια)
1220 With the foolish (μωροις)
1221 Ruin; corpse (πτωμα)
1221 Wonderful (Isaiah 9:6)
(θαυμαστος)
1222
1223 Abominated (στυγνος)
1223 Favorable (ευφημος)
1224 The creation of God (κτισις
Θεου)
1224 Fishes (ιχθυες)
1224 The net (το δικτυον)
1224 Sea-nurtured (αλιοτρεφης)
1225
1226
1227

1228 An undertaking, beginning;
attack (επιχειρησις)
1229 Bound together (συνδετος)
1230 Thought; reflection
(φροντις)
1230 Confirmation (Philippians
1:7) (βεβαιωσις)
1231 Swift (ταχινος)
1231 The confirmation (το
βεβαιωμα)
1232 Foundation of the World
(Καταβολη Κοσμου)
1233 To prepare (Revelation 19:7)
(ετοιμαζω)
1234 To keep secret (κευθω)
1234 Twelve (δυωδεκα)
1234 Tongue, speech (γλωσσα)
1235 To accomplish; to perform
ritual (επιτελεω)
1236
1237
1238 The Power of God (η
Εξουσια Θεου)
1238 The confirmation (η
βεβαιωσις)
1239
1240 Secret, mystical (μυστικος)
1240 To be closed, be shut, cease
(μυω)
1240 Hippolytus (Ιππολυτος)
1241 The Chaos (το χαος)
1241 The tongue (η γλωσσα)
1243
1244 Hierophant, initiating priest
(ιεροφαντης)
1245 To initiate into the Mysteries
(μευω)
1246 Strong, mighty (ρωμαλεος)
1247 Killer of Argus; epithet of
Hermes (Αργει–φοντης)

1247 To suck (μυζω)

1248 Of the king (βασιλευως)

1249 To enchant; to be a magician (μαγευω)

1250 Incense (θυωμα)

1250 Erect phallus (ιθυ φαλλος)

1251 Juggler; magician (θαυματο ποιος)

1251 To whip, scourge (ιμασσω)

1251 Purple (πορφυρα)

1251 Eighteen (οκτω–και–δεκα)

1252 Manifestation, proof (δηλωσις)

1252 To suck (μυζεω)

1253 To speak the truth (Ephesians 4:15) (αληθευω)

1254 That which cannot be understood (Romans 11:33) (ανεξερευνητος)

1255 To set free; to abrogate (εκλυω)

1255 Inspiration, ecstasy (ενθουσιασμος)

1255 Justification (Romans 5:18) (δικαιωσις)

1256 Life-giving (βιο δωρος)

1256 To mix together (διακυκαω)

1257

1258

1259

1260 Letter name of *upsilon* (υψιλον)

1260 Superior, more excellent (υπερτερος)

1260 Solomon (Σολομων)

1261 Vengeance (τιμωρια)

1261 The fixed star Arcturus (Αρκτουρος)

1262 To transmute (αλασσω)

1263 The Sun; beaming (ηλεκ–τωρ)

1263 Excess; excellence (υπεροχη)

1263 Gnosis; wisdom, knowledge (γνωσις)

1264 Geometry (γεωμετρια)

1264 The knowledge; the sign (το γνωμα)

1265

1266 Prophet (προφητης)

1267 Sorcerer (φαρμακευς)

1268 To cleanse (ραντιζω)

1269 Shame (αισχυνη)

1270 Dog; dog-star (κυων)

1270 To fall (Revelation 4:10) (πιπτω)

1270 In a circle, around (κυκλω)

1271 The Gnosis (η γνωσις)

1271 Thy name (το ονομα σου)

1271 Cross (σταυρος)

1271 Perseverence (συνεχεια)

1271 Delightful (χαρτος)

1272

1273 To search out, understand (Matthew 6:28) (καταμαν–θανω)

1274

1275 Orpheus (Ορφευς)

1275 Boast; glory; vow; wish (ευχος)

1276 Fourth (Revelation 6:7) (τεταρτος)

1277

1278 Power of the Word (Δυναμις Λογου)

1278 Distinguishing (διαγνωσις)

1279

1280 Guardian; avenger (μελετωρ)

1280 Intermingled; promiscuous (συμμικτος)

1280 Of the circle (κυκλωι)

1281 Great; wealthy (παχυς)

1282 Fatherless (Hebrews 7:3) (απατωρ)

1283 To grow together (Matthew 13:30) (συναυξανομαι)

1284

1285 Keeping silence (ευστομος)

1285 Decreed by God; made by God (θεσφατος)

1285 Babylon (βαβυλων)

1286

1287

1288

1289 The fish (ο ιχθυς)

1289 The god Poseidon (ο Ποσειδων)

1289 Hephaestus, Vulcan (Ηφαιστος)

1290 Strong (σωκος)

1290 Battle (φυλοπις)

1290 His own mother (of God; Lactantius, *Divine Institutes*, IV 8) (αυτομητορα)

1290 The egg (το ωον)

1291

1292

1293 Bending down (κατακαμψις)

1294 The seven vowels, representing the seven planets (ΑΕΗΙΟΥΩ)

1295 Old man (πρεσβυτης)

1296

1297 Fourfold (τετραπλασιος)

1298

1299 To banish (ανδρηλατεω)

1299 Vengeance (τιμωρημα)

1300 The egg (το ωιον)

1300 Epithet of Demeter (Ουλω)

1301 To shine (φαω)

1302 To bud, sprout; to cause to come forth (βρυω)

1302 Hard to be understood (2 Peter 3:16) (δυσνοητος)

1303

1304 Water (υδωρ)

1304 High-spirited; generous (υπερθυμος)

1305 Proud (υπεροπτος)

1305 Given of all (πανδωρος)

1306 Last (εσχατος)

1307

1308 Luxury; pride (τρυφη)

1308 Chance; fate (τυχη)

1309 Sword (σφαγευς)

1309 Throat (τραχηλος)

1309 To catch (Mark 12:13) (αγρευω)

1309 All-Mystery (Πανμυστηριον)

1310 Man (ανθρωπος)

1310 Universe; nature; origin (φυσις)

1310 To rule (Colossians 3:15) (βραβευω)

1310 Epithet of Demeter (Σιτω)

1311 Chance (συμφορα)

1312 Wanton, luxurious (υβριστικος)

1313

1314 The hierophant (ο ιεροφαντης)

1315 First matter (στοιχειον)

1315 Delight (τερψις)

1315 To fear (τρομεω)

1316 To fast (ασιτεω)

1317 Lying, false (ψευδης)

1318

1319 The veil (το καταπετασμα)

1320 To sacrifice, slaughter (ιερευω)

1320 Resistance (τριψις)

1321

1322

1323 True, real (ετητυμος)

1323 His own father (of God; Lactantius, *Divine Institutes*, IV 8) (αυτοπατορα)

1324

1325 To weep (John 11:35) (δακρυω)

1326 Crown; circle (στεφανος)

1327

1328

1329

1330

1331 To endure (Hebrews 11:27) (καρτερεω)

1332 The Gnostic deity Chnoubis (Χνουβις)

1332 Emperor Nero (= 666 in Hebrew) (Νερων Καεσαρ)

1332 666 x 2 (1332)

1333 Fleshy (σαρκωδης)

1333 Suffering (ταλαιπωρια)

1334

1335

1336 To keep secret (κατασιγαω)

1336 The prophet (ο προφητης)

1337 To overthrow, destroy (2 Timothy 2:18) (ανατρεπω)

1338 To shine, flame (φλεγω)

1339 Python (πυθων)

1340 Intense (συντονος)

1340 Wheel, disc; revolution (τροχος)

1340 Hermopolis, City of Thoth (Herodotus, *Histories*, II 67) (Ερμεω πολις)

1340 Of the temple (του οικου)

1341

1342

1343 Renewing (Titus 3:5) (ανακαινωσις)

1343 Sagittarius (Τοξευτης)

1344 Way of the Lord (Οδος Κυριου)

1344 The Word of Heaven (ο Ουρανιος Λογος)

1344 The Holy Spirit of Truth (το Αγιον Πνευμα Αληθειας)

1344 To corrupt (2 Corinthians 2:17) (καπηλευω)

1345

1346

1347

1348

1349 To receive the Law (Hebrews 7:11) (νομοθετεω)

1350 Light, lamp (λυχνος)

1351

1352 The Teletarchs, an order of divine beings (*Chaldean Oracles*) (τελεταρχαι)

1353

1354

1355

1356

1357

1358 Altar (θυσιαστηριον)

1358 Perfect knowledge (επιγνωσις)

1358 Of the Sun (Ελιωτις)

1358 Voice, word (φωνη)

1358 The Great Gnosis, the Mighty Knowledge (η Μεγαλη Γνωσις)

1358 Knowledge and Truth
(Γνωσις και Αληθεια)
1359
1360 To sacrifice (αποθυω)
1361
1362
1363
1364
1365 Overmuch (υπερπολυς)
1365 Shining (φαεθων)
1365 Of midnight (μεσονυκτιος)
1366 O phallus (vocative) (Ω Φαλλε)
1366 Phallus + kteis (φαλλος + κτεις)
1366 The voice (η φωνη)
1367 Circular (τροχο–ειδης)
1368
1369 Image of God (εικων Θεου)
1369 To make unseen, annihilate (αφανιζω)
1370 Returning (υποτροπος)
1370 Sublimity; height (υψος)
1371 Foretold (προφαντος)
1371 Whirling (στροφας)
1371 Face (υπωπια)
1372
1373
1374 To enslave (δουλοω)
1375 Flashing (στεροψ)
1376 Beget; bring forth (James 1:18) (αποκυεω)
1376 Angels of God (αγγελοι του Θεου)
1377
1378
1379 Falsehood (ψευδος)
1380 Line (στιχος)
1381
1382

1383 Triangle (τριγωνον)
1384 *Alpha + Omega*; Beginning and End; First and Last (Αλφα + Ωμηγα)
1385 Most excellent (φεριστος)
1386 To show forth, appear, reveal (εκφαινω)
1387
1388
1389 Inspiration of God (2 Timothy 3:16) (Θεοπνευστος)
1390 Cup (σκυφος)
1391 Love of wisdom, philosophy (φιλοσοφια)
1392 Pleasant; thanksgiving; the Eucharist, sacrament (ευχαριστος*)
1393
1394
1395
1396
1397
1398 Thread (στημων)
1399
1400 Natural (φυσικος)
1400 Of the Law (του Νομου)
1401 To act according to one's will (ιδιοβουλεω)
1402 Priest (κληδουχος)
1402 Ark of the Covenant; chest (κιβωτος)
1403 Sin (παραπτωμα)
1404 Lion-hearted (θυμο–λεων)
1405 To bring forth; to desire (σευω)
1405 To follow (Revelation 6:8) (ακολουθεω)
1405 To bear (φερω)
1405 To have (εχω)

1406

1407 Vital, full of life (ζωτικος)

1408 Savior, redeemer (Σωτηρ)

1408 Echo, lament (Ηχω)

1408 Away all evil demons (phrase from liturgy of Greek Orthodox Church) (Απο παντος κακοδαιμονος)

1409 The Python (ο πυθων)

1410 Force, strength (ισχυς)

1410 The wheel, disc (ο τροχος)

1411 The body (το σωμα)

1412 To write in (2 Corinthians 3:2) (εγγραφω)

1412 *Alpha* and *Omega*; Beginning and End; First and Last (Αλφα και Ωμεγα)

1413

1414 Excellent (υπερηφανος)

1415 Girdle (ζωστηρ)

1415 Cruel, wicked (σχετλιος)

1416 Savior, redeemer (Σωτειρα)

1417 To be reverent (ευσεβεω)

1418 The Hebrew god Jehovah (Ιεχωβα)

1419 Salvation (σωτηρια)

1420 To be silent (φιμοω)

1420 By chance (τυχον)

1420 To have compassion (Hebrews 5:2) (μετρι– οπαθεω)

1420 To set on fire (James 3:6) (φλογιζω)

1421 To walk about (1 Peter 5:8) (ωρυομαι)

1422

1423

1424

1425

1426 To walk in (2 Corinthians 6:16) (εμπεριπατεω)

1427

1428

1429 The Pleroma; the fullness (το Πληρωμα)

1430

1431 Double-mouthed; double (αμφι–στομος)

1432 Avenger; Alastor (Αλαστωρ)

1433

1434

1435

1436

1437

1438 Thrice-greatest; epithet of Thoth (τρισμεγιστος)

1439 To be watchful (Hebrews 13:17) (αγρυπνεω)

1440 Rope, cord (στροφος)

1440 Archer (τοχοφορος)

1440 Watcher; guard (φρουρος)

1441 Tomb (χωμα)

1441 Hidden, secret (Colossians 2:3) (αποκρυφος)

1442

1443

1444

1445

1446

1447

1448 To exceed (υπερβαλλω)

1448 To reign (Revelation 5:10) (βασιλευω)

1448 Forty (τεσσαρακοντα)

1449

1450 To be neutral (μεσευω)

1450 Countenance; mask (προσωπον)

1451 Firmament (στερεωμα)
1452
1453 A filling-up, completion (εκπληρωσις)
1454
1455
1456
1457 Life-giving (φυσιζοος)
1457 To act with free will (επελευθεριαζω)
1458
1459 Rest, ease (ραστωνη)
1459 Earth; name of the goddess Gaea (Χθων)
1460 One in eight (εις εν οκτω)
1461 Foundation; matter (υποστασις)
1461 Apollyon, Abaddon (Απολλυων)
1462 Excess (αναχυσις)
1462 To interpret (μεθερμηνευω)
1463 Continuous (συνεχης)
1464 With God (common Coptic inscription (συν Θεω)
1465 Knowing, intelligent; warlike (δαιφρων)
1465 A uniting; synagogue (συναγωγη)
1465 Holy water (χερνιψ)
1466 To more than conquer (Romans 8:37) (υπερκιναω)
1467
1468 Life-destroying (θυμοφθορος)
1469 To be wanton (στρηνιαω)
1470 Smoke, mist; vanity (τυφος)
1471 Last, extreme (υστατος)
1472

1473
1474
1475 Builder (τεκτων)
1476
1477
1478 To come together (συνηκω)
1478 Righteous, good (χρηστος)
1478 The Savior (ο Σωτηρ)
1479 Odysseus (Οδυσσευς)
1480 The Star of Love (ο Αστηρ της Αγαπης)
1480 Throne of Wisdom (Θρονος Σοφιας)
1480 The Host (ο Πανδοχευς)
1480 The Holiness (Romans 1:4) (η Αγιωσυνη)
1480 The Goodness (η Αγαθωσυνη)
1480 Christ; anointed (Χριστος)
1480 Sodom and Egypt (Σοδομα και Αιγυπτος)
1481 Throat; stomach (στομαχος)
1481 Abominated (στυγητος)
1482
1483
1484 Simon Magus (Σιμων ο Μαγος)
1484 The Omnipotence (η Αυτοδυναμις)
1485
1486 Fourfold (τετραπλους)
1486 Most high, highest (καθυπερτατος)
1487
1488 Master (σοφιστης)
1489
1490
1491

1492 Paths of the Lord (Τριβοι Κυριου)

1492 One crying (βοωντος)

1492 The last Adam (1 Corinthians 15:45) (ο εσχατος Αδαμ)

1493 To perform sacred rites (ιερ–ουργεω)

1494 Bound by an oath (διωμοτος)

1495

1496

1497

1498

1499 Messenger (σημαντωρ)

1500 Light, life (Revelation 22:5) (φως)

1500 The Egyptian god Horus (Ωρυς)

1500 Unseen, secret; blind (τυφλος)

1500 Eye; countenance (ωψ)

1500 Robe of the Lord (Ενδυμα Κυριου)

1500 Destruction, ruin (κατασ–τροφη)

1501 Frequent (ταρφυς)

1501 Swift (ταχυς)

1501 Space (χωρα)

1502 Everywhere (πανταχου)

1504 Word of the Aeon (Λογος Αιωνος)

1510 Blood of the gods (ιχωρ)

1525 The Synoches, a group of Chaldean divinities (*Chaldean Oracles*) (Συνοχες)

1527 The True Gnosis (η Αληθης Γνωσις)

1549 The First Mystery (το Α Μυστηριον)

1549 Great Light (Μεγα Φως)

1549 Founder of Mysteries (Orphic) (Τελεταρχης)

1560 Perfection (τελειωσις)

1560 The eight (το οκτω)

1570 Gold (χρυσος)

1580 Strong (ισχυρος)

1601 Lights; wisdom (φωτα)

1601 Of the death (του θανατου)

1700 Body (Acts 19:12) (χρως)

1708 Psyche; soul (Revelation 12:11) (Ψυχη)

1724 Sword (κνωδων)

1730 Pluto, Hades (Πλουτων)

1815 United (συμφερτος)

1828 To keep the feast of Bacchus; to be in ecstasy (βακχευω)

1886 Eucharist, sacrament (ευχαριστος)

1910 Happy, lucky (ευτυχες)

1913 Happy, lucky (ευτυχης)

1919 The Word of the Law (το Ρημα του Νομου)

1945 Lucifer, light-bringer (Εωσφορος)

1984 Light of God (Φως Θεου)

1984 The Will of the Father (το Θελημα του Πατρος)

1990 The whole of the Law (το Ολον του Νομου)

2050 Typhon (Τυφων)

2150 Title of Hermes and Priapus (Τυχων)

2200 Hurricane (τυφως)

2220 I, the *Alpha* and *Omega*; I, the Beginning and End (Εγω Αλφα και Ωμεγα)

2220 The Nature of the Father (η Υποστασις Πατρος)

2220 Osoronnophris (*Papyri Graeci Magicae*) (Οσοροννωφρις)

2368 Jesus Christ (Ιησους Χριστος)

2368 And his number is 666 (Revelation 13:18) (και ο αριθμος αυτου χξς)

2440 Day-star; light-bringer (2 Peter 1:19) (φωσφορος)

2488 The Form of the Lord (Μορφη του Κυριου)

2488 The Universe is the Word of the Lord (Κοσμος εστι Λογος Κυριου)

2683 Almighty Aeon (Αιων Παντοκρατωρ)

2683 The Pleroma of God, the Fullness of God (το Πληρωμα του Θεου)

3663 Bainchoooch, soul of Khukh, god of darkness (*Papyri Graeci Magicae*) (Βαινχωωωχ)

3999 Sum of the 24 letters of the Greek alphabet (3999)

appendix III

ANCIENT AUTHORS CITED

THE CENTRAL THEME OF THIS BOOK HAS BEEN to collate and present the evidence for an original and independent philosophy of Greek alphabetic mysticism. That evidence includes graffiti, papyri, inscriptions and amulets; but a very large and important part is also the testimony of many reknowned ancient authors whose works are known to us. Their writings not only carry the weight of authority, but also allow for easy and firm placement of various developments on the historical continuum. In any work seeking to draw historical conclusions, it is also impossible to overemphasize the importance of returning and referring to original sources. Apart from simple negligence or ignorance, subsequent historical discovery can make even the most reputable authority unreliable or incorrect. In this book, a number of serious mistakes were rectified by not accepting the statements or conclusions of later writers, and instead checking the earliest cited and available evidence whenever possible. By this practice also, anyone willing to familiarize themselves with original sources, can be confident that their own views are as soundly based as may be. The ancient authors and works cited in this book are listed here in one place, so that anyone who wishes can easily locate and then refer to the original sources in the area for their own verification or research.

Aeschylus, *Eumenides*.
Aristophanes, *Birds*.
Aristophanes, *Lysistrata*.
Aristophanes, *Peace*.
Aristotle, *Metaphysics*.
Aristotle, *On the Heavens*.
Artemidorus, *Interpretation of Dreams*.
Augustine, *The City of God*.
Augustine, *Tractates on the Gospel of John*.
Celsus, *True Doctrine*.
Cicero, *On Duties*.
Cicero, *The Dream of Scipio*.
Clemens Alexandrinus, *Miscellanies*.
Demetrius, *On Style*.
Dionysius Thrax, *Art of Grammar*.
Heliodorus, *An Ethiopian Story*.
Herodotus, *Histories*.
Hesiod, *Works and Days*.
Hippolytus, *Refutation of All Heresies*.
Homer, *Iliad*.
Homer, *Odyssey*.
Hyginus, *Fables*.
Iamblichus, *The Life of Pythagoras*.
Iamblichus, *The Theology of Arithmetic*.
Irenaeus, *Against Heresies*.
Jerome, *On Amos*.
Jerome, *Homilies*.
Johannis Lydus, *On the Months*.

Josephus, *Antiquities.*
Justin Martyr, *Apologia.*
Lactantius, *The Divine Institutes.*
Livy, *History of Rome.*
Lucian, *Alexander the False Prophet.*
Lucian, *Hermotimus.*
Lucian, *Philosophies for Sale.*
Lucian, *The Consonants at Law.*
Macrobius, *Commentary on the Dream of Scipio.*
Martianus Capella, *The Marriage of Philology and Mercury.*
Nicomachus, *Manual of Harmony.*
Olympiodorus, *Prolegomena.*
Origen, *Against Celsus.*
Persius, *Satires.*
Philo Judaeus, *Questions and Answers on Genesis.*
Philo Judaeus, *On the Creation.*
Plato, *Republic.*
Plato, *Timaeus.*
Pliny the Younger, *Letters.*
Plutarch, *Life of Pompey.*
Plutarch, *Moralia.*
Plutarch, *On Isis and Osiris.*
Proclus, *A Commentary on the First Book of Euclid's Elements.*
Proclus, *A Commentary on Plato's Timaeus.*
Pseudo-Callisthenes, *Life of Alexander.*
Ptolemy, *Tetrabiblos.*
Servius, *On Virgil's Aeneid.*
Suetonius, *Nero.*
Tacitus, *Annals.*
Virgil, *Aeneid.*
Virgil, *Fourth Eclogue.*
Xenophon, *Memorabilia.*
Xenophon, *The Education of Cyrus.*
Zosimus, *Upon the Letter Omega.*

SELECTED
BIBLIOGRAPHY

Allen, R. E.(ed.). *Greek Philosophy—Thales to Aristotle*. New York: The Free Press, 1991.

Babbit, Frank Cole (trans.). *Plutarch's Moralia*. London: William Heinemann, Ltd. 1969.

Bartlett, J. R. *Jews in the Hellenistic World*. Cambridge: Cambridge University Press, 1985.

Bate, H. N. *The Sibylline Oracles—Books III-V*. London: Macmillan, 1918.

Bernal, R. M. *Cadmean Letters*. Winona Lake, IN: Eisenbrauns, 1990.

Berthelot, M. *La Chimie des Anciens et du Moyen Age*. Paris: 1893.

Berthelot, M. and Ruelle, C. *Collection des Anciens Alchimistes Grecs*. Paris: 1888.

Betz, Hans D. *The Greek Magical Papyri in Translation*. Chicago: University of Chicago Press, 1986.

Boardman, J., Griffin, J., and Murray, O. (eds.). *The Oxford History of the Classical World*. Oxford: Oxford University Press, 1986.

Brown, S. *The Origins of Christianity—A Historical Introduction to the New Testament*. New York: Oxford University Press, 1993.

Burkert, W. *Lore and Science in Ancient Pythagoreanism.* Cambridge: Harvard University Press, 1972.

Bullock, P. (trans.). *The Dream of Scipio.* London: Aquarian Press, 1983.

Burn, A. R. *The Pelican History of Greece.* London: Pelican Books, 1966.

Butterworth, G. W. (trans.). *Clement of Alexandria.* London: William Heinemann, Ltd. 1919.

Cahill, Thomas. *How the Irish Saved Civilization.* New York: Anchor Books, 1995.

Cary, Ernest. *The Roman Antiquities of Dionysius of Halicarnassus.* London: William Heinemann, Ltd. 1978.

Cook, B. F. *Greek Inscriptions.* Berkeley: University of California Press, 1987.

Cross, F. L. *The Early Christian Fathers.* London: Gerald Duckworth, Ltd. 1960.

De Vogel, C. J. *Pythagoras and Early Pythagoreanism.* Assen: Van Gorcum and Co., 1966.

Diringer, David. *The Alphabet.* London: Hutchinson, 1948.

———. *Writing.* London: Hutchinson, 1962.

Doresse, Jean. *The Secret Books of the Egyptian Gnostics.* Rochester, VT: Inner Traditions International, 1986.

Dornseiff, Franz. *Das Alphabet in Mystik und Magie.* Leipzig: Teubner, 1925.

Encyclopedia Judaica. Jerusalem: Keter Publishing House, 1972.

Eisenman, R. and Wise, M. *The Dead Sea Scrolls Uncovered.* New York: Penguin Books, 1992.

Ewald, M. L. (trans.). *Homilies of St. Jerome.* Washington: Catholic University of America Press, 1948.

Falls, T. B. (trans.). *Writings of St. Justin Martyr.* Washington: Catholic University of America Press, 1966.

Farbridge, M. H. *Studies in Biblical and Semitic Symbolism.* Hoboken, NJ: Ktav Publishing House, 1970.

Fideler, David. *Jesus Christ, Sun of God.* Wheaton, IL: Quest Books, 1993.

Fideler, David (ed.). *The Pythagorean Sourcebook and Library.* Grand Rapids, MI: Phanes Press, 1988.

Frazer, James G. *The Golden Bough—A Study in Magic and Religion.* London: Macmillan Press, 1922.

Gettings, Fred. *The Arkana Dictionary of Astrology.* London: Penguin Books, 1985.

Gibbon, Edward. *The Decline and Fall of the Roman Empire.* London: Chatto and Windus, 1960.

Godwin, David. *Light in Extension—Greek Magic from Modern to Homeric Times.* St. Paul, MN: Llewellyn Publications, 1992.

Godwin, Jocelyn. *The Mystery of the Seven Vowels.* Grand Rapids, MI: Phanes Press, 1991.

Grant, Robert M. *Irenaeus of Lyons.* London: Routledge, 1985.

Gwynn Griffths, John (trans.). *Plutarch—On Isis and Osiris.* Cardiff, Great Britain: University of Wales Press, 1970.

Graves, Robert. *The White Goddess.* London: Faber & Faber, 1961.

———. *The Greek Myths.* London: Pelican Books, 1955.

Guthrie, K. S. (trans.). *The Message of Philo Judaeus of Alexandria.* Kila, MT: Kessinger Publishing Co., 1997.

Harmon, A. M. (trans.). *Lucian.* London: William Heinemann, Ltd., 1925.

Hayward, C. T. (trans.). *Saint Jerome's Hebrew Questions on Genesis.* Oxford: Clarendon Press, 1995.

Healy, John F. *The Early Alphabet.* London: British Museum Press, 1990.

Hennecke, Edgar and Schneemelcher, Wilhelm (eds.). *New Testament Apocrypha.* Cambridge: James Clarke and Co. Ltd., 1992.

Hilgard, A. *Scholia in Dionysii Thracis Artem Grammaticam.* Leipzig: Teubner, 1901.

Hoffman, R. Joseph. *Jesus Outside the Gospels.* New York: Prometheus Books, 1984.

Horner, George (trans.). *Pistis Sophia.* London: Macmillan Co., 1924.

279

Hopper, V. *Medieval Number Symbolism*. New York: Columbia University Press, 1938.

Imhoof-Blumer, F. W. and Gardner, Percy. *Ancient Coins Illustrating Lost Masterpieces of Greek Art—A Numismatic Commentary on Pausanias*. Chicago: Argonaut, 1964.

James, Jamie. *The Music of the Spheres*. London: Abacus, 1995.

Jan, Carl (ed.) *Musici Scriptores Graeci*. Leipzig: Teubner, 1895.

Janowitz, Naomi. *The Poetics of Ascent—Theories of Language in a Rabbinic Ascent Text*. Albany: State University of New York, 1989.

Jeffrey, Lilian. *The Local Scripts of Archaic Greece*. Oxford: Oxford University Press, 1961.

Kingsley, P. *Ancient Philosophy, Mystery and Magic*. Oxford: Clarendon Press, 1995.

Lea, Simcox and Bond, Bligh. *The Apostolic Gnosis*. Great Britain: RILKO, 1979.

———. *Gematria*. Orpington, Kent, Great Britain: RILKO, 1977.

McDonald, M. F. (trans.). *Lactantius—The Divine Institutes*. Washington D. C.: Catholic University of America Press, 1948.

McGinn, Bernard. *Antichrist*. New York: HarperCollins, 1994.

McManners, John (ed.). *The Oxford Illustrated History of Christianity*. Oxford: Oxford University Press, 1992.

Maas, M. *John Lydus and the Roman Past*. London: Routledge, 1992.

Mansfield, J. *The Pseudo-Hippocratic Tract ΠΕΡΙ ΕΒΔΟΜΑΔΩΝ Ch. 1–11 and Greek Philosophy*. Assen: Van Gorcum & Co., 1971.

Marcus, Ralph (trans.). *Philo—Questions and Answers on Genesis*. London: William Heinemann, Ltd. 1953.

Meyer, Marvin (ed.) *The Ancient Mysteries—A Sourcebook*. San Francisco: HarperSanFrancisco, 1987.

Meyer, Marvin and Smith, Richard (eds.). *Ancient Christian*

Magic—Coptic Texts of Ritual Power. New York: Harper-Collins, 1995.

Michell, John. *The Dimensions of Paradise*. London: Abacus, 1988.

———. *City of Revelation*. London: Garnstone, 1972.

Moeller, W. *The Mithraic Origin and Meaning of the Rotas-Sator Square*. Leiden: Teubner, 1973.

Moorhouse, A. C. *The Triumph of the Alphabet*. New York: H. Schuman, 1953.

Morrow, G. R. (trans.). *Proclus—A Commentary on the First Book of Euclid's Elements*. Princeton: Princeton University Press, 1970.

Murray, Gilbert. *Five Stages of Greek Religion*. London: Watts and Co., 1935.

Neugebauer, O. *The Exact Sciences in Antiquity*. New York: Dover, 1967.

Patai, Raphael. *The Jewish Alchemists*. Princeton: Princeton University Press, 1994.

Pearson, B. (ed.). "Nag Hammadi Codices X and XI," in *Nag Hammadi Studies*, Vol. XV. Leiden: Brill, 1981.

Pennick, Nigel. *The Secret Lore of Runes and Other Ancient Alphabets*. London: Rider Books, 1991.

Philip, J. A. *Pythagoras and Early Pythagoreanism*. Toronto: University of Toronto Press, 1966.

Potok, Chaim. *Wanderings—Chaim Potok's History of the Jews*. New York: Fawcett Crest Books, 1980.

Powell, B. *Homer and the Origin of the Greek Alphabet*. Cambridge: Cambridge University Press, 1991.

Prentice, W. K. *American Journal of Archaeology*, Vol. X (1906).

Rettig, J. W. (trans.). *St. Augustine—Tractates on the Gospel of John*. Washington: Catholic University of America Press, 1948.

Rhys Roberts, W. (trans.). *Demetrius—On Style*. London: William Heinemann, Ltd., 1973.

Robbins, F. (trans.). *Tetrabiblos*. London: William Heinemann, Ltd., 1940.

Rohmer, John. *Testament—The Bible and History*. London: Michael O'Mara Books, 1988.

Ronan, Stephen. *Theodorus of Asine and the Kabbalah*, in McLean, A. (ed.), *The Hermetic Journal*, No. 42. London: privately published, 1988.

Rudolph, K. *Gnosis—The Nature and History of Gnosticism*. San Francisco: HarperSanFran-cisco, 1987.

Runia, D. *Philo of Alexandria and the Timaeus of Plato*. Leiden: Brill, 1983.

Rutherford, W. *Pythagoras—Lover of Wisdom*. London: Aquarian Press, 1984.

Scholem, Gershom. *Kabbalah*. Jerusalem: Keter Publishing House, 1974.

———. *Origins of the Kabbalah*. Princeton: Princeton University Press, 1990.

Scott, Walter (trans.). *Hermetica*. Boulder: Hermes House, 1982.

Stahl, W. H. (trans.). *Martianus Capella and the Seven Liberal Arts*. New York: Columbia University Press, 1971.

Stone, M. (ed.). *Jewish Writings of the Second Temple Period*. Assen: Van Gorcum and Co., 1984.

Taylor, Thomas (trans.). *The Commentaries of Proclus on the Timaeus of Plato*. London: A. J. Valpy, 1820.

———. *The Arguments of the Emperor Julian Against the Christians*. Kila, MT: Kessinger Publishing Co., 1997.

Uhlig, E. (ed.). *Dionysii Thracis Ars Grammatica*. Leipzig: Teubner, 1884.

Waddell, W. (trans.). *Manetho*. London: William Heinemann, Ltd., 1964.

Walker, Benjamin. *Gnosticism*. London: Aquarian Press, 1983.

Waterfield, R. (trans.). *The Theology of Arithmetic*. Grand Rapids, MI: Phanes Press, 1988.

Westcott, William W. (ed.). *The Chaldean Oracles of Zoroaster*. London: Aquarian Press, 1983.

Wilken, Robert L. *The Christians as the Romans Saw Them.* New Haven and London: Yale University Press, 1984

Wolohojian, Albert (trans.). *The Romance of Alexander the Great by Pseudo-Callisthenes.* New York: Columbia University Press, 1969.

Woodard, R. D. *Greek Writing from Knossos to Homer.* New York: Oxford University Press, 1997.

Wuensch, Richard (ed.). *Ioannis Laurentii Lydi Liber De Mensibus.* Leipzig: Teubner, 1898.

INDEX OF NUMBERS

INDEX

KIEREN BARRY WAS BORN IN TAURANGA, New Zealand. As a student at Auckland University he won awards for his work in Ancient History and Latin. He received a grant to study Mandarin in China, a scholarship in Law, and a position as Editor in Chief of the *Law Review*. He graduated from Auckland University in 1993 with two degrees; the first in Law and the second in the Arts, specializing in Classics and Ancient History. He currently practices law and lives in Hong Kong with his wife, Michelle.